Setting the Virgin on Fire

Setting the Virgin on Fire

Lázaro Cárdenas, Michoacán
Peasants, and the Redemption
of the Mexican Revolution

Marjorie Becker

UNIVERSITY OF CALIFORNIA PRESS

Berkeley / Los Angeles / London

University of California Press
Berkeley and Los Angeles, California

University of California Press, Ltd.
London, England

© 1995 by
The Regents of the University of California

Library of Congress Cataloging-in-Publication Data

Becker, Marjorie, 1952–
    Setting the Virgin on fire : Lázaro Cárdenas, Michoacán peasants,
and the redemption of the Mexican Revolution / Marjorie Becker.
        p.   cm.
    Includes bibliographical references and index.
    ISBN 0-520-08419-5 (pbk. : alk. paper)
    1. Cárdenas, Lázaro, 1895–1970—Relations with peasantry.
2. Mexico—Politics and government—1910–1946.   3. Mexico—
History—Revolution, 1910–1920—Social aspects.   4. Peasantry—
Mexico—Michoacán de Ocampo—History—20th century.
5. Indians of Mexico—Mexico—Michoacán de Ocampo—
Government relations.   6. Political culture—Mexico—Michoacán
de Ocampo—History—20th century.   I. Title.
    F1234.C233B43   1995
    972'.37—dc20   94-40327
                                                                  CIP

Printed in the United States of America

08   07   06   05   04   03   02   01   00
9   8   7   6   5   4   3

To the memory of my great-aunt,
Lillian Lavine

Index

Aceves, Jesús, 20, 26
Acosta, Angelina, 42, 42, 47, 51–53, 80
Agraristas, 127–28
Anguiano, Matilde, 91
Anticlericalism: demonstrations, 108, 109, 110; destruction of icons, 77, 78
Ario Santa Monica, 23n43, 24, 26, 77, 85; torching and dance, 93–100, 120, 122, 129, 130
Ascencia, Ramón, 24
Aztecs, 5

Barosa, María Guadalupe, 93
Barragán, Carmen, 97, 98
Barragán, Soledad, 99, 100
Bautista, Antonio G., 113–15
Brading, David, 4n15

Caciques, 119–23
Calderón, José, 137
Calles, Plutarco Elías, 6, 56, 62
Campesinos: and Catholic restoration, 159–60; conflict among, 25–26; and construction of postrevolutionary government, 8–9; and Cristero revelations, 7; cultural knowledge of, 157, 160–61; daily routines of, 22–23; health as government concern, 90; and land redistribution, 158; military defeats of, 161, 162; as participants in governing, 76; resistance to Cardenista education

efforts, 123–28; and Unión Nacional Sinarquista, 146–47
Cárdenas, Lázaro, 1–4; Callista heritage, 49, 62; cultural inheritance of, 161; and cultural myopia, xiv, 8; governorship, 40, 49, 50–51, 55–56; and making of postrevolutionary government, 155–62; obstacles to presidency, 62; on school boycott, 127; threats to government of, 156–57; use of caciques, 50, 85, 105–6
Cárdenas's cadre: composition, 9, 49; Confederación Revolucionaria Michoacana de Trabajo, 49–50; Protestants, 42
Cardenistas: anticlericalism of, 68–69; and campesinos, 63, 64, 66–67, 72, 75–76; and Catholicism, 45–47, 65–66; concepts of culture, 72–73; critique of elite excesses, 64–65; and cultural myopia, 9, 40, 44; cultural roots of, 3, 8, 9, 41, 42; divisions among, 67–69; and health concerns, 88–90; on Indians, 4, 47, 69–72, 103, 104, 111–12, 115; and liberalism, 41, 47, 48; and mestizos, 44, 46–47, 70, 72–74; missionary tradition of, 61, 62–64; and new ritual forms, 110–15; and reconstruction, 44–61; religious conflict among, 68–69; responses to Catholic revival, 80, 81–83; role in Indian liberation, 94, 99, 104–5, 136–37; and state making as hegemonic project, 4–5

185

Catholicism: belief, and science, 66; and
community, 79; and hierarchy, 47;
message of humility, 38; restoration,
158, 159–60; rituals of, 45, 46; social,
in Michoacán, 84
Cervantes, Carlos, 25
Charapan, 149–50
Chilchota, 108, 109, 133–34, 150–52
Church: desecration of, 93–100; destruction of icons, 77, 78; Sunday mass, 15
Coastal region (*región de la costa*), 11
Colonialism, 71
Confederación Revolucionaria Michoacana del Trabajo, 49–50
Contepec, 125
Corona Núñez, José, 43, 45, 47, 48, 50,
69, 81, 110, 143; agrarian leader, 53;
background, 42; as seminary rebel, 46;
as secular priest, 53
Cristeros: attacks on teachers, 124–25;
and Cárdenas, 39, 40, 49; and Consti-
tutionalist governing problem, 7; rebellion by, 6, 100
Cuevas, Ramón, 120–21

Daughters of Mary (Hijas de María),
27–31. *See also* Women
Domingo Cultural (Cultural Sunday) programs, 112

Economic relations, northwestern Michoacán: land ownership, 19–20; system of
domination, 26–32
Education, Cardenista: resistance to, 123–
28; school boycott, 126–28; socialist,
143–44. *See also* Campesinos; Cardenistas
Ejido, and ejidal lands, 73
Elizalde, Francisco, 80, 126
Enríquez, María, 27
Espitia, Ignacio, 23n44, 145

Feminine Socialist Congress, 113–15

Gallardo González, Gustavo, 151–52
García Verduzco, Vicente, 120
Garrido Canabal, Tomás, 68
Geertz, Clifford, 7–8
Gender, and military force, 100–101
Guaracha, 24
Guerra, François-Xavier, 59n66
Gutiérrez, Juan, 86–87, 91, 123, 148

Hacienda system, 19–23, 24, 43
Hay, Eduardo, 159
Hegemony, construction of, 5, 76, 161
La Huerta, 74

Indianism: and Prado, 107; revolutionary,
135–38, 142; and Tarascan renaissance,
111–12
Indians, 75, 103: as Cardenista reinventions, 72, 76; and handicrafts, 107; and
mestizos, 54–55, 73; and reform laws,
103n2. *See also* Campesinos; Tarascans

Jarácuaro villagers, 139–41

Knight, Alan, 3n9, 82n17, 156n2

Ladislao, Teresa, 29
Lake Pátzcuaro, 12
Land redistribution, 82, 83–84, 117–19,
128
Land tenure. *See* Tarascans, land tenure
Le Duc, Alberto, 113
Liberalism: and Cardenista critique of
rural life, 66, 67; and Catholicism, 42;
in Michoacán, 47–48; and privatization
of Tarascan communal property,
33–34, 103
Literacy, in Michoacán, 1940, 42
López, Odilon, 136–37

Maestro Rural, 113, 114, 137
Magaña, Gildardo, 144–45
Manso, Maximino, 25–26
Martínez, Carlos, 98
Méndez, Concepción, 77, 78, 96, 97, 98
Mendoza, Antonio, 27
Meseta tarasca, 11, 12
Mestizas, 28–30, 31. *See also* Women
Mestizos: culture, 19–31, 130–31; and
landlessness, 83–85; reconstruction of
land reform, 118, 119; response to rev-
olutionaries, 116–17, 123, 124; and
underground Catholic restoration, 128,
129–31
Mexican governmental reconstruction,
157–62
Mexican revolutionary culture, 1–2n3,
5–9
Mexican women's movement, 54–45
Meyer, Jean, 6n20, 38n89, 39n1
Michoacán: and Cárdenas' political exile,

Contents

List of Maps

Preface

As readers will immediately discover, this book utilizes metaphors with great liberality. This is partly because it has long struck me that the separation between history and poetry is a false and damaging one. It is also because, as poets understand with great intuition, metaphors enable us to cut to the heart of the matter. In a historical literature encrusted with official representations of peasantry and state, such a method seems useful.

The metaphors used here should all be recognizable to Latin Americans and to Latin Americanists because they speak of and to Latin American realities. I wish to take this opportunity to speak of the metaphor, rooted in my personal life, that in conscious and unconscious ways has guided the investigation that led first to my dissertation and then to what has become a very different book. My maternal grandfather, a lawyer in the Depression South, was paid in kind for his legal services, but *kind* embraced a wide variety of items. What interested me as a child was his collection of antique glass paperweights, a collection that began with such a payment. I kept wondering, "What is underneath the glass outer shell?" While this would appear to be obvious—encased within were millefiore flowers, multicolored mushrooms, marzipanlike pieces of fruit, the occasional person—my concerns were slightly different. Although I was alert to the great beauty of the paperweights, I kept asking myself how the things within—the people, the apples and pears—in fact differed from the ways they were presented. I wondered about the will to transform reality, to beautify it or coarsen it, and then to arrest its motion, trapping it forever in glass.

I do not believe that my concern with objects encased in glass was innocent. On the contrary, in the Georgia town where I was raised there was a powerful demand for conformity, and distortion was everywhere. A wealthy white elite dominated economic and social relations. I remember being struck as a child by the seemingly curious resemblance between racist allusions to people I knew and the paperweights. The analogy was imprecise, and yet both the glassblowers and racists removed people from their contexts, portrayed them as embodiments of a limited range of characteristics, and undermined the possibilities of self-representation. It seemed important to somehow break through these misrepresentations, to observe these people as they represented themselves in their everyday lives.

The most considerable evidence that this task was worth undertaking comes from my great-aunt, the late Lillian Lavine. Although she was herself at times misrepresented, she taught me an approach to the problem. For those who knew her inadequately, in her guises as spinster at a time when marriage mattered intensely, as a low-paid assistant to a superior court clerk, she "never amounted to anything." But they were wrong. Closer engagement, closer observation of what she said and what she did, revealed a woman of abiding honesty, persistence, and sweetness of heart. It also revealed the hazards of underestimating her. This book is dedicated to her.

Acknowledgments

We found ourselves together in the agrarian reform archive, a dank room located in one of Mexico City's poor barrios. Papers spilled over the wooden tables and onto the floor. Peasants had come from distant villages only to wait, shuffling around, sometimes for days. Bureaucrats barked out names of villages, then handed out dusty folders. I was sitting in a chair taking notes on the agrarian history of northwestern Michoacán when a woman dressed in black tugged at my arm. Although I was a stranger—no, because I was a stranger—she seemed intent on engaging me. "You are so lucky," she said. "I had to pay a man to come with me from my village. He knows how to read and write, so he can help me find out something about my family's land. You don't have to do that. You can do your own work."

Then again, Pancho Elizalde tried to head off my too innocent sympathy. The son of a labor leader, devout in his Catholicism, he had offered me an acute reading of the agrarian reform in Zamora, Michoacán. He stressed the disarray, even the dishonesty. "There are people who took five, six plots of land. It wasn't even peasants who got the land. And I have to say, if there were any peasants who were unable to get anything out of the land reform, who were nothing more than cannon fodder, people forced to do nothing but beg for a little clothing, a mouthful here or there, well, nobody could have been that ignorant." It took me some time to make sense of his warning, to realize that he was not deriding the woman's ability to choose just the word to elicit sympathy, that he was alert to the conditions that induced poor people to deal with unfair conditions, conditions they sometimes had participated in making, that a too ready sympathy would obscure that point every time.

I bring this up with some reluctance, partly because while this book touches on issues of land, it is principally a study of cultural nearsightedness. It examines the ways that passionate liberals and equally ardent Catholics misunderstood one another. Those troubled perceptions took on concrete, at times murderous, forms. From a series of conflicts, from a series of negotiations leading to a recognition of the commonplaces they might share, these people joined with Cárdenas in making the postrevolutionary Mexican government.

For some time I had been thinking and writing about the intimate bonds between culture and power, how Mexicans forged those bonds, how they experienced them. It had seemed to me that peasants, particularly peasants engaged in spiritual endeavors, deserved greater respect than scholars had accorded them. I felt that at times I had gone too far, however, simply turning scholarly disdain for campesinos on its head, thus revealing a continuously benign peasantry. In fact my intellectual discomfort was such that while I had been encouraged to publish my dissertation with relatively minor revisions, I determined to develop a new conceptual framework.

To be sure, if I was to use the language of architecture to evoke my thought, there were certain mental blueprints I would need to discard, particularly because the Mexicans' concern was with the remaking of governing institutions—all right, the state. However pervasive the idea of states as immobile, built on elements designed to endure, it was a dubious idea to apply to a time when Mexicans contested prerevolutionary understandings of government. Also, the thought that governing institutions are designed according to some neutral, interchangeable plan would have to be dismissed. As the activities of a wide variety of Mexicans would demonstrate, states are structures possessed of a point of view, a perspective suggestive of the balance of power current in society.

I recognized, of course, the potential iconoclasm of my work. To train a scholarly lens on Lázaro Cárdenas, a man whose status approached sainthood, might have proved hazardous in Cárdenas's home state of Michoacán, a state whose traditions of liberalism and conservatism engendered ardent allegiances. I was wrong to worry. Somehow, through their generous reception of my work and their sometimes provocative questions, a number of friends and colleagues at the Colegio de Michoacán dispelled my concerns. This was especially true of Jean Meyer. Although he may well disagree with some of my interpretations, his own work serves as a model of humanism and complexity. A number of other scholars in Michoacán also offered me intellectual companionship and warm hospitality. I would particularly like to thank Beatrice Rojas, Luis González and Armida de la Vara, Andrés Lira and Cecilia Noriega, Carlos Herrejón, Heriberto Moreno, Nelly Sigaut, and Martín Sánchez. The friendship and companionship of Ellen Kennedy, Rebeca de Sierra, and Susana de Sierra afforded me a respite from my archival and anthropological work.

Whatever its problems, Mexico City remains a splendid city, an appropriate capital for a country with this astonishing history. I am sure my enthusiasm emerges in part from the unstinting support I received from an array of colleagues there. At the Colegio de México, where I was a visiting researcher, I would like to single out Romana Falcón, Clara Lida, Engracia Loyo, and Alicia Hernández Chávez. I would also like to thank Adolfo Gilly and Roberto López at the Universidad Nacional Autónoma de México (UNAM), Carlos González and Arnulfo Embriz, who were then at the Centro de Estudios Históricos del Agrarismo en México, Susana Glantz, Eugenia Meyer, Luis Prieto, and Salvador Rueda. In understated ways the Toledo family, in particular Lila Toledo, has taught me much of what I know and cherish about the Mexican past.

Without archivists we are lost. I especially enjoy remembering Socorro Alonso Hurtado. Tough-minded, full of *gracia,* she was intent (if unsuccessful) on plying me with tequila as I worked in the Agrarian Reform Archives in Morelia. I would be remiss, however, if I stopped there. In Mexico City Guillermo Bermejo and the staff of the Archivo General de la Nación proved enormously helpful. Federico Lazarín Miranda of the Archivo Histórico de la Secretaría de Educación Pública was never too busy to participate in my seemingly endless quests for documentary information. I also appreciate the cheerful competence of the staffs at the Archivo de Reforma Agraria, the Hemeroteca de la Ciudad Universitaria, the Instituto de Geografía of the UNAM, the Biblioteca de la Dirección General de la Economía Agrícola, and the libraries of the Instituto Nacional de Antropología e Historia and of the Colegio de México.

In Morelia I would like to thank Angel Gutiérrez at the Universidad Michoacana de San Nicolás de Hidalgo, as well as the staffs of the Archivo General del Poder Ejecutivo, the Archivo del Poder Judicial, the Archivo Judicial del Estado de Michoacán, and the Archivo Histórico Manual Castañeda Ramírez. In Zamora I am grateful to two archivists, Alvaro Ochoa and then Martín Sánchez, who provided me with almost continual access to the Archivo Municipal de Zamora. I would also like to thank Don Alfonso Sahagún, who kindly granted me access to the Archivo de la Purísima Corazón in Zamora. And in Zamora Antonio Gobea allowed me to use uncatalogued agrarian reform documents.

Several people in Zamora graciously permitted me to utilize private documents, including Luis Vargas, José Lomelí, and the Castro Ramírez family, who allowed me to examine the private documents of their uncle, Juan Gutiérrez. In Jiquilpan at the Centro de Estudios de la Revolución Mexicana "Lázaro Cárdenas," A.C., Juan Ortíz Escamarilla was quite helpful. I am also grateful to Enrique Soto at the Archivo Municipal in Pátzcuaro and to Carmela Valadéz for arranging access to the disordered documents that constitute the municipal archive in Ario de Rayón.

Although this book is but distant kin to my 1988 Yale University dissertation, I would have been unable to grow as an intellectual without either my graduate training at Yale or the support of numerous granting agencies. It is a pleasure to acknowledge, then, the Yale University Fellowship, which funded my graduate study, two Inter-American Foundation Fellowships, and two fellowships granted by the Yale University History Department, which funded my initial research in Mexico. I am also very appreciative of the Woodrow Wilson Foundation's Charlotte Newcombe Doctoral Dissertation Fellowship, which supported the writing of my dissertation.

The generous support of a number of other granting agencies was absolutely crucial to the research and writing of this book. I am exceedingly grateful to the agencies that awarded me a Faculty Fulbright Research Fellowship, an American Council of Learned Societies Grant-in-Aid, a National Endowment for the Humanities Summer Stipend, and a University of Southern California Faculty Research and Innovation Fund grant. A visiting research fellowship at the Center for U.S. Mexican Studies at the University of California, San Diego, enabled me to write the book and to participate in a wonderful intellectual community.

While the woman in the agrarian reform archive knew little about me, I have come to feel that she was prescient regarding my good fortune. Certainly in the United States I have been blessed with remarkable teachers. Nobody who has studied with her at Yale could have failed to be inspired by either the brilliance or the courage of Emilia Viotti da Costa. I would also like to thank Friedrich Katz for his kindness in serving on my dissertation committee and for his generous comments on my work. If it is true that I first went to Jim Scott as something of a supplicant, there was a peculiarity to my request. In fact, I disagreed with one of his formulations regarding culture and secretly hoped he would bless my disagreement. Surprisingly enough, he did. Though Jim was never formally my teacher, his willingness to treat my ideas respectfully has meant a great deal to me. In particular I appreciate his refusal to treat dogma dogmatically, his willingness to discard his own previous perspectives, and his compassion for the peasantry. I have long benefited from Gil Joseph's keen grasp of the intricacies of the Mexican revolution and his gift for collegiality. It was his generous praise and probing questions that encouraged me to develop an even greater openness toward my readers. I can only hope that the result is a richer book.

Notwithstanding the contemporary prattle about "learning smart," there is something ineffable about the process of teaching, and, for that matter, about the process of friendship. That does not mean that there is nothing to be said about two of my teachers at Yale, Florencia Mallon and Steve Stern. Florencia possesses a special blend of empathy and intellectual poise. One of the things I most appreciate about her is her ability to listen intuitively. I frequently have sensed that she really heard what I was saying as I struggled to develop an empathic grasp of the complex peoples I write about. This was never truer than at a certain point during the writing of this book. The struggle to hear Mexicans' muted voices, to resist the forces from within and without that silenced them and threatened to silence me, had become acutely painful. I don't feel that I can adequately express my thanks for the ways Florencia encouraged me to hone the edges of my thought that felt most dangerous and controversial. In a related (!) sense, on many occasions Steve has been kind enough to train his acute, deeply humane intellect on my work. I have always found his comments at once reassuring and thought-provoking.

When it came time to write this book, it became clear that the story and its characters had somehow invaded me, had become a part of me. The task was to coax them out. I bring this up (and not without mixed feelings, since historians have become accustomed to viewing the literary process as somehow unmentionable) because the solitude required for such a process would have left me lackluster and depleted were it not for a number of very special friends and relatives. It is hard to resist the thought that one's friends are the warmest, most talented, and most sustaining group of people ever made. In the case of Alice Bullington-Davis, Clara Eschmann, Dana Frank, Velma García, Peter Guardino, Rebecca Horn, the late Bill Maynard, Daniel Nugent, and Sharon Reese, it is true. I also have been blessed with colleagues and friends who could be persuaded to share my fascination with the dancing women, with Ernesto Prado. It was gratifying to watch people like Joe Boone, Charlotte Furth, Lisa Silverman, and Dale Wall turn minds honed on other kinds of material to my work. I am grateful to five other exceptional USC colleagues, Elinor Accampo, Carolyn Dewald, Nora Hamilton, Philippa Levine, and Mauricio Mazón, for their continuing concern for my intellectual well-being. While I was writing this book I was somehow fortunate enough to stumble onto Carolyn Gurman. A tough-minded, compassionate teacher, she displayed an immense kindness as she listened to my multiple efforts to understand the puzzling ways Michoacanos' incomplete apprehensions of one another resulted in charged, sometimes damaging encounters. And I will never forget that even when my own confidence flagged, she believed in my work.

At the University of California Press, a number of editors eased the inherently difficult process of letting go of a manuscript that had come to feel like skin. Eileen McWilliam's excitement about this book was infectious. Her impressive editorial judgment and ample insights regarding cultural history lured me to Berkeley in the first place. When she left the press, I feared my book might become an orphan. That this did not occur is largely due to the intelligence and skill of my editors, Joanne Allen, Monica McCormick, and Erika Büky.

My family. I was fortunate enough to have this book accepted for publication by a number of presses, but before that occurred the book might as well have been an underground manifesto. I had talked about some of my ideas with a few friends and had presented one lonely chapter at a meeting of the American Historical Association and at the Program in Agrarian Studies at Yale. Otherwise the work remained unseen. In this nerve-racking period my sister, Joan Becker (who actually belongs in the category of beloved friend, as does my brother, Simon Becker), showered me with her characteristic humor, loyalty, and stylishness. And my parents, Carrie Popper Becker and Marvin Jerome Becker, not only provided me with models of gentleness, courage, and wit. They also nurtured my interest in people and places far from home.

Finally, there must be a special room in the afterlife for the Michoa-canos who shared their versions of history with me. I fear, however, that the room would house a wrestling match. One of the contestants would enter the room armed with reams of archival information. The others would have experienced the events themselves. There would be a level of contention, not about what really happened, for we are not destined to know that, but about the many possible occurrences. All of the participants, it seems, would recognize the danger of misrepresent-ing their histories. Yet without the conviction that histories are among the few things we have to offer one another, none of the contestants would have participated. The fear of misspeaking, of mishearing, would have overtaken them. Weighed against that kind of courage, my gratitude seems paltry indeed.

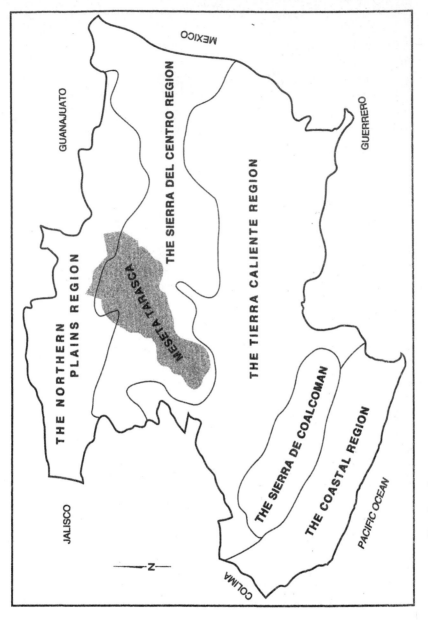

1. Regions of Michoacán

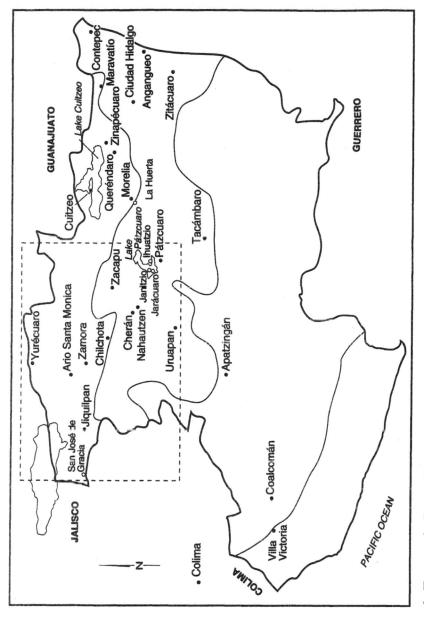

2. Towns and villages of Michoacán

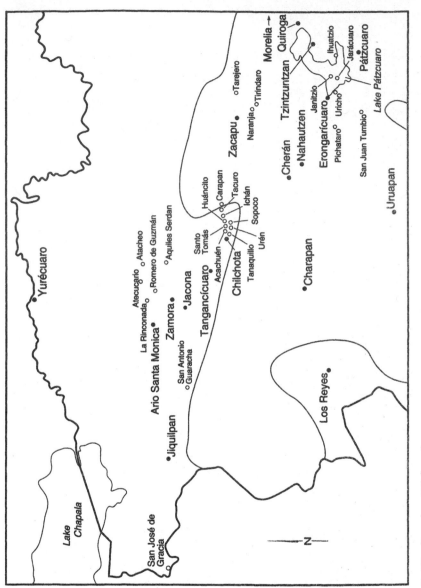

3. Northwestern Michoacán

CHAPTER ONE

Introduction

*Official History and the Myth
of Secular Redemption*

In the northwestern corner of prerevolutionary Michoacán, social abandon at times took on an almost biblical cast as women
trailed after reapers, gleaning spilled and forgotten stalks of wheat.[1] At
times, too, peasants foraged in nearby woods for roots and berries to
feed their children.[2] Yet when Mexican President Lázaro Cárdenas
promised to·deliver peasants from this heritage of social neglect, the
poor hardly embraced him. Rather, while Michoacán men accepted
lands offered by Cárdenas's cadre of revolutionaries, Michoacán
women often clung to their rosaries, as if to amulets dispelling evil.
Together these rural men and women (campesinos) came to forge
alliances with Cárdenas that transformed Mexico's postrevolutionary
state.

This story has not been told. Instead, Mexican governmental ideologues have offered up a myth of secular redemption.[3] In this myth,
Cárdenas is styled as something of a latter-day Jesus. As a redeemer, he
traveled from village to village performing wonders. Like no Mexican

1. Interviews with Mari Elena Verduzco de Peña, lifelong resident of Ario de Rayón
(formerly Ario Santa Monica), Michoacán, April 1990.
2. José Ventura González, Profesor inspector federal, Michoacán, caja 412, Archivo
Histórico de la Secretaría de Educación Pública.
3. Cardenistas drew on a variety of techniques to convey this mythology. They constructed an official revolutionary iconography, an official literature, and an official art.
Official themes filled pages of textbooks, such as Ignacio Ramírez, *El niño campesino:
Libro tercero, escuelas rurales* (Mexico City: Editorial Patria, 1939), and G. Lucio,

1

head of state since the hapless emperor Maximilian, he listened as campesinos detailed their troubles. Most spectacularly, while Cárdenas multiplied no loaves or fishes, he divided large estates into peasant plots. In response, campesinos crowded around to pay homage to him and his government.

A luminous image and a generous one, it has proved compelling to scholars. This is probably because Cárdenas's land redistribution—on paper, at least—appears to coincide with the radical hope at the heart of Emiliano Zapata's agrarian revolution.[4] And however important it has been to decry the easy romanticism of this portrait,[5] to ponder the psychological confusion that has led non-Mexicans and nonpeasants to take comfort in community struggles far from their doors,[6] the importance of such peasant struggles persists. Expressed simply, efforts to forge relatively egalitarian communities speak to deeply felt human needs for connection to neighbors, for a just return on labor.[7] To the

---

Simiente: Libro segundo para escuelas rurales (Mexico City: Editorial Patria, n.d.), and novels, including Gregorio López y Fuentes, *El indio,* José Rubén Romero, *Mi caballo, mi perro y mi rifle* (Barcelona, 1936). Statues of official heroes graced village squares. A revolutionary calendar commemorated official dates. For an extended analysis of this mythology, see Marjorie Becker, "Lázaro Cárdenas and the Mexican Counter-Revolution: The Struggle over Culture in Michoacán, 1934–1940" (Ph.D. diss., Yale University, 1988), ch. 1.

Just as the French revolutionaries established a revolutionary tradition that has endured to this day, so too the French were pioneers in the effort to create revolutionary culture. See Lynn Hunt, *Politics, Culture, and Class in the French Revolution* (Berkeley: University of California Press, 1984). For a provocative critique of the time-bound provincialism that leads historians of the French revolution (like their Mexican cousins) to reproduce the assumptions of the revolutionaries themselves, see François Furet, *Interpreting the French Revolution,* trans. Elborg Forster (Cambridge: Cambridge University Press, 1981).

4. As I attempt to demonstrate both in "Lázaro Cárdenas" and below, the implementation was a different matter.

5. Frans J. Schryer, *The Rancheros of Pisaflores: The History of a Peasant Bourgeoisie in Twentieth Century Mexico* (Toronto: University of Toronto Press, 1980); Alan Knight, *The Mexican Revolution,* 2 vols. (Cambridge: Cambridge University Press, 1986). For a particularly scathing attack on peasant hopes and ideals, an attack nurtured in the old battles pitting Stalinism against assorted leftist alternatives, see E. J. Hobsbawm, *Primitive Rebels: Studies in Archaic Forms of Social Protest in the Nineteenth and Twentieth Centuries* (New York: W. W. Norton, 1959).

6. For a sophisticated version of this approach, see Roger Bartra, *La jaula de la melancolía: Identidad y metamorfosis del mexicano* (Mexico City: Editorial Grijalbo, 1987). See also Guillermo Bonfil Batalla, *México profundo: una civilización negada* (Mexico City: Editorial Grijalbo, 1987).

7. These needs have been expressed politically in movements as geographically disparate as the U.S. Populist movement, the largest third-party movement ever to sweep

extent that scholarly work has recognized the diverse political expression of those needs, it has revealed a deeply humanistic face.[8]

At the same time, this image of Cárdenas delivering a human flock from hunger has led scholars to reproduce the official story.[9] While a debate surrounds Cárdenas's involvement with the peasantry, the controversy tends to focus on Cárdenas's motivation in redistributing the land. Was Cárdenas a rural democrat, as Frank Tannenbaum and Silvia and Nathaniel Weyl insisted so long ago?[10] Or was the Cárdenas period Nora Hamilton's "experiment with quasi socialist forms of ownership and control of the means of production" or Adolfo Gilly's second phase of a socialist revolution?[11] Or yet again, was Cárdenas the

---

the United States, Spanish anarchism, and the second phase of the U.S. feminist movement. On the Populists, see Lawrence C. Goodwyn, *Democratic Promise: The Populist Moment in America* (New York: Oxford University Press, 1976). On Spanish anarchism, see Clara Lida, *Anarquismo y revolución en la España del XIX* (Madrid: Siglo XXI de España, 1972), and Temma Kaplan, *The Anarchists of Andalusia, 1868–1903* (Princeton: Princeton University Press, 1977). On U.S. feminism, see Sara Evans, *Personal Politics: The Roots of Women's Liberation in the Civil Rights Movement and the New Left* (New York: Knopf, 1979).

8. See, for example, G. M. Joseph, *Revolution from Without: Yucatán, Mexico, and the United States, 1880–1924* (Cambridge: Cambridge University Press, 1982); Frank Tannenbaum, *Mexico: The Struggle for Peace and Bread* (New York: Knopf, 1950); John Womack Jr., *Zapata and the Mexican Revolution* (New York: Vintage Books, 1968); Friedrich Katz, *The Secret War in Mexico: Europe, the United States, and the Mexican Revolution* (Chicago: University of Chicago Press, 1981); even, notwithstanding the normative nonsense regarding "normative nonsense," Knight, *The Mexican Revolution*, 2:518.

9. Traditional practitioners of official history include Leslie Byrd Simpson (*Many Mexicos*, 4th ed. [Berkeley: University of California Press, 1966]); Charles Cumberland (*Mexico: The Struggle for Modernity* [New York: Oxford University Press, 1968]); Howard Cline (*Mexico: Revolution to Evolution* [New York: Oxford University Press, 1962]); and Daniel Cosío Villegas ("Mexico's Crisis," in *Is the Mexican Revolution Dead?* ed. Stanley Ross, 2d ed. [Philadelphia: Temple University Press, 1975]). The most recent rendition of this approach is Alan Knight's *The Mexican Revolution*, a sophisticated work whose great merit is to remind us of the popular nature of the revolution. And yet for all his sophistication, Knight shares with traditional historians a limited appreciation of the political cultures that led both to rebellion and to consolidation of postrevolutionary governments. As a result, Knight at times suggests, first, that peasants' economic suffering in and of itself was sufficient to produce rebellion and, second, that Constitutionalist leaders and peasant fighters automatically shared identical interests.

10. See Frank Tannenbaum, *Peace by Revolution: Mexico after 1910* (1933; reprint, New York: Columbia University Press, 1966); idem, *Mexico;* and Silvia Weyl and Nathaniel Weyl, *The Reconquest of Mexico: The Years of Lázaro Cárdenas* (New York: Oxford University Press, 1939).

11. Nora Hamilton, *The Limits of State Autonomy: Post-Revolutionary Mexico* (Princeton: Princeton University Press, 1982), 140; Adolfo Gilly, *La revolución interrumpida* (Mexico City: El Caballito, 1971).

populist demagogue described by Arturo Anguiano and Arnaldo Córdova?[12]

Preoccupied by this image of Cárdenas as either redeemer or tarnished messiah, scholars have shared an insufficiently political image of the peasantry. Out of a diverse and contentious population repeatedly rising to rectify a varied array of grievances,[13] a stripped-down image of the land-hungry peasant emerges. In response to their need for sustenance peasants enact a single political sensibility. Rising out of hunger, they flock to the leaders who feed them.[14] The suggestion is that once their nutritional requirements have been met, peasants no longer participate in the construction of the state. State making, in turn, is portrayed as fairly aloof from peasant concerns.[15] In short, there is a strange, exponential Pavlovianism here, the state responding to peasants responding to their bellies.

Clerical imagery seems appropriate for a place as deeply and variously Catholic as northwestern Michoacán. Yet in examining the Cardenista effort to remake Michoacán peasants, we find that Cardenismo

12. Arturo Anguiano, *El estado y la política obrera del cardenismo* (Mexico City: Editorial Era, 1975); Arnaldo Córdova, *La política de masas del cardenismo* (Mexico City: Serie Popular Era, 1974).

13. For the late colonial period, see William B. Taylor, *Drinking, Homicide, and Rebellion in Colonial Mexican Villages* (Stanford: Stanford University Press, 1979). For the nineteenth century, see Jean Meyer, *Problemas campesinos y revueltas agrarias, 1821–1910* (Mexico City: SEP, 1973); and Leticia Reina, *Las rebeliones campesinas en México* (Mexico City: Siglo XXI Editores, 1980). And in Jarácuaro Michoacán some peasants sought to remedy spiritual, political, and economic grievances in a series of encounters with Lázaro Cárdenas. For an analysis highlighting peasant ideological flexibility in this instance, see Marjorie Becker, "Black and White and Color: *Cardenismo* and the Search for a *Campesino* Ideology," *Comparative Studies in Ideology and History* 29 (1987): 453–65.

14. The emphasis on campesino "creaturely" characteristics is strongly reminiscent of Domingo Sarmiento in *Civilización y barbarie* (Buenos Aires: Librería El Ateneo, 1952).

15. This has been particularly true of David A. Brading and some of the scholars who joined with him to produce *Caudillo and Peasant in the Mexican Revolution* (Cambridge: Cambridge University Press, 1980). For them, the only relevant historical actors are the leaders of the victorious Constitutionalist coalition. Indeed, if the official storytelling technique is to minimize campesino interests, the caudillo scholars' strategy is to ignore them entirely. While the careers of caudillos are amply documented, campesinos' demands, their ideology, the nature of their leverage with caudillos, even the campesinos themselves, disappear entirely. Of particular interest in this regard, all in Brading's volume, are Brading's introduction, "National Politics and the Populist Tradition," and his preface; Ian Jacobs, "Rancheros of Guerrero: The Figueroa Brothers in the Revolution," 76–91; Linda B. Hall, "Alvaro Obregón and the Agrarian Movement, 1912–1920," 124–39; and Dudley Ankerson, "Saturnino Cedillo: A Traditional Caudillo in San Luis Potosí," 140–68.

should not be compared to lightning-bolt messianic activity. Rather, a comparison to the work of the sixteenth-century Spanish missionaries seems more apt.[16] For, like the sixteenth-century friars, the Cardenistas in Michoacán determined to undermine the previous ideological order and to create institutions reflecting their state-making project. And again like the early friars, Cardenistas sought popular identification with their program.[17] Expressed in more contemporary terms, the Cardenista effort to bring revolution to Michoacán might be called a hegemonic project.[18]

Yet how were Cardenistas to construct hegemony? Just as it has been a troublesome, if dimly perceived, historical question, so too it was a troublesome historical inheritance for Cárdenas. The issue first emerged for the leaders of the victorious Constitutionalist armies of the 1910–20 Mexican revolution. Led by members of the middle and the upper class, the Constitutionalists defeated the popular armies of Emiliano Zapata and Pancho Villa. Nonetheless, the specter of the popular armies was to haunt the Constitutionalist victors for two decades. What would it take to gain peasant allegiance to the postrevolutionary government?

16. Some of the Cardenistas themselves compared their work to that of the early missionaries. For an analysis of this tendency see Becker, "Black and White and Color," and chapter 4 below.

17. To be sure, the literature of the so-called spiritual conquest of the Aztecs yields far more concern with the friars' dogged determination to create identification with their soul-saving project than with the more power-laden effort to develop alliances. This is because the project has widely been conceptualized as an encounter between two homogeneous peoples embodying the spirit of their respective cultures. Based on scholarly determinations that a single moment in time represented Aztec and Spanish cultures—as though any photograph ever encapsulates human life—the resulting studies reveal limited appreciation for the cultural exchanges that occurred and specifically for the ways the Indians *always* affected, and at times transformed, the terms of domination. For the classic example of this tendency, informed by considerable identification with the Christianization project, see Robert Ricard, *The Spiritual Conquest of Mexico: An Essay on the Apostolate and the Evangelizing Methods of the Mendicant Orders in New Spain, 1523–1572*, trans. Leslie Byrd Simpson (Berkeley: University of California Press, 1966). Reversing Ricard's bias, Tzvetan Todorov develops a morally sophisticated meditation on the encounter between Spaniards and Indians in *The Conquest of America: The Question of the Other*, trans. Richard Howard (New York: Harper Colophon, 1985). Nonetheless, for Todorov, Spanish brutality emerges as an inevitable realization of what he posits as a Spanish mental superiority over the Aztecs. For a fascinating example of the Yucatán Mayas' ingenious yet tragic responses to spiritual conquest, see Inga Clendinnen's elegant *Ambivalent Conquests: Maya and Spaniard in Yucatán, 1517–1570* (Cambridge: Cambridge University Press, 1987).

18. I have always viewed theory as intellectuals' efforts to grapple with complex realities. This means that the notion of seizing a theory and applying it to the object of

Dogged by old images of a barbarous peasantry, stunned by the persistence and the longevity of the peasants' clamor, throughout the twenties Constitutionalist leaders recognized only that peasants called for sustenance. This was particularly true of Alvaro Obregón and Plutarco Elías Calles, Constitutionalist leaders who dominated the Mexican presidency from 1920 through 1934.[19] Then came the 1926–29 Cristero rebellion. Responding to governmental anticlerical legislation and priestly exhortation, peasants throughout western Mexico rose to the cry *¡Viva Cristo Rey!* (Long Live Christ the King!). Notwithstanding the conflicts that historically threatened peasant solidarity, ragtag bands of diverse campesinos had managed to unite. As though the figure of Cristo Rey on their banners lent courage and solace, they fought to heal an array of spiritual, economic, and political wounds. Turning the anger often directed toward neighbors against peasants fighting for the government, Cristeros mounted a three-year guerrilla war. Before it was over, perhaps as many as eighty thousand peasants died.[20]

---

study has been an alien approach. There is a dialectical relationship between historical subjects and their activities and the ways of ordering them. In regard to hegemony, some of those ways have been stimulated by the work of the Frankfurt school, Gramsci, Genovese, Marcuse, Laclau, and Mouffe. See, for example, Antonio Gramsci, *Selections from the Prison Notebooks,* ed. and trans. Quintin Hoare and Geoffrey Nowell Smith (New York: International Publishers, 1971); Ernesto Laclau and Chantal Mouffe, *Hegemony and Socialist Strategy: Towards a Radical Democratic Politics* (New York: Verso, 1989); Eugene Genovese, *Roll, Jordan, Roll: The World the Slaves Made* (New York: Vintage Books, 1976); and Herbert Marcuse, *One-Dimensional Man: Studies in the Ideology of Advanced Industrial Society* (Boston: Beacon, 1966). For an often poetic rendition of the effects of hegemony, see Walter Benjamin, *Illuminations,* trans. Harry Zohn (New York: Harcourt, Brace & World, 1968).

I would particularly like to single out Laclau and Mouffe's work for its appreciation of subordinate classes' capacities to forge alliances that can at times affect the terms of domination. Moreover, their work serves as a corrective to many scholars' reflexive tendency to grant priority to economic causality. In addition, in "The Conflictual Construction of Community: Gender, Ethnicity, Hegemony," ch. 3 of *Peasant and Nation: The Making of Post-Colonial Mexico and Peru* (Berkeley: University of California Press, 1995), 63–88, Florencia E. Mallon uses the concept of hegemony in a provocative and inspiring way.

19. For a fine analysis of the political culture from which the victorious Sonoran revolutionary leaders emerged, see Héctor Aguilar Camín, "The Relevant Tradition: Sonoran Leaders in the Revolution," in Brading, *Caudillo,* 92–123. On Obregón's efforts to activate that culture in response to peasants' battles over land, see Linda Hall, "Alvaro Obregón and the Politics of Mexican Land Reform," *Hispanic American Historical Review* 60:2 (1980): 213–38.

20. In *La Cristiada,* trans. Aurelio Garzón del Camino, 2d ed., 3 vols. (Mexico City: Siglo XXI Editores, 1974), a work of great sensitivity and courage, Jean Meyer

What the Cristeros forcefully demonstrated was that the problem had been misconstrued. Constitutionalists faced no economic problem in the narrow sense.[21] Although the problem has not been conceptualized in these terms, Cristeros, like the revolutionary campesinos before them, presented Constitutionalists with an intellectual problem. Postrevolutionary governmental hegemony would rest on knowledge of campesino cultures.

Campesino cultures? What can this mean? A term misunderstood by the Cardenistas themselves,[22] *culture* refers to a people's evolving interpretation of the world and the way that interpretation shapes the contours of everyday life. To be sure, "a people's interpretation" connotes images of a homogeneous peasantry, placid as silk, and *culture* has long suggested shared values.[23] Indeed, it is difficult to resist Clifford Geertz's insistence that culture is the public practice of those values. A sober, limited definition, it refuses the temptation to read the heart of the other.[24]

However, for historians pondering Geertz, a central problem per-

---

provides much of the evidence for this interpretation. In addition, *La Cristiada* reveals Meyer's passionate identification with his historical subjects. It is this kind of love for ordinary people, rather than a shared ideology or culture, as Meyer insists (2:96), that links Meyer's work with that of Womack. Yet for all its originality, *La Cristiada* is flawed by Meyer's insistence that campesinos shared an identical understanding of Catholicism, itself a perfect reflection of reality (3:307, 310). Meyer's response to the strongest evidence to the contrary—the fact that campesinos fought for the government against the Cristeros—is a masterpiece of Manichean thought. Progovernmental campesinos, Meyer maintains, were manipulated (3:82), whereas Cristeros embodied authentic Catholic purity, even—perhaps most fully—when they cut off their foes' genitals.

21. There is a deep irony to the *way* Latin Americanists have misconstrued this problem. Men and women whose stock in trade is the mental universe have persistently shrunk peasants' mental universes to issues of subsistence. See for example, John Tutino, *From Insurrection to Revolution in Mexico: Social Bases of Agrarian Violence, 1750–1910* (Princeton: Princeton University Press, 1986). Among non–Latin Americanists, even a scholar as creative as Pierre Bourdieu conceptualizes culture as a transposition—in the musical sense—of material needs. See Bourdieu, *Distinction: A Social Critique of the Judgement of Taste,* trans. Richard Nice (Cambridge: Harvard University Press, 1984) and idem, *Outline of a Theory of Practice,* trans. Richard Nice (Cambridge: Harvard University Press, 1977).

22. See chapter 4 below.

23. For a deeply pessimistic view of the possibilities of subordinate classes' creativity in the light of just such shared values, see Sidney W. Mintz, *Sweetness and Power: The Place of Sugar in Modern History* (New York: Viking Penguin, 1985).

24. Clifford Geertz, *The Interpretation of Cultures* (New York: Basic Books, 1973), 10. It should be remembered that this is a retreat, not something to be glorified. Praxis may be all that we can know or guess about, but it should not be mistaken for all that there is.

sists: how do people come to share values? While Geertz acknowledges the existence of diverse and conflicting cultural behavior—there are those sheep stealers, after all—the conflicts tend to be waged between cultural adepts and outsiders.[25] Yet for scholars of Mexican peasant communities, this dichotomy will not do. The premise of colonialism is extraction, and the common scenario has been one of outsiders bullying insiders into submission. Nonetheless, campesinos confined within village boundaries have not proved immune to the temptations of theft and exploitation of their neighbors. In short, Mexican peasant cultures can in no way be viewed as static oases of calm.

Moreover, Spanish colonialism also created—and partially reproduced—a welter of sociological distinctions. It is common to refer to such variations among population groups as mosaic tiles, but in thinking of Michoacán's rural population, the image of puzzle pieces seems more useful. For in Michoacán the divisions were so extensive that elites, whether priests or Cardenistas, would again and again ponder how campesinos could fit together. Geography flung them into dozens of small villages. Ethnic variation was a factor, for while most campesinos were mestizos, one-fifth of the 1920 population was classified as Tarascan Indians.[26] Almost all were poor, but the population was marked by hundreds of minute economic distinctions. Similarly, while most men worked on large estates, their jobs ranged from water carrier to cowboy. Not least, men and women were assigned different lots in life. While such variations would seem to guarantee conflict, it is still pertinent to consider the specific sources of dispute among neighbors. What precisely fueled their persistent strife? And how could they come to share cultural perspectives?

Inheriting the task of pacifying the smoldering west, Cárdenas urgently needed to understand the peasant cultures that fueled both conflict and consensus. It was just as important that he recognize that any effort at rural pacification would itself be culturally driven. Yet these notions eluded him. And as the problem of ignorance, even partial ignorance, is that it refuses to recognize itself, Cárdenas plunged ahead. Oblivious to the cultural nature of his response, he called for what amounted to the cultural transformation of the countryside. He

---

25. Ibid., 8–9, 18.
26. These population figures are based on the 1921 Mexican census and are drawn from Fernando Foglio Miramontes, *Geografía económica agrícola del estado de Michoacán*, 4 vols. (Mexico City: Editorial cultura, 1936) 2:138.

mobilized a cadre—teachers, agricultural agents, rural political bosses (caciques). They were to overhaul land tenure arrangements, to dispel illiteracy, to remake campesino habits. In addition, they were to revise peasant assessments of the world—that amorphous realm of allegiance, hope, desire. Most importantly, Cárdenas called on his cadre to develop peasant acceptance of this human reconstruction.

The result was that the countryside was turned into a schoolroom. Far from another dowdy foray into the history of teachers instructing children in their first letters, Cardenistas constructed lessons out of their own cultural perspectives. More precisely, Michoacán Cardenistas were a diverse group of men and women, mestizos and Indians touched by the historically rooted cultural clash between liberalism and Catholicism in Michoacán. Because of their diversity, Cardenistas would develop sundry approaches to forging revolution. However, as renegades from Catholicism, Michoacán Cardenista leaders set an anti-clerical tone that dominated the approach to cultural transformation.

This meant that many Cardenistas stumbled—without fully appreciating their clumsiness—onto a peasantry trained in a very specific form of Catholicism. It was a symbolic system largely based on gender that called for a self-denial that the priests referred to as purity. That is, Catholic elites had developed a symbolic system that depended on an understanding and acceptance both of women's actual abnegation and of that abnegation as a metaphor designed to restrain the potential nonconformity of Indians, peasants, workers, all subordinate groups. In return, priests held out an infinite array of consolations. However painful the wound, the church promised the balm of redemption.

Baffled by Catholic enthusiasms, Cardenistas developed an awkward form of government, here liberating, there grievously exploitative. This posed a grave challenge to the campesinos. Hardly immune to the exploitation, campesinos were also alert to the benefits of allying with Cárdenas. The price would be revealing knowledge of their cultures, knowledge that to an extent had served as a final refuge against abuse and misunderstanding. In a series of sober, premeditated moves, campesinos relinquished part of their knowledge. Schooling the revolutionaries in their cultures, they attained greater participation in the national political arena. At the same time, they enabled Lázaro Cárdenas to bind them—and peasants all over Mexico—more securely to the postrevolutionary government.

CHAPTER TWO

A Culture of Purity
and Redemption

*Not common speech . . . but the uncommon speech of paradise,
tongue in which oracles speak to beggars and pilgrims.*
Denise Levertov

*Seek for food and clothing first, then the Kingdom of God shall be
added unto you.*
Hegel

To wander into the state of Michoacán in any season is
to be seized by the prominence of mountains. Relentless, imposing,
their peaks define the skyline. From east to west burnt-out craters of
the central volcanic axis dissect the state. In the southwest the mountains of the Sierra Madre parallel the Pacific Ocean. Toward the north,
the shadows of the pine-covered ranges dwarf stalks of corn growing
along their slopes. Although at times it seems that the state's numerous lakes have eclipsed the mountains' visual significance, suddenly the
ridges' images reappear upon the water. Even the valley floors are
punctuated by stray hills, constant reminders of the mountainous presence. There is a ponderous attraction to all this, as the jagged ridges
cut off and displace access to light. Where the mountains cluster
together, they create thick, foreboding shadows. Where they loosen
their grip, retiring to the background, they soften and whiten the light
after the region's persistent summer rains.

Yet for all their grandeur, the mountains have been cumbersome
neighbors. For centuries they made the business of living on a small
scale difficult for the state's native Tarascan Indians. Even today some

of these difficulties persist. As arbiters of the state's climates, they force the Tarascan women living among them to drape themselves in woolen shawls against the cold. They dictate the state's growing patterns, willingly sharing their slopes with corn, stubbornly refusing the cultivation of wheat. They are equally cranky regarding settlement patterns, occasionally allowing a wooden hut to perch along a ledge, more frequently pushing campesinos to build small communities in their recesses.

Neither the Tarascans' living arrangements nor the mountains' beauty preoccupied the sixteenth-century Spanish conquerors. They had come to subdue the land and its people. There was Nuño de Guzmán, the conqueror who has found his place in the annals of cruelty. And however exceptional he may have been, his companions were frequently rapacious. At best, they were universally out for a profit, and they intended to make nature their accomplice.

The mountains proved a worthy match. Cutting up the state, defining the geographic regions, they determined where profit would come easily and where it would not. As the Spaniards soon discovered, only the state's northern plains region would serve their purposes. There the land is relatively flat and well watered. Beyond, the mountains recur, bordering the region to the south with the central mountain range, the *sierra del centro,* which extends from the eastern to the western boundaries of the state. South of the sierra lies Michoacán's third geographic region, the tropical hot lands of the *tierra caliente,* bordered by the Sierra Madre to the southwest. Finally, a strip of coastal land is located between the Sierra Madre and the Pacific Ocean in the state's extreme southwest.[1]

By the eve of the Cardenista effort to reconstruct the state, the Spaniards and their descendants had long since learned to use the mountains as permeable fences. Making the northern plains area a sort of headquarters, they had constructed lucrative haciendas out of what once had been Tarascan land. This was particularly true of the northwestern corner of the state, dominated by the town of Zamora. Yet they refrained from building haciendas on a nearby plateau, the *meseta tarasca.* Located across the mountains, the plateau was studded with old volcanic cones running into basins or long depressions. By the

1. For information on Michoacán geography, see Claude Bataillon, *Les regions geographiques au Mexique* (Paris: Institut des Hautes Études de L'Amerique Latine, 1967); and Genaro Correa Pérez, *Geografía del estado de Michoacán,* 3 vols. (Morelia: Gobierno del Estado de Michoacán, 1974).

early twentieth century, Tarascan Indians had taken refuge in this remnant of their former lands, living in three areas of the *meseta:* the mountain villages, the villages surrounding Lake Pátzcuaro, and the villages of the Zacapu marsh.

In other words, over time social relations in the northwestern region of the state had taken on that poignant, circuslike quality that writers such as Gabriel García Márquez have evoked so well.[2] In the center ring were the main performers, the wealthy landowners. Owners of the large estates that dominated the state economy, these people lived in the best houses, fronting on the plazas. Their homes were spacious, frequently sporting two kitchens, always staffed by a number of servants and supplied with bountiful foodstuffs—chicken, eggs, chocolate, tamales.[3] But the further one went from the plaza, the sparer lives became. Behind the most conspicuous houses were the dour homes of the middling mestizos, men who were muleteers, hacienda administrators, merchants, and the wives and servants who performed domestic chores. If the memory of Cardenista teacher Tomás Rico Cano is reliable, they may have owned a few chairs, a table or so, but little else.[4] These were people who ate reasonably well but whose children, the daughters in particular, regularly lacked shoes.[5]

---

2. See, for example, Gabriel García Márquez, "La increíble y triste historia de la cándida Eréndira y de su abuela desalmada," in *La increíble y triste historia de la cándida Eréndira y de su abuela desalmada* (Barcelona: Barral Editores, 1972), 95–163; and idem, *One Hundred Years of Solitude,* trans. Gregory Rabassa (New York: Harper & Row, 1970). For a darker rendition of this thematic approach, see Juan Rulfo, *El llano en llamas,* 2d ed. (Mexico City: Fondo de Cultura Económica, 1980).

3. For the material culture of regional elites, I interviewed members of that group, including Concepción Méndez, Mari Elena Verduzco de Peña, and Francisco González Esquivel. Persuaded that outsiders can be alert to certain aspects of cultural life that are obscure to insiders, I cross-checked through interviews with Tomás Rico Cano and Jesús Múgica Martínez, members of Michoacán's diffuse lower middle class. Interviews with Concepción Méndez, Ario de Rayón, Michoacán, June 1990; Mari Elena Verduzco de Peña, Ario de Rayón, April 1990; Francisco González Esquivel, Zamora, Michoacán, August 1985; Tomás Rico Cano, Morelia, Michoacán, June, August 1990; and Jesús Múgica Martínez, Morelia, June, August 1990. See also Luis González's description of the dietary habits of the Mexican rural bourgeoisie in *San José de Gracia: Mexican Village in Transition,* trans. John Upton (Austin: University of Texas Press, 1972), 88.

4. On the material culture of middling mestizos, I interviewed Múgica Martínez, Rico Cano, and Constantino Murillo, informants who identified themselves in those terms. I cross-checked by interviewing elite campesinos Verduzco de Peña and Méndez. Interviews with Constantino Murillo, Morelia, July 1985, March 1990; Rico Cano, June, August 1990; Múgica Martínez, June, August 1990; Verduzco de Peña, April 1990; and Méndez, June 1990.

5. Interviews with Verduzco de Peña, April 1990; and Rico Cano, August 1990.

Past this tentative middle class lived the mestizo men and women who had been cast adrift, styled sideshow acts. Please understand that this is no metaphoric flourish. On the eve of Cardenismo, numerous Michoacán men and women "lacked the barest security that their children would be nourished," as a school inspector put it.[6] Even the everyday domestic arrangements reveal significant disparities in wealth. Crowded in the alleys or adrift toward the estates were the homes of the peons. Their sons wore the minimal white pajamalike outfits and the huaraches so prevalent in the period.[7] In even worse straits, as we shall see, were the Tarascans, wandering into town, then returning to their sparse homes across the mountains.

The Marriage of Piety and Property

Michoacán campesinos were heirs to traditions of popular insurgency. As recently as the nineteenth century their ancestors had waged energetic battles against outsiders threatening their landed and religious prerogatives. Particularly in the regions populated by Tarascan Indians, these grievances were fresh. And yet by the twentieth century many campesinos had been reduced to tatters and subservience. Relegated to a set piece, they performed the same motions with dreary monotony. What led to such woodenness?

In the absence of inborn humility, landlords and priests had devised a host of inducements to look upward. To follow that gaze is to find that towering over this tawdry collection of sideshows was the plaza, dominated by a central building, the church. Even in a country where such connections were routine, the constancy of the marriage between piety and property in the Zamora area was remarkable. From the early years of the Porfiriato (1876–1911) profits gleaned from agriculture were plowed into the church in the form of alms, loans, tithing.[8] For

---

6. Pablo Silva, Profesor inspector federal, Michoacán, caja 412, Archivo Histórico de la Secretaría de Educación Pública (AHSEP), Mexico City.

7. Interviews with Múgica Martínez and Rico Cano, August 1990.

8. Gustavo Verduzco, "Zamora en el Porfiriato: Una expresión liberal de los conservadores," in *El dominio de las minorías: República restaurada y Porfiriato,* by Anne Staples et al. (Mexico City: El Colegio de México, 1989), 60–61. Notwithstanding scholarly reticence on this point, there is no small irony in the fact that Michoacán hacendados, staunch supporters of the conservatives in the 1858–61 Reform War, themselves profited from the Reform Law provisions that privatized Indian lands.

its size Zamora boasted an exceptionally large number of clerical institutions—churches, orphanages, and schools. Landowners received
their formal education in clerical institutions. So did incipient priests,
men often related to the hacendados.[9]

The revolution did not undermine this connection. In fact, both
clerical and landed property remained largely intact. Yet while Michoacán was no major revolutionary theater,[10] it was scarcely innocent of
revolutionary hope and bitterness. Local conditions bred at least two
strains of revolutionary conflict. In the north, where the majority of
the population was submerged in landlessness, a handful of rebels promoted a shadowy liberalism.[11] In the nearby Tarascan regions, the revolution in Michoacán rekindled the nineteenth-century liberal effort to
privatize Indian land. Then too, when Michoacanos looked beyond
their boundaries they saw a country awash in rebellion.[12]

More than actual Michoacán skirmishes, the specter of revolution
triggered a longstanding clerical anxiety. With the arrival of liberal soldiers in the 1858–61 War of the Reform, priests hastened to the ideological battlefield. In their determination to defend an inequitable status quo against the liberal challenge, they plucked up the Virgin Mary
and outfitted her for battle. Stressing her alleged purity, they remade
her into a guardian of the status quo. The campaign climaxed with her
1851 coronation as the patron saint of Zamora.[13]

The revolution evoked similar pastoral panic. Once again Michoacán priests responded with a fervent yet contradictory effort to reproduce stasis over time. Their strategy, expressed in pastoral letters, fies-

9. Ibid., 61.
10. In this regard, the work of Gerardo Sánchez, Alvaro Ochoa, and Angel Gutiérrez seems miscast. It appears that their sympathy for the politics of the minority of
socialists in the state has led them to exaggerate socialism's popular significance during
the period. See Alvaro Ochoa, *Los agraristas de Atacheo* (Zamora: El Colegio de Michoacán, 1989); and Angel Gutiérrez, José Napoleon Guzmán Avila, and Gerardo Sánchez
D., *La cuestión agraria: Revolución y contrarrevolución en Michoacán (tres ensayos)*
(Morelia: Universidad Michoacana de San Nicolás de Hidalgo, 1984).
11. Heriberto Moreno García, *Guaracha: Tiempos viejos, tiempos nuevos* (Zamora:
Colegio de Michoacán/FONAPAS Michoacán, 1980), 49.
12. See Alan Knight, *The Mexican Revolution,* 2 vols. (Cambridge: Cambridge University Press, 1986).
13. For a discussion of the nineteenth-century establishment of the cult of the
Purísima, see Jesús Tapia Santamaría, "El culto de la Purísima: Un mito de fundación"
(paper presented at VII Reunión de historiadores mexicanos y norteamericanos, Oaxaca,
Mexico, 23–26 October 1985).

tas, articles, and Sunday Mass, was to draw on a series of characters understood as eternally the same, eternally responsive to the same dilemmas. The Catholic roster provided alternatives for these figures, including God, Jesus, and a wide variety of saints. But because priests sought an image that could convey both authority and mercy, they often remade and celebrated the Virgin.

The Virgin was a woman of many faces.[14] Michoacán priests at times referred to the Virgin of Guadalupe, the Virgin considered distinctively Mexican because of her miraculous sixteenth-century appearance to an impoverished Mexican Indian, Juan Diego.[15] But just as frequently this woman who had originally been dark, Semitic, and poor was recast. Painting her skin in tones of ivory, icon makers whitened her, presenting a striking contrast to her real-life appearance, and to the dark-skinned Tarascans and mestizos of the area.[16] In her new life she appeared as a delicate blonde. As they dressed her in the finest silks and crowned her in delicate gold, her poverty became a thing of the past.[17] She no longer had to work, unless riding in processions through the dusty streets of Michoacán villages and towns is to be considered work.

Come Sunday, priests and villagers created a setting conducive to the role she would play. During these weekly celebrations of Mass, many priests attempted to place God's seal of approval on the hierarchical organization of the towns. For the wealthy would arrive, dressed in their best clothing. Refusing to leave ritual to chance, the rich crowded their way to the front, establishing themselves closest to the

14. For a perceptive exploration of the ambivalence surrounding the Virgin as a female model, see Marina Warner, *Alone of All Her Sex: The Myth and Cult of the Virgin Mary* (New York: Knopf, 1976).

15. See, for example, "Acta de consegración a la Santísima Virgen de Guadalupe"; Othón Núñez y Zarate, circular 52, 20 November 1921; and Luis E. García, Vicario Gen. to V. Cabildo, sacerdotes y fieles de la diócesis de Zamora, 1 November 1917, all in caja 13, Sacramental y Disciplina, 1901–30, Archivo de la Purísima Corazón (APC), Zamora, Michoacán.

16. In *Imagined Communities: Reflections on the Origin and Spread of Nationalism* (London: Verso, 1983), 28–29, Benedict Anderson suggests that the medieval Italian and Flemish artistic renditions of the Virgin reflected the surrounding society in terms of skin tone and costume because Catholics understood God's coming as a present-day event, lacking a historical past. Still, considering the Catholic Church's history of racism in Latin America, it is hard to shy away from the conclusion that white men could understand God—and his relatives—only if he had a white face.

17. This iconographic evidence is based on participant observation of the churches in Zamora, Ario, Pátzcuaro, Morelia, and Jarácuaro, Michoacán, in 1984, 1985, and 1990.

priest and to the image of the Virgin. Poor people, if they were able to come at all—and if their frequent lack of shoes did not embarrass them in such a setting—congregated in the back. Visually, at least, wealth was immediately transformed into proximity to the men who designated themselves God's representatives and to the woman they would use to defend the status quo.[18]

For in their texts—the sermons and pastoral letters they delivered to their listeners—the priests seemed to bring Mary to life as sort of a spiritual La Malinche, a woman who shed her rags to console the rich.[19] There she was presented as La Purísima, the Virgin Mary in her most chaste aspect.[20] In sermon after sermon priests re-created an image of purity and obedience. As the "immaculate daughter of God, the Virgin mother of God, the purest wife of God the Holy Spirit," she was chaste. As a woman who allowed the male God to have his way with her, she was portrayed as a model for women, who were to be "submissive to their husbands."[21] Then too, she was generous beyond generosity. As she reputedly told the faithful, "I am a loving and tender mother for whomever asks my help in their pain and suffering."[22]

18. Interviews with Verduzco de Peña, April 1990; and Méndez, June, November 1990.

19. Notwithstanding Tzvetan Todorov's intriguing reconstruction of Malinche as the mother of Mexican and Western biculturalism, here I draw on the traditional understanding of Malinche as traitor to her people. See Tzvetan Todorov, *The Conquest of America: The Question of the Other*, trans. Richard Howard (New York: Harper Colophon, 1985), for the argument that Malinche bridged the divide between a certain literal grasp of formula, which could transform the order of things if it was performed with no corruption, and modern efforts to manipulate the universe. For evidence that numerous Indians knew how to use discourse for their own ends, at least in the immediate post-Conquest era, see Charles Gibson, *The Aztecs under Spanish Rule: A History of the Indians of the Valley of Mexico, 1519–1810* (Stanford: Stanford University Press, 1964); Inga Clendinnen, *Aztecs: An Interpretation* (Cambridge: Cambridge University Press, 1991); and on Peru, Steve J. Stern, *Peru's Indian Peoples and the Challenge of Spanish Conquest: Huamanga to 1640* (Madison: University of Wisconsin Press, 1982).

20. I have explored some of these ideas in an article analyzing purity and its discontents as seen by a range of Ario women. See Marjorie Becker, "Torching La Purísima, Dancing at the Altar: The Construction of Revolutionary Hegemony in Michoacán, 1934–1940," in *Everyday Forms of State Formation: Revolution and the Negotiation of Rule in Modern Mexico*, ed. Gilbert M. Joseph and Daniel Nugent (Durham, N.C.: Duke University Press, 1994).

21. Quotation in "Carta pastoral colectiva de los prelados de la provincia de Michoacán," 1920, caja 11, APC. It is important to remember that while this archive houses documents illuminating much about varying clerical perspectives on nineteenth- and twentieth-century events, the documents remain largely undated and unnumbered.

22. Caja 13, Sacramental y Disciplina, 1901–30, APC.

While women's sexual behavior was of considerable concern to the church, clerical messages were not simply for and about women. Rather, the priests used Mary and the message of purity to establish a fence, walling out nonconformity. The priests very clearly manipulated the notion of "purity" to cast the "impure"—the nonconformists—beyond the pale. Most dramatically, the church feared socialism, and in sermons the priests reproduced the Pope's antisocialist stance. Reiterating the doctrinaire view regarding private property, the Pope contended that "as men are naturally unequal in strength and intelligence, so they must be unequal in terms of what they own; the church commands that property rights, rooted in nature, are inviolable."[23]

In addition, a host of everyday delinquencies raised hierarchical hackles. Priests were particularly concerned about deception, and false pretenses seemed to abound. Foreigners, sporting credentials from the Eastern—not the Roman Catholic—church begged for alms.[24] Women, though specifically prohibited from singing in church, "tried to pass themselves off as members of the community by positioning themselves with the faithful and singing their hearts out."[25] And campesinos played sacred music on a host of instruments "never permitted in church, such as kettledrums and tambourines."[26]

A rather conventional Catholicism enabling the rich to hoard up lands and people, relegating the desires of the poor to a shadowy future? To be sure. Indeed, Zamora bishop Manuel Fulcheri was not above touting the Catholic system of reward and punishment. As he frankly put it, such a regimen was the only way to get people to comply with Catholicism's demands. While acknowledging the gravity of hellfire as punishment, he stressed the desirability of the reward. He claimed that "The prize which Catholicism offers is complete eternal happiness, exactly what people who are God's children deserve."[27]

And yet for all her pearls, Mary was constructed as something more

23. "Carta pastoral colectiva de los prelados de la provincia de Michoacán," 1920, caja 11, APC.

24. Luis E. García, "Los ordinarios no permitan en sus diocesas que algún oriental de cualquier orden. . .," circular, caja 13, Sacramental y Disciplina, APC.

25. *Reglamento de la música sagrada que deberá observarse en la provincia eclesiástica de Michoacán* (Morelia: Tipografía del Agustín Martínez Mier, 1921).

26. Ibid.

27. Ilmo. y Rev. Dn. Manuel Fulcheri y Pietra Santa, *Carta Pastoral del Ilmo. y Rvmo. Sr. Dr. Don Manuel Fulcheri y Pietra Santa, Obispo de Zamora* (Zamora: privately printed, 1922).

than the confidante of the wealthy: the priests had created a woman who spoke in hushed but explicit terms to the poor. Her message, rooted in her own serendipitous past, was partly a tease of compensation and redemption, of a miraculous transformation of all that had been cramped and harmful into lives flooded with happiness and light. After all, Mary had been but a Nazarethene peasant silenced because of poverty, religion, and gender. Even her own son had scorned her.[28] But then, out of no particular merit of her own, she was chosen for greatness. In short, her past crystallized hope for unpredictable good fortune. For campesinos reduced to foraging for food in the wild, for those who threw disobedient children out of their homes, for those who murdered their peers for a living, this was a promise of unguarded hope.[29]

There was also the appeal of her plasticity. As the priests stressed tirelessly, she was there for everyone. Putting words in her mouth, they claimed that she would have said, "I am the loving and tender mother for all who turn to me with their needs and afflictions."[30] What they did not say explicitly perhaps did not need saying: if the priests re-created her, and again and again bestowed her upon the entire community, every Michoacano could also re-create her. Consciously or not, priests offered their blessing to the widespread tendency to cradle her image in the hand and to confide to her an array of grievances and longings. They even tolerated the tendency of poor Ario women to imagine the stamped images of the Virgin on paper as the incarnation—rather than the representation—of the Virgin. They loosened the tendency to appropriate Mary, to use her in personal ways for personal problems.[31]

What can it mean to poor people to be constantly dogged by

28. Mark 3:32, 33; John 2:3, 4.

29. On murder for hire, interview with Zamora native Francisco Elizalde, Zamora, July 1985; on disciplining children, Griselda Villegas Muñoz, *Emilia, una mujer de Jiquilpan* (Jiquilpan de Juárez: Centro de Estudios de la Revolución Mexicana "Lázaro Cárdenas," A.C., 1984), 26–28.

30. "Acta de consegración a la Santísima Virgen de Guadalupe," 1901–30, caja 13, Sacramental y Disciplina, APC.

31. On holding fast to images of the Virgin, interviews with Verduzco de Peña, April, May 1990; Esperanza Rocha, the devout Catholic wife of an Ario agrarian leader, Ario de Rayón, May, June 1990; and María de los Angeles Verduzco Gómez, Ario de Rayón, May 1990; as well as Policarpo Sánchez, Profesor inspector federal, Michoacán, caja 412, AHSEP. On the perceived plasticity of the Virgin, interview with Padre Francisco Miranda, historian and Catholic priest, Zamora, March 1990.

images of humility and redemption? Scholars throughout the academy are correctly suspicious of elite exhortations as any accurate gauge of popular behavior. This is not simply because the repetition of harangues suggests that they do not produce the intended inhibitions. It is more deeply because popular responses to elite exhortations have been so unpredictable—conformist, rebellious, here conformist and there rebellious—as various and complex as campesinos themselves have been.[32]

In Michoacán, however, the culture of purity and redemption was scarcely confined to the pulpit: the marriage of piety and property was consummated in the culture of everyday life. It was there that the absence of significant ideological and material alternatives proved telling, as campesino challenges to elite presumptions remained within the confines of the dominant culture. By turning to the daily lives of the men and women who reproduced cultural patterns on the land and in the home, then, we shall see how this culture both enticed and confined its participants.

To Doff the Cap, To Murmur Ave María

On the eve of the Cardenista effort to spark everyday revolution, landlords owned the vast tracts that provided the principal economic options for men and women in northwestern Michoacán. In terms of the extent of their holdings and their approaches to agriculture, the landowners were a diverse group. Perhaps 350 people owned most of the land in the state, with holdings that ranged from ten thousand to thirty-five thousand hectares.[33] Some of them experimented

32. As Raymond Williams pointed out in *Culture and Society, 1780–1950* (New York: Harper & Row, 1958), 320, cultural creations are formed by dominant and subordinate classes. Later participants in this conversation have stressed that subordinate classes use elite formulations in their own—sometimes startling—ways. As Stephen Greenblatt puts it, "Representational practices are ideologically significant. . .but. . .it is important to resist what we may call *a priori* ideological determinism, that is, the notion that particular modes of representation are inherently and necessarily bound to a given culture or class or belief system, and that their effects are unidirectional." See Greenblatt, *Marvelous Possessions: The Wonder of the New World* (Chicago: University of Chicago Press, 1991), 4.

33. For information regarding the size of landholdings, see Fernando Foglio Miramontes, *Geografía económica agrícola del estado de Michoacán*, 4 vols. (Mexico City:

with threshing machines, grinding mills, insecticides. Refusing innovation, others allowed vast stretches of land to go untended.[34] Still,
because of a lack of economic alternatives in this region, almost 80
percent of the male population worked as day laborers on haciendas.[35]
This enabled the landowners to develop a relatively uniform system of
domination. Summarizing the situation in a sort of shorthand, former
peon Jesús Aceves remarked, "The rich man's land stretched, it
seemed like, to eternity, while we lived so poor. And how were we
going to do anything about it?"[36]

In more prosaic terms, landowners rather than workers set the para-
meters of the peons' workaday lives. They determined what their
workers were to do. Though tasks varied, with peons set to work as
cowboys, watchmen, plowboys, and water carriers, the dawn-to-dusk
schedule was fixed and onerous. Even though workers lived as far as

Editorial Cultura, 1936), 3:20–30. In addition, Cayetano Reyes kindly lent me an
intriguing though largely undocumented paper in which he developed this estimate. See
Cayetano Reyes García, "Las condiciones materiales del campo michoacano,
1900–1940" (1987; paper in author's possession), 3.

34. Foglio Miramontes, *Geografía*, 3:82–98; Reyes García, "Condiciones materiales," 13. On the modernization of regional infrastructure, see Verduzco, "Zamora,"
62–69.

35. My calculations are based on information found in Estados Unidos Mexicanos,
Secretaría de la Economía Nacional, Dirección General de Estadística, *Quinto censo de
población—15 de mayo de 1930: Estado de Michoacán*, 11; Foglio Miramontes, *Geografía*;
and Frank Tannenbaum, *The Mexican Agrarian Revolution* (1929; reprint, New York:
Archon Books, 1968). In 1988 I developed an analysis based on Foglio's categories. I
argued that his categories, based on the 1920 census, were confusing, for they lumped
together water carriers, resident peons, day workers, harvesters, trappers, watchmen, and
plowboys under the designation "day laborers." Distinctions such as "resident peon,"
"tenant," and "sharecropper" would afford analysts more precise descriptions of the
agrarian relations the campesinos experienced.

Jean Meyer develops a very different line of attack on the 1910 census. In his longstanding emphasis on the existence of private property owners, he downplays the significance of hacienda domination. A recent rendition of this perspective is his "Haciendas y
ranchos, peones y campesinos en el Porfiriato: Algunas falacias estadísticas," *Historia
Mexicana* 35 (January–March 1986): 477–509. Nonetheless, for the 1920s and 1930s,
survivors, local studies, and the statistical material available confirm that Michoacán day
workers possessed few alternative forms of economic enterprise and that landowners frequently treated them as faceless ciphers. See Moreno García, *Guaracha;* John Gledhill,
"Casi Nada: Capitalism, the State, and the Campesinos of Guaracha" (Ph.D. diss., University College, London, n.d.; reproduced without scholarly apparatus); and Pascale
Pérez Sadrine, "Cambios tecnológicos, dinámica social y sus impactos sobre la organización del espacio: Dos comunidades rurales del Valle de Zamora" (master's thesis,
Colegio de Michoacán, 1989).

36. Interview with Jesús Aceves, Ario de Rayon, May 1990.

fourteen kilometers from the haciendas, there were no exceptions.[37] And during a period when people required a peso a day to fulfill their needs for food and clothing, workers could expect no more than half that wage.[38]

The landowners had managed to lend their pattern of landownership the appearance of inevitability. Indeed, many peasants had come to consider such a pattern (if it could be transferred to them) as desirable. How did this come about? While it has been repeatedly shown that people do not readily engage in violent rebellion, it still takes a certain analytical sleight of hand to insist that Michoacán peons were born hoping to become hacendados. Even in a world where agrarian capitalism was so old that it felt habitual, the Michoacán majority also experienced traditions of conviviality and noncapitalist social relationships. And notwithstanding the Catholic hierarchy's time-worn proclivities to ally itself with the wealthy, in Michoacán history Catholicism had worn many faces.[39] To the extent that men saw privately held property as normal, to the extent that they did not balk at the hierarchical blessing offered an exploitative regime, they must have been carefully taught. But how? How did the men and women who profited from such a regime school their workers in behavior of seeming acquiescence?

One way to dispel the sense that there was anything predictable or normative about peasants' somewhat tentative tolerance of the regime is to observe the system landowners had devised to elicit obedience. It was a system that culled together elements of coercion and persuasion, binding them so intimately as to make it difficult to distinguish between the two. To exemplify the problem, it may be worth remembering the terms of the job itself. Imagine that a man with a family has no economic possibility other than day work on an agricultural estate.

37. Interviews with Aceves, May 1990; Carlos Cervantes, Ario de Rayón, June 1990; Ignacio Espitia, Zamora, August 1985; and Elizalde, July 1985.

38. Economic statistics regarding wages and prices are particularly scanty for this region. This estimate is based on Foglio Miramontes, *Geografía*, 3:242; and interviews with Aceves, May 1990; Espitia, August 1985; and Elizalde, July 1985. In addition, Reyes García claims that during this period peons were paid no more than half a peso daily. See Reyes García, "Condiciones materiales," 12.

39. The social Catholicism of the nineteenth century and campesinos' responses to that movement is one of the more striking examples of Catholic variation in Michoacán history. See Arturo Rodríguez Zetina, *Zamora: Ensayo histórico y repertorio documental* (Mexico City: Editorial Jus, 1952), 216–17, 278, 316–17, 322, 331–36; and Luis González, *Zamora*, 2d ed. (Zamora: El Colegio de Michoacán, 1984), 122–23.

When you offer him a job that will stave off hunger only if his wife stints on food for herself, does the man accept because of your charismatic power? Has he been forced to accept the job? Or do the elements work together, reinforcing one another?

Representatives of the three central institutions of the region—church, hacienda, and family—each disseminated a version of this double message: by virtue of their wealth and power, landowners will dominate the region, but they will also make their control relatively bearable. Relying on Catholicism's twin engagements with hierarchy and ambivalence regarding gender roles, the clerical interpretation of this message called for a measured degree of subservience for peons. Even as it acquiesced in poor men's insufficient earnings and prestige, church representatives demanded that "women submit to men."[40] In their families, poor boys learned that while men and not women were to support the families economically, they would be released from the more persistent and less esteemed tasks assigned to women. To work as a day laborer on an hacienda meant suppressing any hope of utilizing one's intelligence to organize the work unless—and here was the lure—the peon was named to the position of overseer.

To follow the peons' daily routines is to watch these lessons unfold. They began by rising before the sun. Splashing water on their faces, they rearranged the uniform of the laboring agrarian poor—the white cotton shirt and trousers resembling white pajamas, the huaraches, the sombrero. Leaving the image of the Virgin at home, workers met up with friends and relatives and trudged the several miles to the workplace.[41]

There they would meet the overseer. The landlord's bad-guy standins, many of these *mayordomos* had once been peons themselves. Perhaps they had once seen themselves in alliance with poor friends and relatives. But their new jobs transformed them. Now, upon sighting

40. "Carta pastoral colectiva de los prelados de la provincia de Michoacán," caja 11, APC. In addition, various priests expressed concern about the sanctity of the traditional Catholic family. See Fulcheri y Pietra Santa, *Carta pastoral,* caja 8, APC. The "Carta pastoral colectiva de los prelados de la provincia de Michoacán," found in caja 11, APC, describes socialism as a sort of radical democratic threat to "the natural union between men and women."

41. On the clothing of the Mexican laboring poor of the period, see Ezequiel M. García, "Estudio preliminar de la zona agrícola Zamora," 7 September 1934, Biblioteca, Colegio de Michoacán, Fondo Ramón Fernández y Fernández; and interviews with Rafael Ochoa, Ario de Rayón, May 1990, and Múgica Martínez, June 1990.

them each morning, peons were to doff their caps and murmur "Ave Maria" in recognition of their new position.[42] For overseers had become tutors, hired to instruct campesinos in the philosophical boundaries of an agrarian capitalism blessed by the church.

It was a schooling in denial. Peons on many Zamora and area estates were not to think deeply about agrarian problems. Peons learned that while the church celebrated the individual initiative that carved the countryside into lucrative estates, the individual initiative of poor men was to be worn away. Day after day, year upon year, overseers taught the peons to hold in abeyance their ability to make significant decisions regarding farming. On the larger estates, where the hacienda work load was subdivided into myriad individual tasks, peons knew their particular tasks quite well. However, they were denied both knowledge about the larger agrarian picture and practice in making large-scale decisions. The overseers told the peons when and how to farm. They dictated what tools to use, what fields to plant, what crops to cultivate.[43]

Men were united by a number of ties, from bonds of kinship to the shared social geography of village or hacienda.[44] Yet overseers forcefully suggested that campesinos were to suppress any communal tendencies. To make this point, owners and mayordomos employed a combination of mild incentives and frightening disincentives. Drawing on their collective insights, they spread the advantages of limited individualism before the peons. Perhaps the most lucrative incentive was the possibility of being an overseer. Culled from the vast army of

42. Interview with Ochoa, July 1990.

43. On Ario haciendas, interviews with Ario area peons Cervantes, June 1990; Aceves, May 1990; and Ochoa, July 1990. On the Guaracha hacienda, see Moreno García, *Guaracha*, 130–56; and Gledhill, "Casi Nada," 75–84. On Zamora area haciendas, interviews with peon–turned–agrarian leader Espitia; and Zamora agrarian leader Vicente Pérez, Zamora, August 1985.

44. The assertion that kinship spilled over into work relationships is based on a painstaking cross-check of agrarian documentation with informants. In the case of Zamora, the documents include "Censos para la expedición de derechos agrarios," housed in the Archivo de la Secretaría de Reforma Agraria in Morelia (SRA-M). However, the agrarian reform documentation, whether in Mexico City, Morelia, or Zamora, refrains from identifying the former occupations or the kinship ties of land recipients. It was agrarian leader Ignacio Espitia in Zamora who generously granted me interviews that enabled me to place Zamora peons within their webs of kinship. I pursued a similar strategy in Ario, using "Acta de Posesión en definitiva, Santa Monica Ario, Michoacán," expediente 135, 22 September 1927, SRA-M, as the documentary basis. There Rafael Ochoa helped me to develop a portrait of the peons.

peons, these men received better housing, higher wages, and higher status.

In addition, on haciendas throughout the region it was occasionally possible for peons to obtain a mild concession from overseers or even landowners. At Guaracha the sharecropping contracts stipulated the amount of money and corn workers would be paid. Yet by developing personal relationships with the overseers, peons routinely extracted more corn than their contracts stipulated. Peons forced Zamora area landowners to pay their baptismal and wedding expenses. And Jiquilpan and Ario campesinos frequently persuaded landlords to pay for local fiestas.[45]

While the absence of dramatic revolutionary activity in the region enabled landowners to conduct business as usual, during this restive period they were skittish. Concerned that their usual combination of coercion and persuasion might prove inadequate, they heightened the pressure on employees. They began by employing priests, men whom campesinos later denounced as "kept ministers." Landlords fed them, feted them, and paid them, and the priests responded in kind. They lent the church bells for summoning workers to their jobs. They wrote sermons demanding obedience to hacendados. And in one chilling instance a priest used the confessional to gain information about rebellious peons for the landlords. When he passed this information on to the owners, the men were executed.[46]

There is much suspicion that landlords indulged in other forms of repression as well. According to Esperanza Rocha, the wife of a local agrarian leader, landowners in the Ario area converted a tunnel into the underground railroad of the propertied, using it to transport secrets about potential local rebels.[47] In a regionally celebrated court case, the defendant Ramón Ascencia claimed that the rebels' trial for murder reflected nothing more than the landlords' blistering attack on "the few liberals in the area."[48]

---

45. On Guaracha, see Gledhill, "Casi Nada," 81, and Moreno García, *Guaracha*, 147, 155; on Zamora, González, *Zamora*, 71; on Jiquilpan, Alvaro Ochoa, *Jiquilpan* (Morelia: Gobierno del Estado de Michoacán, 1978), 134; on Ario, interview with Aceves, May 1990.

46. On "kept ministers," interviews with Verduzco de Peña, May 1990, and Ochoa, July 1990; on the church bells, González, *Zamora*, 124; on the use of the confessional, Gledhill, "Casi Nada," 79–80.

47. Interview with Rocha, June 1990.

48. Series of documents in trial of Ladislao Alvarado et al., expediente 15, 1923, Justicia, Archivo Municipal de Zamora (AMZ), Zamora, Michoacán. Of particular interest is

Under these circumstances, peons' responses varied. Some devised secretive strategies to oppose treatment they considered unfair. Many fled to the United States. Some men sought out secluded spots on the haciendas to grumble about the mayordomo's abuses. As ex-peon Rafael Ochoa remarked, "We knew how to criticize them right under their noses, on the hacienda itself."[49] Carlos Cervantes and his two brothers confined their complaints to the long walk home.[50]

Other peons appear to have accepted the concept of private property. They did not object to the idea of selling their abilities to work in the fields. When landowners or other peons obstructed that potential, however, they were troubled. For Rafael Ochoa's father, it was the landlord's own unwillingness to abide by the terms of his contract that evoked discontent. Because he was himself a socialist, Ochoa's disappointment that he and his father never shared an ideological perspective may have led him to dramatize his father's stance. "My father believed in the doctrine of Christ, but he also believed in justice," Ochoa declared. Though the terms of the workers' sharecropping contracts stated that workers would receive half of the corn they produced, they believed the landowner was cheating them. Refusing to tolerate the situation, Ochoa's father organized his fellow workers. As Ochoa told it, "There were two men paid by the hacendado to keep a lookout. They never slept. So the men sneaked off, and met on the plain. They made my father the leader, and he went to the hacendado. He told him 'I came to tell you that it's not fair that you cart off our corn, take it away and weigh it in liters. Then you give us our part in liters. How are we supposed to know how much it weighed, and how many liters we get?'"[51]

Other men used a language of individual rights to turn, not on the hacendado, but on one another. A regional court case revealed that campesino Nepomuseno Cuevas assaulted fellow campesino Maximino Manzo. According to Cuevas, it all began innocently enough, with his early morning effort to borrow the landlord's team of oxen. Discovering that the oxen were not grazing in their customary pasture, he

---

the testimony of Ramón Ascencio, Francisco Herrera, and Teresa y Ladislao Alvarado, "procesados injustamente por el delito de plagio y asesinato que no hemos cometido," 4 October 1923, and Manuel Duñas Maciel, Agente del Ministerio Público, to Juez primero de letras, 23 May 1923.

49. Interview with Ochoa, July 1990.
50. Interview with Cervantes, June 1990.
51. Interview with Ochoa, July 1990.

sought out Maximino Manzo. At Manzo's house, Manzo's father denied Cuevas the use of the team. Persisting in his view that "we are all sharecroppers together, and I believe that we all have the same right to use the animals," two days later Cuevas repeated his request to Manzo. Manzo responded by attacking him, leading Cuevas to kill him in what he stoutly maintained was self-defense.[52]

While oral history offers participants an opportunity to use their present vantage point to critique or even prey upon the past, ex-peon Jesús Aceves declined the opportunity. A resident peon on the Ario hacienda of Potrerillos, he had no complaints about the landowner and few about hacienda life. Try as I might, I could elicit no more than resigned acceptance of conditions on the estate. "Tell me about the hacendado," I asked. "What kind of man was he?" Aceves replied that "he was a good person. He knew us. He paid for the fiestas, and if we were sick, he paid for the medicine."

"Did you have any reason to complain about the work?"

"Why complain? It just makes the world worse."

"You never sensed that it was unfair for him to be so wealthy, and you so poor?"

"Yes, but what was I to do? We had lived with this hacendado all our lives. He was a good man."[53]

With no prompting, however, Aceves verbally assaulted the memory of another peon. "We got paid every week in Zamora. To get your money, you signed your name and the mayordomo handed it to you. But this other worker got in line ahead of me and signed my name. When I got to the front they wouldn't give me my money. Because of him I didn't get paid."

As much as a resigned toleration of the status quo, the responses of these men suggest a certain acceptance of the sanctified private property relations that peons knew. Indeed, the landowners' ability to own property and dominate other people probably kindled both desire and frustration among the workers. However, in order to emulate the hacendado or to safely express frustrations based on their landless plight, peons required subordinates. Returning to their wives, those conscientious practitioners of the Catholicism of the poor, the peons would confront them.

52. Expediente 1984, Fondo Zamora, 1934 Penales, Archivo Judicial del Estado de Michoacán (AJEM), Morelia, Michoacán.
53. Interview with Aceves, May 1990.

Daughters of Mary

María Enríquez had done what she could to protect herself. She attended church. She surrounded herself with women—a friend, her sister, strangers. When the assault came that August afternoon, she pulled away, running toward a group of older women on the street corner. Meshing with their group, she fled into the sanctuary of the church.[54]

Nevertheless, she later claimed in court, Antonio Mendoza had grabbed her, hissing, "Now you come with me." And nobody had helped her. Not her sister. Not her friend. Not even the group of older women on the corner.

In trial testimony, witnesses developed excuses for the inaction of Enríquez's friends and neighbors. Enríquez herself reasoned that her sister and her friend may have been "shocked and frightened." Besides, her own sister was very young. Her girlfriend Jesusa was Mendoza's sister and probably experienced divided loyalties. One of the women on the street corner justified her behavior on the grounds that she mistook Enríquez for Pachita la Loca, a "crazy woman who wanders the streets all the time."[55]

While their excuses are distinct, the women all determined that Enríquez—and Pachita la Loca, for that matter—was somehow unworthy of protection, out of bounds. And yet, this is the testimony of Enríquez herself. The woman who claimed she was victimized and unprotected offered excuses in court for the women who deserted her. How did this come about? Why would a woman scorned by friends and neighbors share their mental landscape?

Representatives of northwestern Michoacán's central institutions persistently promoted the view that women were to emulate the Virgin. Indeed, priests and lay people organized female clerical organizations called Hijas de María (Daughters of Mary). Particularly concerned about the "loss of modesty among women subject to the tyranny of fashion, the lack of respect for private property," and the wave of assaults on "conjugal bonds, domestic authority," some priests

---

54. "Instruida en contra de Antonio Mendoza por el delito de rapto," 13 August 1924, expediente 13–923/28, ramo penales, Zamora, Juzgado de primera instancia, AJEM.

55. Ibid.

called on women to stem the tide. They were to see the Virgin as "a model," as Mari Elena Verduzco de Peña put it. "The leaders asked us to be as pure as she was, to avoid errors."[56]

Expressed in these terms, these qualities seem both static and imprecise, worthy of the scholarly disregard they have received.[57] Why, after all, should analysts of revolution and counterrevolution concern themselves with Michoacán women's tendency to ponder clerical abstractions regarding female modesty and self-denial? Do moments of high public intensity not merit greater attention?

One reason that revolutionary and counterrevolutionary activities should not be portrayed in isolation from their social context is that these traits of abnegation and modesty did not remain abstract. Instead, in catechism groups, in the Hijas de María, and in family settings women were asked to transform these characteristics into practices protecting an inequitable social order from the sort of egalitarian behavior that might endanger it. Women might have been denied the possibilities of creating haciendas from Indian lands, of building bridges and monuments. At the same time, they were asked to construct what might be called behavioral architecture. The materials seemed innocuous enough. Physical spaces, language, and activities considered suitable for public then for private life. Out of these materials women were to build a social landscape marked by boundaries. More than that, through their own conduct they were to delineate the boundaries.[58]

56. Ilmo. y Rmo. Sr. Obispo de Zamora, Doctor Don José Othón Núñez, *Edicto XIX del Ilmo y Rmo. Sr. Obispo de Zamora, Doctor Dn. José Othón Núñez* (Zamora, 1921); interview with Verduzco de Peña, May 1990.

57. The separation of "personal" from "political" life has proved dominant in studies of both family life and politics in Latin America. This reflects deeply embedded personal and political assumptions on the part of scholars rather than some conspiratorial determination to exclude women.

It remains true that the culture of everyday life of Mexico's mestizo majority has been deemed unworthy of notice. It has somehow been considered ordinary and therefore not "cultural." Although this book clearly does not focus on men's and women's work relations, it very early became clear that some sense of the nature of men's and women's everyday lives and the interrelations between them would be indispensable to any analysis of their revolutionary and counterrevolutionary activities. By heightening instances of family misconduct, court documents housed in both the AMZ and the AJEM provide a number of important clues regarding family members' expectations of one another.

58. For a provocative attempt to revise interpretations viewing purity rituals as repressive for women, see Mary Douglas, *Purity and Danger: An Analysis of the Concepts*

In the absence of alternatives, women adopted this concern with boundaries. This appears to have been particularly true of poor women, whose alternatives were more limited than were those of wealthier women.[59] In part this meant that poor women took on a shadowy role in the realm of public life. Teresa Ladislao, the wife of a peasant on trial for murder, set the tone by testifying, "I know nothing about anything, for I am only a woman."[60] Women were also effectively banned from public political activities, as the wives of agrarian leaders revealed. Esperanza Rocha pointed out that "I had to guess what was going on, for my husband never told me anything." Even the lower-class *tertulias,* the gatherings that provided information about landlords and political leaders, were confined to men. These included the snatched moments on the hacienda when men complained about the overseers, the night meetings to plan strategy, the meetings of the local liberals, even the walks back and forth from the hacienda.[61]

If the public realm was largely out of bounds for women, the arena of home and family life was considered to be their domain, where they both established boundaries and patrolled them. And here it is important to recognize that within this social context, abnegation offered women certain rewards. As clerical lieutenants women wielded a certain power over children and neighbors who stepped out of bounds.

---

of Pollution and Taboo (London: Ark Paperbacks, 1984). While Douglas attempts to reconstruct the original context for certain purity customs, including those of the traditional Jews and the "new" Christians, in her fervor to portray Paul as revolutionary she obscures the continuities between traditional Jewish and Catholic ambivalence regarding women and virginity.

59. This assertion is based on an extensive examination of court documents for the northwestern Michoacán area in the 1920s and 1930s. This examination revealed that rich women used the legal system to defend their property. Poor women, however, were often named in trial documents as victims of rape or assault. This evidence led me to suspect that poor women may have developed a concern with behavioral fences because the cultural agreement designating women protectors of an inequitable status quo left poor women unprotected in a number of ways. See, for example, "Expedientes relativo a consignas que se hacen al Ministro Público de los delitos cometidos y de los responsables de ellos," in expediente 1, legajo 1, Justicia, 1922, AMZ; "Expediente relativo a las consignaciones que se hacen de individuos y hechos a la autoridad judicial," expediente 6, Justicia 1920, AMZ; expediente 6, Zamora, 1923, Penales, AJEM.

60. "Contra Ladislao Alvarado y socios por calumnia," 23 May 1923, expediente 15, Justicia, AMZ.

61. On night meetings, interview with Ochoa, July 1990. On women's ignorance of male political activities, interviews with agraristas' wives Julia Mayes, Morelia, December 1985; and Rocha, June 1990.

They began by monitoring their children's recreation. Women frequently insisted that their children play only with children who shared their class and ethnic background. As Mari Elena Verduzco de Peña, a woman raised in impoverished gentility, remembered, "I played with Indian children, but all the other Ario mothers forbade it." Such vigilance frequently continued into adolescence. In Jiquilpan Emilia Cárdenas refused her son lodging as long as he courted a woman of indeterminate chastity. Rafael Ochoa maintained that his mother and her friends taught him and his fellow peons to avoid involvement with wealthy women, "who wouldn't want to work and who would want things we couldn't give them."[62]

Women in haphazard and informal communities of relatives and neighbors also produced what can be viewed as a sort of confederation of the disempowered. For women shared their workaday lives with kinfolk and neighbors. Women walked to early morning Mass with friends and relatives. Sisters and neighbors washed clothes together at the stream, or carried the water together back to their homes. Women also visited one another, using pockets of time in their long mornings to construct and refurbish networks of information and gossip.[63]

In addition, throughout the period priests developed special relationships with women.[64] Like much in the Catholic realm, these relationships drew on everyday habits to express elements of both hierarchy and communion. Thus, it is possible to understand why women tended to priests' domestic needs, cooking for them, cleaning their homes, repairing their vestments. In a functional sense, priests' admonitions regarding women's behavior, their sermons glorifying domestic life, might be viewed as poor reward. Yet women seem to have believed there was something to be gained from tending the priest. While the thicket of consciousness is dense, difficult to cut through with surety, it may be that in a society where poor women were relegated to unpaid and unnoticed work, God's earthly intercessors' appreciation of their domestic activities was gratifying.[65]

62. Interviews with Verduzco de Peña, April 1990; Ochoa, July 1990; and José Corona Núñez, Morelia, 1989; Villegas Muñoz, *Emilia*, 26–28.
63. Interviews with Verduzco de Peña, April 1990; Méndez, June 1990; and Rocha, June 1990.
64. Interviews with Zamora agrarian leaders Pérez, Zamora, August 1985; and Maximino Padilla, Zamora, August 1985; Policarpo Sánchez, Profesor inspector federal, Michoacán, caja 412, AHSEP.
65. On women performing priests' domestic chores, interviews with Padre Joaquín Paz, Zamora, August 1985; Padre Porfirio Medina, Zamora, August 1985; and Padre

At the same time, there was a price to be paid for whatever advantages women gleaned from their behavior. For the family was an arena where men could indulge in what they came to know as the entitlements of manhood. Women expressed this principally through their work, a sure token of deference. It is not that men did not work hard. Their work was backbreaking, and it continued from dawn to dusk. But they came home to women who worked harder. Women rose before their families. They worked later. They were always on call to care for the endless children, who, however gratefully received, needed constant attention. They cared for the sick. They were in charge of tending the home and feeding the household, a strenuous job in an era when tortillas were made by hand. In short, through the generosity (or, depending on the perspective, exploitation) of women's work, they took the edge off the agrarian capitalists' exploitation of their husbands.[66]

Francisco Miranda, Zamora, March 1990. On priests offering women advice, interviews with Verduzco de Peña, May 1990; and Villegas Muñoz, *Emilia*, 17–20, proved useful.

66. On women's work, I relied upon interviews with Verduzco de Peña, April, May 1990; Rocha, June 1990; Rico Cano, June, August 1990; and Múgica Martínez, June, August 1990. For analyses of the ways women's unpaid or poorly paid labor has subsidized capitalism, see Lydia Sargent, ed., *Women and Revolution: A Discussion of the Unhappy Marriage of Marxism and Feminism* (Boston: South End Press, 1981). Of particular interest is Heidi Hartmann's article in that volume, "The Unhappy Marriage of Marxism and Feminism: Towards a More Progressive Union," 1–42. For an early effort to move beyond efforts to prioritize *either* gender- or class-based oppressions, see Joan Kelley, "The Doubled Vision of Feminist Theory: A Postscript to the 'Women and Power' Conference," *Feminist Studies* 5 (spring 1979): 216–27.

Analyses pointing to the specific ways women's work has made family subsistence possible in dependent capitalist economies have been more prominent among Latin Americanists than among scholars focusing on gender in the United States and Europe. This is probably because North American and Western European populations have not experienced the widespread, persistent immiseration that Latin American populations, the women in particular, have experienced. But at times this has led Latin Americanists to adopt an overly economistic approach, which has been utilized to the exclusion of approaches pondering other types of exploitation and other possibilities of resistance. See, for example, the essays in June Nash and Helen I. Safa, eds., *Sex and Class in Latin America* (New York: Praeger, 1976). For a very sophisticated example of this approach, see Carmen Diana Deere, *Household and Class Relations* (Berkeley: University of California Press, 1990). For exceptions to this approach, see Ruth Behar, "Rage and Redemption: Reading the Life Story of a Mexican Market Woman," *Feminist Studies* 16 (summer 1990), 223–58; Florencia E. Mallon, "Patriarchy in the Transition to Capitalism: Central Peru, 1830–1950," ibid. 13 (summer 1987): 379–407; and Marjorie Becker, "When I Was a Child, I Danced as a Child, but Now That I Am Old, I Think about Salvation: Soledad Barragán and a Past That Would Not Stay Put" (paper presented at "Narrating Histories: A Workshop," Division of the Humanities and Social Sciences, California Institute of Technology, Pasadena, April 1994).

The Two Faces of the Tarascan

Then there were the Tarascans. By the mid-1920s they had fashioned two styles of being an Indian.[67] In one formulation, wrinkled with age, Indians expressed purity and redemption with great flair. In the other, most profoundly displayed by Primo Tapia, Indians wore a face with many contours—governmental, traditional, revolutionary. While at times these two versions of the Indian coexisted, by our period it was a sullen coexistence, from time to time exploding into violence. To put it baldly, in many Indian villages throughout the meseta two groups, both sporting behavior outsiders had deemed appropriate for Indians, both, we might say, in Indianface, jostled for supremacy.

It was the Franciscan friars arriving in 1526 who originally taught Tarascans how to be Indians. As would-be spiritual conquerors, the friars developed a mode of instruction that graphically expressed both the humbling effects of paternalism and the vital hope of redemption. The terms of Tarascan subordination included acceptance of limited allotments of their once spacious lands: plots assigned to each family,

---

67. In the large body of literature on the Tarascans most of the approaches have been singularly nonanalytical. Certainly the theoretical issue at stake here—that the whole notion of Indianness was an invention that Indians learned to manipulate—has scarcely been pointed out, let alone addressed. Much of the literature is informed by the assumption that the Franciscan paternalism was, in fact, protective for the Indians. See, for example, Cesar Moheno, *Las historias y los hombres de San Juan* (Zamora: El Colegio de Michoacán/CONACYT, 1985); Lucio Mendieta y Núñez, ed., *Los tarascos* (Mexico City: Universidad Nacional Autónoma de México Imprenta Universitaria, 1940); and J. Benedict Warren, *The Conquest of Michoacán: The Spanish Domination of the Tarascan Kingdom in Western Mexico* (Norman: University of Oklahoma Press, 1985). An alternative, less popular approach is that the Franciscans pursued goals entirely consistent with the conquistadores' determination to plunder the colonies. An intellectually sophisticated, if sparsely documented, example of the latter approach is Jesús Tapia Santamaría, *Campo religioso y evolución política en el bajio zamorano* (Zamora: El Colegio de Michoacán/Gobierno del Estado de Michoacán, 1986).

There is an older literature that demonstrates that both paternalism and manipulation of Hispanic cultural imperialism existed. But out of deference to a heightened empiricism, scholars such as Pedro Carrasco and particularly Ralph Beals avoid overt theoretical pursuit of these issues. See Beals, *Cherán: A Sierra Tarascan Village*, 2d ed. (New York: Cooper Square, 1973); and Carrasco, *Tarascan Folk Religion: An Analysis of Economic, Social, and Religious Interactions* (Tulane: Middle American Research Institute, 1952).

surrounded by community holdings.[68] To maintain the productivity of their lands, they learned a strategy of sacred barter. Celebrating God and the saints, they offered up wine, oil, ornaments. They launched rockets and fireworks. They played musical instruments and sang. In return they expected rain at the proper season, a bountiful harvest, familial well-being.[69]

While Tarascans persisted in what one scholar has called their "interested devotion" through most of the twentieth century,[70] the connection between material and spiritual life had long been frayed. Foreshadowing the national Reform Laws of 1855–57, developed by Mexican liberals, early nineteenth-century state legislation in Michoacán curtailed communal property ownership.[71] At least fifty villages lost their lands as panicky Indians entrusted their holdings to local Spanish-speaking elites who could negotiate with the outside world.[72]

The most far-reaching variation on this theme of theft in the name of liberalism and private property was the coming of the Spanish Noriega brothers to Naranja. Striking a deal with the mayor of Naranja, in the 1880s they acquired title to twelve thousand acres of the villagers' lands, leaving the Indians with four hundred acres to remind them of their former possibilities. Draining the swamp, the Noriegas uncovered the rich black soil underneath, and there they established a profitable hacienda. At the same time, by transforming the region's ecol-

68. Carlos García Mora, "El conflicto agrario-religioso en la sierra tarasca," *América Indígena* 36 (January–March 1976): 116; Moheno, *Las historias,* 111–16; Mendieta y Núñez, *Los tarascos,* 279.

69. Moheno, *Las historias,* 55, 57, 156–60; Arturo Chamorro, "Sincretismo y cambio en la formación de la música Purépecha," in *La sociedad indígena en el centro y occidente de México,* by Pedro Carrasco et al. (Zamora: Colegio de Michoacán, 1986), 153, 156–60; Carrasco, *Tarascan Folk Religion,* 27; Paul Friedrich, *Agrarian Revolt in a Mexican Village* (1970; reprint, Chicago: University of Chicago Press, 1977), 39; Mendieta y Núñez, *Los tarascos,* 164–65.

70. The quotation is from Mendieta y Núñez, *Los tarascos,* 161. My evidence on the persistence of this form of worship comes from my own participant observation in Ocumicho in 1990; Beals, *Cherán,* 120–43; Friedrich, *Agrarian Revolt,* 39; and Francisco Miranda, "Ocumicho, una comunidad en fiesta," *Relaciones: Estudios de Historia y Sociedad* 16 (fall 1983): 40–41.

71. Jean Meyer demonstrates that elites all over western Mexico initiated campaigns to privatize communal lands at the state and local level long before the Reform Laws in *Esperando a Lozada* (Zamora: El Colegio de Michoacán, 1984), 36–38. Angel Gutiérrez describes this legal process in his "Investigación y lucha ideológica: El caso de las comunidades michoacanas," in Gutiérrez, Guzmán A., and Sánchez D., *La cuestión agraria,* 17–19.

72. Carrasco, *Tarascan Folk Religion,* 16.

ogy they undermined traditional sources of village income. Naranjeños had once supplemented their income by weaving mats and baskets out of rushes, but after 1900 the rushes dried up. Then the supply of fish, mussels, and aquatic birds shrank. In effect, the Noriegas had destroyed the possibilities of self-sufficiency for a majority of villagers.[73]

In the face of increasing poverty, Naranja Tarascans did not relinquish their celebrations. On the contrary, they worked harder to sustain them, making long journeys to cumbersome work on the sugar plantations in the state's hot lands. But make no mistake: whatever the degree of harmony that originally characterized the fiesta cycle, by the twenties dissension and division between villagers and within families marked both work and festivals.[74]

Take, for example, the workday routines of men and women that made fiestas possible. While most Tarascan men worked land belonging to their communities, and many possessed plots, two cautions are necessary. First, this was a population riddled with economic inequality. While a large landowner might own no more than a three-hectare plot, his possibilities were exponentially greater than those of the peasant trying to feed a family from his two-hectare scrap.[75] At the same time, men reaped the skewed and limited advantages granted their gender by both Hispanic and Tarascan cultures. Unlike women, they sometimes possessed title and frequently enjoyed direct access to land.[76] Tarascan bilingualism was almost completely confined to men.[77] Moreover, unlike the women, Tarascan men toiled at time-bound activities.

73. Paul Friedrich recounts this important history in *Agrarian Revolt*. See also Arnulfo Embriz Osorio, *La liga de comunidades y sindicatos agraristas del estado de Michoacán: Práctica político-sindical, 1919–1929* (Mexico City: Centro de Estudios Históricos del Agrarismo en México, 1984).

74. The doubtful tone here reflects the fact that friars initiated the reciprocity between work and fiesta both as an expression of religiosity and as an effort to placate the victims of colonial land seizures. This perspective flies in the face of the classic, humane, but rather one-sided efforts to see ritual mainly as a constraint against villagers' runaway exploitation of neighbors. See, for example, E. P. Thompson, "The Moral Economy of the English Crowd in the Eighteenth Century," *Past and Present* 50 (February 1971): 76–136; and James C. Scott, *The Moral Economy of the Peasant: Rebellion and Subsistence in Southeast Asia* (New Haven: Yale University Press, 1976).

75. The calculations are from Embriz Osorio, *La liga*, 53.

76. Beals, *Cherán*, 60–61; Friedrich, *Agrarian Revolt*, 23.

77. Friedrich, *Agrarian Revolt*, 47; Beals, *Cherán*, 175; Mendieta y Núñez, *Los tarascos*, 155.

The staple task for Tarascan men was planting corn. In this, Tarascan men shared four unerring duties: they prepared the soil, planted
the seeds, guarded against animal and insect threats to their labor, and
harvested the grain. For the poorest men, compelled to use digging
tools rather than plows, the work was more grueling. At the same
time, their poverty pushed them toward more varied tasks, including
hat and pottery making and fishing.

To enter the kitchen was to find the women, and to observe them
was to see people engaged in domestic routines similar to those of
mestizas. In both traditions women's social value depended on public
passivity alongside domestic competence. The difference resides in the
fact that among the Tarascans, women's demeanor positively trum-
peted these values. In their long skirts arresting movement, their
blouses emblazoned with colorful embroidered birds and flowers, they
literally dressed the part of a people whose restriction was celebrated.
Chatting with one another exclusively in Tarascan in a world where
Spanish was the language of prosperity, they remained linguistically
enclosed.[78]

Then came the work. Tarascan women were assigned tasks essential
to the maintenance of the family, tasks made more difficult by poverty
and inadequate tools. These included bearing and rearing the children,
keeping house, feeding and clothing the family. Each of these tasks
was complex. For example, childbearing in its most basic version
meant kneeling, catching hold of ropes suspended from the house
beam; when the pains started, the woman would be placed on a blan-
ket, lifted by four persons, and twirled around the room for about fifteen minutes to position the child properly and to hasten the birth.[79]
Keeping house required routine trips to the stream or fountain to
draw water into pots. These pots were then placed on the left shoulder
and carried home. Cooking would mean, at least, shelling corn for two
hours, taking it to the mill to be ground, shaping and cooking the tortillas.[80]

The fiestas themselves testified both to the social rifts dividing vil-

78. The observations on women's clothing stem from my fieldwork in Jarácuaro and
Pátzcuaro in 1984 and Zamora and Ocumicho in 1984, 1985, and 1990; see also Beals,
Cherán, 40.

79. Beals, *Cherán*, 167.

80. On women's work, see Friedrich, *Agrarian Revolt*, 13, 15; and Beals, *Cherán*,
60–61.

lagers and to the vivacious efforts to bridge those rifts. Understandably, scholars have been agog at this aspect of ritual life. Not only did it seem to display the community's deeper understanding of itself in festive microcosm[81] but Indians celebrated with such flair. As the practices described by a covey of anthropologists differ little from those I witnessed at a recent Corpus Christi celebration in the Tarascan sierra town of Ocumicho, it seems possible to describe them in similar terms.[82]

By day, women adorned the streets with fresh local flowers. They wandered the village carrying baskets of ceremonial breads, which they distributed to all and sundry. Inside the church, villagers created a pyramid-shaped altar decorated with pottery wares, papier-mâché flowers, dollar bills.[83] Right before the priest began the sermon, villagers burned incense throughout the church. Toward evening, men set first rockets and then a papier-mâché castle afire.

For all the color and conviviality, Catholic fiestas were also occasions for the village's wealthiest men to flaunt their wealth and stature.[84] For months they engaged in competition among themselves to be named *prioste,* the master of religious ceremonies. Victory allowed the incumbent prioste to regale villagers with his hospitality and religious sensitivity. Preparing a niche in his home, he decorated it at times with paper streamers, miniature cooking utensils, and colorful dolls. Then he threw open the house to guests seeking to worship at the shrine. Similarly, during the feast day itself, the prioste characteris-

---

81. This hunch follows Geertz in "Ethos, World View, and the Analysis of Sacred Symbols," in *The Interpretation of Cultures* (New York: Basic Books, 1973), 130.

82. This analysis is based on my 1990 fieldwork; for the anthropological descriptions, see Moheno's particularly affecting description in *Las historias,* 91–94. See also Mendieta y Núñez, *Los tarascos,* 161–72; Carrasco, *Tarascan Folk Religion,* 25–48; and Friedrich, *Agrarian Revolt,* 27–39.

83. June Nash found a similar coexistence of older and newer forms of expression in Bolivia. And this would appear to be true in the Quiché region of Guatemala described by Rigoberta Menchú, notwithstanding Menchú's insistence that peasants there maintain unalloyed pre-Conquest traditions. See June Nash, *We Eat the Mines and the Mines Eat Us: Dependency and Exploitation in Bolivian Tin Mines* (New York: Columbia University Press, 1979); and Rigoberta Menchú, *I, Rigoberta Menchú: An Indian Woman in Guatemala,* trans. Ann Wright, ed. Elisabeth Burgos-Debray (London: Verso, 1984).

84. In *The Fiesta System and Economic Change* (New York: Columbia University Press, 1977), Waldemar R. Smith maintains that lavish reciprocal fiesta spending occurred only as long as lack of capitalist development inhibited more lucrative uses of capital. For a similar approach, elegantly rendered, see Gerald Sider, "Christmas Mumming and the New Year in Outport Newfoundland," *Past and Present* 71 (May 1976): 102–25.

tically pressed rare and expensive foods—whole cheeses, *chapatas*, *menudos*—on his neighbors.[85]

Out of an array of ideological messages Primo Tapia amassed the tools to challenge this Tarascan tradition of inequitable conviviality.[86] From his uncle, a nineteenth-century lawyer and agrarian fighter, he learned of the possibilities the liberals' message of individual well-being held out for the poor.[87] Through observing his bilingual uncle's work with governmental notables and monolingual Tarascans, Tapia glimpsed the possibilities of multilingualism, and before he left the state he had learned both Tarascan and Spanish. Then, in self-imposed exile in the United States, he mastered both English and the anarchist ideology of friends in the IWW, the Industrial Workers of the World.

In the process, Tapia ignited the smoldering village conflict. On one side were the anti-*agraristas*. A group composed of the village majority, they included Naranja's more prosperous and more devout citizens. On the other side was a group of villagers led by Tapia's relatives, people who had shared poverty, illiteracy, and friendships with Tapia since childhood. The conflict became still more complex because, in pursuit of land, Tapia was compelled to seek an alliance with Mexican president Plutarco Elías Calles. In an ideological sense, it is difficult to imagine two more distinct personalities. Calles was all proponent of agrarian capitalism, private property, small family plots for the villagers. He pursued an anticlerical politics with the vigor of a man who had encountered evil incarnate and was determined to vanquish it. Tapia, on the other hand, hoped to establish a quasi-socialist political culture in the villages of Michoacán. And his response to Catholicism appeared to combine political expediency with sentimental affection for the movement and emotion bound up in popular Catholic ritual.

In pursuit of his program, Tapia found himself compelled to placate opposition at every turn. Was the devout village majority reluctant to support his agrarian politics? He would mobilize his lingering credibility as a man who sang at traditional religious fiestas.[88] Drawing up what he called a petition for a priest, he obtained villagers' signatures, which he forwarded to Morelia in support of the land redistribution.

---

85. Friedrich, *Agrarian Revolt,* 38.

86. The following discussion reflects Friedrich's and Embriz Osorio's empirical data, though not their analyses. See Friedrich, *Agrarian Revolt;* and Embriz Osorio, *La liga.*

87. Alan Knight, "El liberalismo mexicano desde la reforma hasta la revolución (una interpretación)," *Historia Mexicana* 35 (June–September 1985): 59–86.

88. Friedrich, *Agrarian Revolt,* 88–90.

Was Calles aggrieved at Tapia's efforts to establish quasi-socialist experiments with communal farming among the Tarascans? Perhaps by mobilizing Indians and leading them in anticlerical demonstrations, he could appeal to Calles' religious antipathies.

Tapia's highly original ideological meandering combined governmental largess, popular agrarian practice, Catholic images of comfort. Out of this combination of courage, conniving, chicanery, and manipulation of the national government, Tapia and his Indians successfully recovered the lands. His streak of independence ran too wide for Calles, who had him shot for it. Yet Tapia understood the inadequacies of both liberalism and Catholicism and resolved them in a way that proved prescient, as we shall see.

Premonitions of Impurity

By the 1920s, priests and agrarian capitalists had shaped an institutional order that apparently reflected their insistence that God himself blessed the marriage of piety and property. Indeed, to gain access to the Michoacán social landscape in the 1920s is to find that the churches and the haciendas had blended into the mountainous background. Like the mountains and the plains, the endurance of these social forms evoked a sense of permanence and inevitability. Throughout the region, Catholic peasants responded to these intimations of eternity with respect. If their devotion to the Virgin differed markedly from elite spirituality, it hardly challenged the articles of the faith.

However, there was something labored, even wistful, in the clerical insistence that this marriage was holy. For clearly disbelief roamed in the land. There were those who were mean enough to believe that the women following the reapers represented, in their humility and their humiliation, the true creatures of Catholicism.[89] If the priests and the capitalists overstated their case, it was because they sensed the fragility of the regime. And in this they proved to be correct.

89. It is this aspect of clerical experience that Jean Meyer, for all his brilliance and sensitivity, refused to acknowledge. The same might be said of François Xavier Guerra. See Jean Meyer, *La Cristiada*, trans. Aurelio Garzón del Camino, 2d ed., 3 vols. (Mexico City: Siglo XXI Editores, 1974); and François-Xavier Guerra, *México: Del Antiguo Régimen a la Revolución*, trans. Sergio Fernández Bravo, 2 vols. (Mexico City: Fondo de Cultura Económica, 1988).

CHAPTER THREE

From the Margins of Purity to the Margins of Danger

For now we see through a glass, darkly; but then face to face.
1 Corinthians 13:12

In the midst of the 1926–29 Cristero rebellion Lázaro Cárdenas asked a handful of Michoacán residents to remake campesinos caught up in the culture of purity and redemption.[1] While it was a ramshackle, poorly funded effort, it was also boldly experimental. Campesinos saw neighbors—people who wandered the same streets, experienced the same summer flooding—come to personify the government. They experienced what government could mean when it took seriously the hunger and illiteracy of the poor. Yet in the most elementary terms the experiment failed, as Cardenistas were thrown out of office and their opponents reinstated.

This turn of events could be explained in the terms of conventional political history. It could be said that forces rallying around the church and around the landowning elite overwhelmed Cárdenas's cadre, the Cardenistas.[2] A rather muscle-bound perspective drawing its strength

---

1. Jean Meyer reconstructs the history of the Cristeros with passion and courage, and I make no attempt to rewrite that story here. See Jean Meyer, *La Cristiada*, trans. Aurelio Garzón del Camino, 2d ed., 3 vols. (Mexico City: Siglo XXI Editores, 1974).

2. In "El surgimiento del agrarismo cardenista—una revisión de las tesis populistas," *Historia Mexicana* 27 (January–March 1978): 333–56, Romana Falcón expends her considerable historical talent to develop such an approach. See also Lorenzo Meyer, *El*

from the political clout of ex-president Plutarco Elías Calles and the old Michoacán elites, it does not capture the tenuous realities the Cardenistas confronted. Just as the revolutionary winds that swept Mexico had subsided, a vigorous Catholic breeze had blown through Michoacán. Indeed, more Cristeros came from Michoacán than from any other state. Inexplicably, campesinos who once had endured insults in relative tranquility repeatedly sought to destabilize the government.[3]

Faced with campesinos who seemed wanton in their rebelliousness, Cárdenas sorely needed men and women who understood Michoacán culture. More than that, because of his determination to forge campesinos anew, Cárdenas required people who possessed a critical distance from that culture. His ideal Michoacán cadre, then, would have resided *alongside* the culture of purity.

And in a certain, halting way this came to pass. Most of the men and women who responded to Cárdenas's invitation had grown up in Michoacán villages and towns.[4] Attending church, spending days in the countryside, they had witnessed Indian rituals in the plazas and participated in routine Michoacán pastimes. Despite all this, they emerged as outsiders. While their vision was sometimes acute, in significant ways it glazed over. It recognized little about the festive and workaday experiences of campesinos, and even less regarding the devout Catholics who fashioned individual hope from the Virgin's slender crown. Immune to the most transcendental forms of Catholic culture, Cardenas's followers

---

conflicto social y los gobiernos del maximato, vol. 13 of *La historia de la revolución mexicana,* ed. Luis González (Mexico City: El Colegio de México, 1978), 256–57. For a work with a similar approach but championing a very different viewpoint, see Victoriano Anguiano Equihua, *Lázaro Cárdenas, se feudo y la política nacional* (Mexico City: Editorial Eréndira, 1951).

3. *Relative* is an important qualifier here, as campesinos deployed numerous forms of underground protest. This protest, as Gramsci saw, was part and parcel of a system whose stability depended both on that protest and on its containment. See Antonio Gramsci, *Selections from the Prison Notebooks,* ed. and trans. Quintin Hoare and Geoffrey Nowell Smith (New York: International Publishers, 1971), 52, 161. For a provocative exploration of subordinate classes' relative *resistance,* see James C. Scott, *Weapons of the Weak: Everyday Forms of Peasant Resistance* (New Haven: Yale University Press, 1985). I question the utility of this model in a case where cultural knowledge is at stake in "Cardenistas, Campesinos, and the Weapons of the Weak: The Limits of Everyday Resistance in Michoacán, Mexico, 1934–1940," *Peasant Studies* 16 (summer 1989): 233–50.

4. Interview with Cardenista leader Jesús Múgica Martínez, Morelia, Michoacán, December 1984; personal tabulation based on Jesús Múgica Martínez, *La Confederación Revolucionaria Michoacana del Trabajo* (Mexico City: EDDISA Ediciones, 1982), 98.

found the ways that ordinary people fashioned and refashioned images for their own personal relief difficult to fathom.

What the Cardenistas came to instead was a certain cramped liberalism. A creed that would prove compatible with a detached, sympathetic view of campesinos, their liberalism espoused individual liberty, the surety of existential equality, the possibility of social advancement. It declared that people were not destined to remain huddled and destitute. In the Michoacán of the late twenties and early thirties this must have served as a challenge to the beneficiaries of the old order, a challenge that led the Cardenistas from the margins of purity to the margins of danger.

To Scale the Walls

If we continue the exploration in the sociological and architectural terms we have employed here, we find the church to be a walled fortress. Inside, parishioners encountered a God determined to shut out other presences, demanding conformity. However, the presence of a handful of liberals in the area who were trying to revolutionize the peasantry leads to doubt. The walls must have been more permeable than they appeared. What accounts for this seeming paradox? And how can we come to understand it?

In summary terms, the liberals shared much with their neighbors. Like most Michoacanos—four-fifths of the population, to be exact[5]—they were mestizos. Family conventions conformed to practices long common among mestizos and Tarascans. Fathers were viewed as the principal breadwinners, while women were assigned domestic chores. Still, at least three aspects of their backgrounds were unusual during that time and place. There was, for example, the matter of money. While their family backgrounds varied somewhat, they all described themselves as members of a tentative and downwardly mobile lower middle class. Jesús Múgica Martínez's father owned a carpentry shop, where he worked during the dry season. When the rains came, he "dedicated himself to working the land."[6] His mother was a house-

---

5. Fernando Foglio Miramontes, *Geografía económica agrícola del estado de Michoacán*, 4 vols. (Mexico City: Editorial Cultura, 1936), 2:138.

6. Interview with Múgica Martínez, November 1989.

wife. Tomás Rico Cano's father was a farmer before he became a small shopkeeper. Rico Cano placed his family squarely in "the lower middle class."[7] José Corona Núñez's father held a position as an administrator of tithes, a job that provided his family with a house Corona remembered as "palatial." But when Corona was five years old his father died, leaving his mother dependent on the charity of relatives.[8] Similarly, Angelina Acosta's father, an hacienda administrator, died during her youth.[9] Constantino Murillo's muleteer father was murdered by the bandit Inés Chávez García.[10]

It is also true that in this region characterized by widespread insistence on ideological conformity, a few of the parents maintained doubts. Catholic ritual was of course alien to the families of Protestants who would work as Cardenista teachers, men and women like Moisés Sáenz and Evangelina Rodríguez Carbajal. Yet even in some Catholic families liberalism had gained a toehold. Characteristically, these families were divided, with mothers devoted to Catholic tenets and fathers flirting with free thought. But this division should not be overstated: even liberal fathers might also view themselves as Catholic. As their sons proclaimed, coexistence was possible. Rico Cano described his father as "Catholic, but liberal also." Hilario Reyes echoed this view, pointing out that his father was "Catholic, but he was not a fanatic."[11]

The liberals' educational backgrounds also distinguished them from most people in the region. Indeed, they would later discover that even teachers had barely "taken their first letters," in Rico Cano's despairing phrase. He had a point. Despite twelve years of relatively strenuous governmental efforts to promote basic literacy, census takers found 73 percent of the male population and 76.6 percent of the women illiterate in 1940. In fact, 14.7 percent of the male population and 13.2 percent of the women had never entered a classroom.[12]

Within this context, their formal educational backgrounds were

7. Interview with Tomás Rico Cano, Morelia, August 1990.

8. Interviews with José Corona Núñez, Morelia, July 1985, July 1989.

9. Interview with Angelina Acosta, Zamora, Michoacán, November 1990.

10. Interviews with Constantino Murillo, Morelia, July 1985, March 1990.

11. Interviews with Hilario Reyes, Morelia, July 1985, June 1990; and with Rico Cano, August 1990.

12. My calculations are based on Estados Unidos Mexicanos, Secretaría de la Economía Nacional, Dirección General de Estadística Sexto censo de población, 1940: Estado de Michoacán (Mexico City, 1943–48), 13, 28.

impressive. Tomás Rico Cano and Hilario Reyes attended preparatory school, then the Morelia normal school, the teacher training school. Jesús Múgica Martínez attended the University of San Nicolás de Hidalgo in Morelia. Upon completing primary school José Corona Núñez enrolled first in the Colegio de San Pablo in Yiriria, then in the Seminario Tridentino of San Luis Potosí. Angelina Acosta graduated from primary school and completed courses of study at both the "normal" pedagogical normal school in Zamora and a commercial normal school as well.[13]

Another way to proceed would be to rummage through dusty photograph albums and haunt abandoned movie theaters. Behind these means of exploration lies the fact that Cardenistas learned particular ways of seeing the dominant culture in the relatively slow-moving towns of their youth. Later, by summoning his followers to political action, Cárdenas enabled them to bring their visions to life.

Handling the verbal "photographs" is the more tentative process. Lodged in the memories of the more active Cardenistas, this collection became accessible through repeated forays into anthropological history. Admittedly, as memoirs collected years after the facts, these documents lead to a specific methodological concern. Historians, who by trade are committed both to envisioning and explaining the moment as ephemeral, correctly suspect any efforts to push anthropology's photographic emphasis on fleeting social relations and social values beyond their limited temporal frames.[14] To be blunt, the anthropological historian routinely confronts the fact that outside pressures that alter perspectives multiply over time.[15] In Michoacán, however, docu-

13. Interviews with Múgica Martínez, June 1990; Corona Núñez, July 1985; and Acosta, November 1990.

14. For thoughtful analyses of the new cultural history, see Peter Burke, *The Historical Anthropology of Early Modern Italy* (Cambridge: Cambridge University Press, 1987), 3–22; and Aletta Bierstack, "Local Knowledge, Local History: Geertz and Beyond," in *The New Cultural History,* ed. Lynn Hunt (Berkeley: University of California Press, 1989), 72–96.

15. It is worth remembering that for the disenfranchised, the favored method of recollection is to enter the banks of memory and withdraw verbal accounts of the past. Those who have reproduced this method with great success seem to believe that the political significance of the stories recaptured overrides the epistemological concerns the method raises. See, for example, Peter Winn, *Weavers of Revolution: The Yarur Workers and Chile's Road to Socialism* (New York: Oxford University Press, 1986); Elena Poniatowska, *La noche de Tlatelolco* (Mexico City: Biblioteca Era, 1971); and Theodore Rosengarten, *All God's Dangers: The Life of Nate Shaw* (New York: Knopf, 1974).

mentary research yielding the same biases and blindness during the twenties and thirties tempered this concern.[16]

Rather than a methodological tension between present and past, oral historical and documentary research with Cardenistas led to a more sobering problem: for all their proximity to the world they hoped to redeem, these Cardenistas developed a peculiar blindness to certain campesino values and ways of being. Notice that this blindness was not the result of insularity or provincialism. The Cardenistas were not persuaded that only one perspective existed. Rather, while they recognized that they differed from the campesinos, they misconstrued the nature of the difference. Out of a confused determination to rise above poverty and a spiritualism they tagged "fanaticism," they stressed the class dimension.[17] One false step and they could descend into the world of faceless campesinos. As the Cardenista José Corona Núñez expressed it, "We were poor, but we were of cashmere. They were of huarache and despised."[18] While class and psychodynamics doubtless played a crucial role, while issues of origins remain seductive, they are of minor significance here. What matters more is that for people determined to address and undermine the *mentalité* of the campesinos, from a very early age they developed social patterns that heightened their roles as bemused observers.

A Collection of Sidelong Glances

Parents and priests tirelessly directed the Cardenista gaze along conventional paths. Cardenistas, in turn, strained to see what others did. Yet they could not. Time and again they either saw reality differently or saw nothing at all. Hoping to explain the emptiness and substitutions, they offer up a thin collection of photographs. Focusing on their encounters with Catholicism, with campesinos, and with local liberals, in each case the camera captures a sidelong glance.

16. See chapters 5 and 6 below.
17. A number of Cardenistas branded peasant religiosity "fanaticism," as revealed in interviews with Cardenistas Murillo, July 1985; Rico Cano, August 1990; and Reyes, July 1985. This tendency persisted throughout the 1930s. See, for example, Policarpo L. Sánchez, Profesor inspector federal, Michoacán, 12 February 1936, caja 412, Archivo Histórico de la Secretaría de Educación Pública (AHSEP), Mexico City.
18. Interviews with Corona Núñez, July 1985, July 1989.

Although their trajectory was hardly linear, we can discern a certain movement away from the safest places toward the more dangerous. Begin, then, with the church. Mexican novelists often have developed characters practicing a stilted, rigid Catholicism supposedly endemic to western Mexico. Yet the multifaceted genius of Catholicism, the fact that its rituals can appear to be both routine and alluring, was not lost on Michoacanos. In fact, most of the people who would become Cardenistas saw Catholicism as daily bread. Denounced as conservative "whites" by the Cardenista socialist José Corona Núñez, they saw teaching as a job or an avocation, not as an opportunity to promote anticlericalism or challenge social inequities.[19]

Those who most interest us, however, were some of the Cardenista leaders. They include Jesús Múgica Martínez, who would lead the Cardenista program for educating the children of soldiers, and Evangelina Rodríguez, one of the first women school inspectors. They also include José Corona Núñez, Tomás Rico Cano, Hilario Reyes Garibaldi, Constantino Murillo, a fistful of teachers who led the political organization Cárdenas devised.

These men and women found Catholic belief both compelling and elusive. We see them together in a photograph we might label "The Power and the Glory." At the edge of the photograph is a young boy. He is surrounded by a group of women who stare at him covetously. They wear expressions of people determined to transmit their own Catholic devotion to their children.

These parents proved energetic in their attempts to proselytize. As Múgica Martínez mused, "Our mothers tried to make us feel that there was nothing else, only Catholicism."[20] Molding their daily routine to Catholic dictates, women led their families in daily prayers.[21] They set their lives by the Catholic calendar.[22] To tame remarkable events such as birth, marriage, and death, they surrounded them with incense, priestly utterances, the rituals of festive life.

Similarly, they styled the church as a hedge against natural or supernatural mysteries. In their prayers they sometimes murmured,

19. Interview with Corona Núñez, July 1985.
20. Interviews with Múgica Martínez, August 1989, June 1990.
21. Interviews with Múgica Martínez, July, August 1989, and Reyes, July 1985; Griselda Villegas Muñoz, *Emilia, una mujer de Jiquilpan* (Jiquilpan de Juárez: Centro de Estudios de la Revolución Mexicana "Lázaro Cárdenas," A.C., 1984), 20.
22. Villegas Muñoz, *Emilia*, 17–21; Luis González, *Zamora*, 2d ed. (Zamora: El Colegio de Michoacán, 1984), 123–27.

"Mother of Guadalupe, our sufferings are immense. Oh you who have sheltered everyone, shelter us now."[23] In times of drought or sickness, they joined together in processions to request supernatural attention. Then, in an attempt to seal the bargain, they purchased household replicas of gold-encrusted church statues. "We were trying to get God on our side," explained Ario resident Esperanza Rocha.[24]

Some mothers spread before their sons the advantages of the priesthood. Such positions offered status in an uncertain universe. Women would shower them with attentions ranging from confidences to cooked meals. And the priesthood promised a free, if cloistered, education and a bookish life.[25] Powerful inducements, but their effect on some of the Cardenistas-to-be was ambiguous. As a boy Rico Cano found the church entrancing, full of "beautiful saints and images." Noticing that he went to church "constantly," his mother and her friends began to envision "Tomasito, the little priest." Yet Rico Cano refused the priesthood. "I couldn't do it. I began to study and learned that that kind of fanatic thought had to be overcome. As I studied, I improved the way I thought."[26] Finding the miracles baffling, Múgica Martínez tried to decipher them intellectually. "Miracles seemed so hard to understand that I tried to puzzle them out. The Bible told much about Jesus's cures, so maybe they believed a miracle was a cure for their sicknesses."[27]

Corona Núñez went so far as to enter a seminary. "I wanted to study, so I told my mother that I wanted to be a priest." Upon discovering that the intellectual pursuit was laden with perspectives and commitments with which he disagreed, he baited the priests. "I insisted that if dogs have souls, they have souls, and as faithful as they are, they should go to heaven rather than be tossed in the garbage."[28] Unable to persuade the priest of the immortality of canine souls, Corona left the seminary.

Adrift in a depopulated land of dubious belief, they took no comfort from the mestizo campesinos. Indeed, there could be no comfort,

23. Interview with Reyes, June 1990.
24. Interviews with Múgica Martínez, July 1988; and Esperanza Rocha, Ario de Rayón, Michoacán, June 1990.
25. Interviews with Corona Núñez, July 1989; and Rico Cano, August 1990.
26. Interview with Rico Cano, August 1990.
27. Interview with Múgica Martínez, July 1988.
28. Interview with Corona Núñez, July 1989.

for the mestizos amounted to poor relations. As such, they inspired an unspoken fear of economic decline. Although impoverished mestizos were everywhere, Cardenistas did not fraternize with them. In a photograph of Cardenistas watching campesinos trudging home from work, the mestizos have been relegated to the edges. Peering at them, the Cardenistas' eyes glaze over with disinterest. The photograph might have been labeled "Faceless Campesinos." For Constantino Murillo and Hilario Reyes, mestizos "just did not have a culture."[29] Other Cardenistas knew little about mestizos' work lives. As Múgica Martínez admitted, "We revolutionaries knew almost nothing about farming."[30] This was probably particularly true of women like Angelina Acosta. Even though her father was an overseer on an hacienda employing solely mestizos, she never visited the estate.[31]

The Indians affected them differently. In the photograph labeled "A Brush with the Exotic," Cardenistas watch Indians performing the Tarascan Dance of the Little Old Men. And here the Cardenistas' eyes glimmer with an expression that is frankly acquisitive. The Indians lived in mysterious alternative worlds, worlds they hoped to appropriate. For Corona Núñez, the Indians beckoned, tempting him with forbidden knowledge. "My mother absolutely prohibited my associating with them. But they knew so much. They taught me to trap squirrels. They taught their legends, the Tarascan language itself."[32] As a child Rico Cano's parents summoned family members, prepared food, and altogether treated Indian rituals as occasions for outings. He experienced the Indians as "living representations of anthropology, history, of tradition itself."[33]

The last photo of the men was hard to come by. Labeled "The Promise of Free Thought," it depicts a boy and a man caught in earnest conversation over a book. It seems little enough, but the boys had stumbled outside the church's thoroughgoing efforts at classification. Central to this system was the conceit that physical appearance would readily reveal a person's identity. Thus priests wore special clothing, lepers displayed their sores. Even a hint at free thought from

29. The comment comes from Constantino Murillo, but Hilario Reyes expressed similar doubts regarding the existence of a mestizo culture (interviews, July 1985).
30. Interview with Múgica Martínez, December 1984.
31. Interview with Acosta, November 1990.
32. Interview with Corona Núñez, July 1989.
33. Interview with Rico Cano, August 1990.

a person who to the uninitiated eye appeared to be a devout Catholic was suspect.

This meant that the few liberals afoot had to be scorned. Jesús Múgica Martínez and José Corona Núñez learned why when they entered liberals' homes. Though initially the houses seemed like other homes—spaces bound by walls and ceilings—there were no domestic replicas of the church, replete with images of Jesus and the Virgin. Instead, Morelos, Matamoros, Juárez, and Occampo hung on the walls.[34] Books censored by the church rested on the shelves.[35] And at the table they found "their first real teacher," the man who would reveal the history of Mexican liberalism they had been denied. In ad hoc comments about strangers long dead, they evoked the image of a Juárez gathering up the tokens of distinction, the rags of the mestizos, the rebozos of the Indians, and setting them afire. Then something happened. Tying together words about men separated by time and space, evoking unknown presences of "people nobody had told me about,"[36] they managed to open their students' eyes to the idea of human equality.

In a separate album we come upon a very different kind of photograph. A woman in the front room peers out. Compared with the men's experiences, her encounters with danger are infrequent. Men could be recruited for the priesthood, but the nunnery lacked the monastery's élan. Sor Juana's heyday had long passed, and nobody fussed over nuns as they did priests. Men left their homes to peer at the Indians, but women were more sheltered. Indeed, liberalism itself remained a male-dominated enclave.

An Invitation to Animation

It would seem that they were stuck. They visited the people and the ideas that most attracted them, studied them in half-light, and then returned home. However much they idealized the

---

34. Interview with Corona Núñez, July 1989; José Corona Núñez, *A través de mi vida: Historia de mi pueblo* (Morelia: Universidad Michoacana de San Nicolás de Hidalgo, 1984), 28.

35. Interview with Múgica Martínez, July 1989.

36. Ibid.

Indians or longed for justice, they were confined by an environment in which relations of equality with the poor were taboo. And however much they railed against those conventions, they profited from them. This might have doomed them to loneliness, to whistling their hopes in the provincial wind until they grew brittle with age. They might have continued muting their complaints about the priests, privately spinning their shadowy dreams of companionship with the Indians.

Cárdenas and the Cristero rebellion changed all that. The rebellion had engulfed the state, transforming Cárdenas's 1928–32 governorship into an uncertain proposition. The work of war overshadowed the construction and maintenance of governmental institutions, as the skirmishes frequently put a stop to the government's nascent land reform and educational program.[37] In fact, Cárdenas himself took a leave of absence from his duties as governor to lead the government's forces against the Cristeros in Michoacán's Coalcomán region.

As if that were not enough, Cárdenas's power was makeshift and illusionary. As governor, he appeared dominant, and he bartered this appearance to gain adherents. However, his power ultimately came from Calles, the man who had provided him with military tutelage during the revolution. For all of Cárdenas's painstaking loyalty to Calles, the Jefe Máximo's blessing was secure only as long as Cárdenas maintained Calles-style policies. Cárdenas responded to those challenges by forging a cadre out of students in the Morelia teacher training school, Morelia university students, and local caciques. Enveloping his plan with an aura of clannishness, Cárdenas invited the students from the Morelia schools for Saturday morning coffee at his home.[38] There he and his lifelong political colleague Francisco J. Múgica imparted what the Cardenista Hilario Reyes remembers as "crucial political instruction." Indoctrinating them into the intricacies of low-level espionage, Múgica charged them with gathering information about the ebbs and flows of local political life. "He made us confidential agents. We were to watch the basketball or baseball team, or go to the fiestas to capture the thinking. Then we were to submit monthly reports to Múgica."

To formalize these efforts, at Pátzcuaro in 1929 Cárdenas established the Confederación Revolucionario Michoacano del Trabajo, the

37. David Raby, *Educación y revolución social en México, 1921–1940* (Mexico City: SEP, 1974), 199–204.
38. Interview with Reyes, June 1990.

CRMDT. Organized as a vanguard party, it boasted a central committee and a hierarchical structure with Cárdenas as president and ultimate arbiter.

At the local level, Cárdenas mobilized his temporary power as governor to place rural strongmen in local leadership positions. These men included both prerevolutionary political bosses and revolutionary comrades in arms like Ernesto Prado of the Once Pueblos and Pedro Talavera of Zurumutaro.[39] To groom followers, caciques offered campesinos land and arms. In return, they expected campesinos to enlist in the government's anticlerical crusade, fighting Cristeros on demand. As Corona Núñez put it, "We manipulated the pueblos. The majority was not with us. The people who followed us were minorities."[40]

Much about the CRMDT seems forbidding in its authoritarianism. If democracy implies that citizens possess meaningful say over their political destinies, the CRMDT machinations clearly were not democratic. At the same time, as an organization born of insecurity, it tended to be contradictory. This was particular true because Cardenista educators, who often were vigorous CRMDT leaders and members, determined to empower the campesinos.

Peripheral Visions Come to Life

As solitary villagers, the Cardenistas had shared a problem recognizable to poets or lovers in the early throes of courtship. The problem was not absence of affection. The revolutionaries viewed campesinos with concern and longing. Yet their vision was fragmentary in two ways. First, they did not see what the peasants saw. Second, their romanticism and lack of regular contact with peasants lent their vision a peripheral quality. Now, however, Cárdenas had encouraged them to animate their visions. As he put it at the first CRMDT convention, they were to "seek the emancipation of the worker from their conditions as pariahs" and to tackle "the moral, intellectual, and physical education of the campesinos."[41] In specific terms, his followers

39. Interviews with Múgica Martínez, December 1984; and Corona Núñez, July 1985.
40. Interview with Corona Núñez, July 1985.
41. Múgica Martínez, *La confederación*, 98.

were to teach basic literacy and to mobilize adults to solicit land. They were to marshal support for a secular government rather than an international church.

Notwithstanding Cárdenas's hope of regulating this effort to repair the world, a number of factors made this an era of improvisation. There was the nebulous but palpable fact that the revolution had cut both government and social relations adrift from earlier certainties. The relationship between the governors and the governed remained uncertain. Then too, inadequate funding meant that teachers were infrequently supervised, lending a certain freedom of expression to their encounters with students. Cárdenas was forced to rely on his followers' ideas, no matter how flawed.

Whatever their shared marginalities, these people had experienced social reality differently, and they had developed different views of rural Michoacanos. Still, as we enter the schoolrooms, we will find that the revolutionary visions conformed to two loose patterns. In the first, the Cardenistas' hope to bridge the social distance separating them from their neighbors jostled with a darker tendency to compensate for their personal social marginality by exhibiting their class and educational advantages. In the second pattern, Protestants such as Evangelina Rodríguez Carbajal and Moisés Sáenz combined the conviction of their cultural superiority with a tireless will to share their cultural wealth with campesinos.

Young, unmarried, and determined, Angelina Acosta created a classroom on Zamora's outskirts in which her drive to overcome the looming status of spinsterhood collided with a sense of belonging among the poor.[42] Without question, she had been trained for something else. The daughter of an hacienda overseer and a housewife, she was reared in conventional Zamora fashion. Her parents instructed her in the articles of the faith. They taught her that women were to revel in domesticity, marry young, and maintain public modesty. Then her father died, and for whatever reason—she focused on the fact that "I was just so tall"—no fiancé appeared.

Forced by circumstance to flaunt tradition, Acosta sought a job as a rural teacher. Within the confines of Zamora's Catholic culture, it was a job replete with risks to her social standing. As she would be teaching in a village on the outskirts of town, friends and neighbors could

42. The following analysis draws on the interview with Acosta, November 1990.

not readily monitor her behavior. While the curriculum in Catholic schools included instruction in the catechism, Acosta's work for an anticlerical government precluded such lessons. Most important, despite the cultural expectation of female silence on public issues, her job demanded that she speak outside the domestic setting on a range of worldly issues.

To avoid the sidelong glance or stray remark, she resorted to the most conventional defense, her mother. Together they made the weekly journey to the village of La Rinconada. "She went with me out of affection and to protect me," Acosta said. In La Rinconada her mother kept house and cooked, and she accompanied Angelina back to Zamora every weekend.

Once she was in the village, the risks turned private. They began when Acosta claimed her position as teacher. Lacking the social armor that either wealth or marriage would have lent, she entered the schoolroom alone. Then the strangers shuffled in, one by one. When she saw them staring at her, she realized how they differed from her. Some were adults, while she was but a girl of fifteen. Some were men. All were poor, and all worked in ways that were foreign to her.

As Acosta tells it, the awkwardness passed. If she had once considered campesinos, and particularly campesino men, as alien, a subtle transformation occurred. In Zamora at fifteen she was approaching spinsterhood, but here her youth enabled her to fill the schoolroom with students. "I was teaching boys who were older than me. But we got along, because they were young and I was so young. You know, every week they would be waiting for me when I came back from Zamora." For her part, she "felt I had found a place where I belonged."

Both campesinos and teacher had reasons to risk their unusual relationship. For campesinos, Acosta was an agent of a government promising them benefits. In return, while she maintains that they were "only campesinos and a little backward at that," they offered Acosta the possibility of an acceptance denied her in Zamora.

Carrying a certain social edginess into the schoolhouse, Acosta developed a curiously open classroom. Bent on demonstrating her superiority, she offered campesinos reams of advice. "I told them how to improve their lives, how to take care of their health. I told them to plant vegetables, domesticate wild birds, raise pigs." But in some ways her ignorance of the subject matter forced her to relinquish her pretensions of superiority from time to time. She begged her adult students to "eat your eggs. Don't sell them. You need them for your health." When they responded that they needed the money to dress themselves, she backed down.

In the second schoolroom we find José Corona Núñez, but he is not alone.[43] From his boyhood efforts to befriend the Indians and his adolescent rejection of the church came the demons of early manhood. In fact a fragment of the seminary boy quarreling with the priest lived on in Corona Núñez. The boy so sure of the dog's eternal destiny became the man persuaded of the correctness of his views. In his work in Cuitzeo he came to revel in manipulation, the tools of the self-styled enlightened few. "I stayed up late at night figuring out how to control and dominate the CRMDT congress. For the majority was white. Eight of us dominated the whole congress."

Corona's teaching might be viewed in the same light. Viewing campesinos as "intelligent, but in that way of untrained campesinos," he was something of the secular priest imparting fragments of a wider vision that only he understood in full. It is worth remembering his work with the men soliciting governmental land. "We manipulated the pueblo, filling out the forms, advising them on what they had to do. But most people were against us."

It will not do, however, to dismiss Corona's awkward boyhood attempts at companionship with people he misunderstood but still sought out. That longing for fellowship with Indians and campesinos persisted throughout Corona's life as a revolutionary. In Cuitzeo he expressed it not simply through the work with the agraristas but also through the early morning hours he spent teaching children their first letters. Then in the afternoon he was off to organize a cooperative for the fishermen. And he opened a night school for men.

Then there were teachers destined by their Protestantism to be the ultimate outsiders. Consider Evangelina Rodríguez Carbajal, that portrait of a rebel. Where women of a certain age were trained to temper their charms, Rodríguez consistently presented herself as "a beautiful woman who knew how to dress."[44] Where conventional women culti-

43. The following analysis draws on the interviews with Corona Núñez, July 1985, July 1989.

44. While Michoacanos' perspectives on Rodríguez Carbajal varied widely, all agreed regarding her appearance. This included her champions, such as colleague Jesús Múgica Martínez, employees like Angelina Acosta, and critics like Zamora native Francisco Elizalde. Interviews with Francisco Elizalde, Zamora, June 1988; Múgica Martínez, July 1988; and Acosta, November 1990.

vated a housebound aspect, she thought nothing of riding hours to remote villages to set things aright. And despite Catholicism's relentless assertion of its universality, she was no Catholic.

Against villagers' recognition of her cultural idiosyncrasies, Rodríguez had developed allies in key places. Like other women who were active in public life during the postrevolutionary era, she had come to see government figures as potential allies against misunderstanding villagers.[45] Rodríguez became a slavish adherent of the political line of the government at hand. During Calles's pro-hacienda administration, she persistently cultivated landowners' assistance in her educational designs.[46] Assessing this interaction for her superiors, she reported that "since I began my job, I have encouraged an ample interchange of ideas with many people of good will who, for their wisdom, economic or political power have the destinies of this pueblo in their hands; I have received interesting suggestions and promises of cooperation which will soon become realities."[47] Rodríguez's approach to Cárdenas's presidential policies would be equally reverential.

Her classrooms, on the other hand, were a maze of cultural incomprehension. As a non-Catholic, she claimed to find the most routine observances of Catholicism anachronistic and peculiar. She portrayed the Morelia campesinos as "complete fanatics in their manner of observing their religion. I was surprised to find that they still retain many of their antique traditions. They have the custom of celebrating what is called Holy Week or Lent, reliving days of yore."[48]

Finally, there is a room in the meseta tarasca village of Carapan. On a Sunday afternoon in 1932 a caravan arrived. Inside were men and women from Mexico City determined to make Tarascan Indians into ornaments of western civilization. Considering the scope of the project and the growing fame of its participants, including director Moisés Sáenz, ethnologist Carlos Basauri, school director José Guadalupe Nájera, and psychologist Ana María Reyna, their initial approach to

45. I explored this fragile women's movement in research leading to Marjorie Becker, "The Mexican Women's Revolution" (seminar paper, Yale University, 1982).

46. Though Obregón and Calles redistributed some land, the centerpiece of their agrarian policy was the protection of agricultural capitalists producing for the export market. See Enrique Krauze, Jean Meyer, and Cayetano Reyes, *La reconstrucción económica*, vol. 10 of González, *La historia de la revolución mexicana* (1977), 162, 164.

47. "Año 1925 Michoacán/Asuntos escolares del estado," expediente G, 12–3–9–64, AHSEP.

48. Ibid.

the Indians was quite tentative.[49] As though they feared descending into a cauldron of exoticism, they fabricated a niche filled with ethnic security. Speaking only Spanish, they limited household contact with Tarascans to conversations about the food a handful of Indians fetched and cooked for them.[50]

Establishing themselves in an enclave, the Carapan team revealed both their discomfort with the Indians and their assumptions regarding their own culture. Nonetheless, these men and women were more than city-bred tourists out for an air with the Indians. Along with their unswerving view of western preeminence, they held the conviction that Indians could be westerners. As Sáenz told a group of Tarascans, "We are trying to get you to understand that incorporation means putting you in an equal cultural, political, and economic position with the rest of the Mexicans, which requires instruction, learning Spanish, and learning to work better."[51]

Persuaded that western culture spoke to the Indians, Sáenz developed what might be called a democratic exercise in cultural imperialism. In the classroom Sáenz invited Tarascans to respond to a variety of western representations of reality. He read them news of Gandhi's hunger strike from a Mexico City newspaper. He taught them the song "Indian of my soul, delight of my heart, return to me, gaze at me with those black eyes of yours." Finally, he read them a modernist poem about a frog, a toad, and the moon.[52]

Counterrevolutionary Winds

The Cardenistas did not manage to remake the world between 1928 and 1932. Since Cárdenas never had the political capital to redistribute significant amounts of land, the strength of the landlords remained daunting. Indeed, the agrarian panorama is sobering. Landed inequity in Michoacán was greater in 1932 than it had been in 1915, for medium-sized properties were subject to greater relative

49. Moisés Sáenz, *Carapan: Bosquejo de una experiencia* (Lima: Librería e imprenta Gil, 1936), 33.
50. Ibid., 39–41.
51. Ibid., 142–43.
52. Ibid., 141.

expropriation than the large estates.[53] In the spiritual domain, while here and there a Cardenista hoped to displace the priests, in fact the priests encountered relatively few schoolhouse rivals.

Unable to repair much of the world, Cardenistas nonetheless questioned the inevitability of the status quo. It was a question destined to unnerve a number of people. Cárdenas's agrarian policies proved untenable for Calles, who was committed to an economic order dominated by agrarian capitalists. Landlords possessed a stake in the lopsided distribution of wealth. For priests, the culture of purity and redemption was an earthly enactment of a celestial drama. And many campesinos claimed the right to fabricate and refabricate their connections to God.

People who had been buffeted by the revolutionary winds soon found the winds blowing in a different direction. At the end of Cárdenas's governorship, Benigno Serrato was designated governor of the state. A man who remains an enigmatic figure—and must remain so until the Mexican national defense archives are fully open to researchers[54]—he has been cast as a Calles puppet.[55] What seems entirely likely is that Calles demanded an end to Cárdenas-style agrarianism. Lacking the power to topple Calles, Cárdenas proved amenable to the idea of placating him.

Yet what of the fact that Serrato almost immediately embraced the church? This may not have endeared him to men as anticlerical as Calles and Cárdenas. Calles, however, had hired Serrato for the job of conservative restoration. And Cárdenas? A Cardenista detractor once claimed that "Cárdenas was a man who knew how to throw the rock and hide the hand,"[56] but, in fact, Cárdenas's options were limited. Outmaneuvered by Calles, he could not yet implement his program in Michoacán. He proceeded to sacrifice both the anticlerical campesinos he had mobilized and his own cadre.

For as the Cardenistas would find, Serrato had designs on the CRMDT. As we have seen, Cárdenas believed in grooming campesinos to participate as subordinate members of government. Critical Cardenista methods in promoting that aim had been the development

53. Foglio Miramontes, *Geografía*, 3:221; Manuel Diego Hernández, *La confederación revolucionaria michoacana del trabajo* (Jiquilpan de Juárez: Centro de Estudios de la Revolución Mexicana "Lázaro Cárdenas," A.C, n.d.), 41.

54. At present they are sporadically open to selected researchers.

55. Meyer, *El conflicto social y los gobiernos del maximato*, 257.

56. Interview with Ario de Rayón resident Salvador Peña, Ario de Rayón, September 1985.

of a vanguard party and the mobilization of large numbers of campesinos. The Serratistas began to employ identical techniques.[57] Serrato disarmed the agraristas and the CRMDT members.[58] He replaced Cardenista municipal authorities with officials loyal to him.[59] Finally, he fabricated a parallel CRMDT to enforce his new rural order.[60]

Clearly, this was no orderly transfer of power. Rather, the Serratistas utilized the Cardenista state-making techniques to reinforce the entrenched economic and political interests, which four years of Cardenismo had barely begun to dismantle. Not surprisingly, the newly powerless Cardenistas immediately recognized both the personal and the political implications of their position. The fact that the rise of Serratismo meant the demise of local Cardenismo and a consequent loss of employment colored some of the Cardenistas' initial responses to Serratismo. Sra. Aurelia Carbajal, the mother of school inspector Evangelina Rodríguez Carbajal, wrote to President Abelardo Rodríguez expressing her fear that Zamora Municipal President Guillermo Vargas might dismiss her daughter. Sra. Carbajal suggested that the very "revolutionary and constructive" nature of her daughter's work might provoke her dismissal. After all, she said, "along with being a fanatic," Vargas "sides with the bourgeoisie."[61]

Other local Cardenistas protested the restoration of the old order. Felipe Anguiano R. and Teófilo Pizaro Hernández, officers of the district federation of the CRMDT, described the reinstatement of the old elites. "The clergy, collaborating with the capitalists and the self-serving politicians, have established over thirty priests in their service; . . . they tried to destroy the system of ejidal grants. . . . The congressional representative José Valdovinos Garza, a well-known 'Cristero' is definitely allied with the enemies of the proletariat."[62]

57. Expedientes 541.5/2, 524/331–1, 525.3/61, 525.3/56, Abelardo Rodríguez, Fondo Presidentes, Archivo General de la Nación (AGN), Mexico City, are illuminating regarding the political techniques of the Serratistas. Manuel Diego Hernández and Romana Falcón illustrate the link between Serrato and the Michoacán hacendados in Diego Hernández, *La confederación;* and Falcón, "El surgimiento del agrarismo cardenista."

58. Expediente 541.5/2, Abelardo Rodríguez, Fondo Presidentes, AGN; Hernández, *La confederación.*

59. Expediente 524/331–1, Abelardo Rodríguez, Fondo Presidentes, AGN.

60. Expedientes 541.5/2, 524/331, 525.3/61, 525.3/56, Abelardo Rodríguez, Fondo Presidentes, AGN.

61. Expediente 543.21/4, Lázaro Cárdenas, Fondo Presidentes, AGN.

62. Expediente 524/331–1, Abelardo Rodríguez, Fondo Presidentes, AGN.

Despised by the old elites and lacking a clear mandate from the peasantry, the Cardenistas had found their only political home in the Cardenista government. Now the Serratistas had cast them out. Serratismo had so effectively undercut Cardenista control in Michoacán that even when Cárdenas announced his presidential candidacy on June 5, 1933, the Cardenistas could not muster political resilience.

Instead, events in the weeks following Cárdenas's announcement revealed the Cardenistas' continuing weakness. A major test of strength took place on June 11 in Zitácuaro, in northeastern Michoacán. There the Serratista CRMDT and the skeletal Cardenista group met in separate locations with the mandate to either unite or determine which group controlled the largest bloc of campesinos and workers in the district. The confederation with the most support would be allowed to represent campesinos and workers in Morelia.[63] With their ranks diminished, there was little hope for the Cardenistas, and they realized it. Their principal speaker, J. Jesús Rico, spoke of the "hunger and persecutions" they were suffering.[64]

Seeking to represent the campesinos in Morelia but lacking political clout, the Cardenistas resorted to the traditional weapons of the peasantry. Armed with rocks and knives, they marched to the building where the Serratistas were meeting. There Cardenistas pelted Serratistas with stones and clods of dirt.[65] That the Cardenistas, who had once collaborated in shaping rural destinies, were forced to rely on guerrilla tactics was just another indication that their political fortunes were depleted.

Not Yet Face to Face

In seeing the campesinos through a glass, darkly, the Cardenistas committed no more than a commonplace insensitivity.

63. "Varias constancias que obran en la causa que se instruye en los sucesos sangrientos desarrollados en esta ciudad de Zitácuaro, el día 11 de 6 de 1933," in "Juzgado de primera instancia de Zitácuaro, Michoacán," expediente 524/331–1, Abelardo Rodríguez, Fondo Presidentes, AGN.

64. "Varias constancias," 18, 22 (testimony of Salvador Jiménez Hernández and Aurelio Olivares).

65. "Varias constancias"; Benigno Serrato to Abelardo Rodríguez (copy to General de División Plutarco Elías Calles), 6 June 1933.

People routinely misunderstand their neighbors, and little comes of it. In Michoacán the political landscape had long been organized so that people's encounters would display neither political demand nor personal yearning, but the trappings of class and ethnicity.[66]

The revolution and the Cristero rebellion changed that, but in a way that has been misunderstood. It is customary to view peasant violence as a window into the lives of the poor. The recurrent scholarly perception has been that most of the time peasants are mired in dull lives, unworthy of comment. Only when they burn bridges, murder elites holed up in granaries, or mutilate teachers do they merit analytical notice.[67]

On purely historical grounds, such thinking is suspect. Since at least the sixteenth-century Conquest, Mexican Indians and peasants have had every reason to guard their belongings. Long before Mexican elites, long before Foucault, campesinos recognized that this included access to their consciousness.[68] Thus, Mexican peasant rebellions are not precisely the orgies of psychosocial revelation that analysts have imagined.[69] What Mexican peasant rebellions do reveal, on the other hand, is a heightened version of their political demands. In part, the Cardenistas' failure to understand those demands either in their quiet everyday version or in their violent rendition cost them their jobs.

However, neither the Cardenistas nor Cárdenas was yet prepared to see this as a failure of understanding. In part this was because other

66. In this regard, François-Xavier Guerra's insistence that Catholicism is universal and constructed around an organic community should be viewed as a sentimentalization. See *México: Del Antiguo Régimen a la Revolución,* trans. Sergio Fernández Bravo, 2 vols. (Mexico City: Fondo de Cultura Económica, 1988), 1:127, 128, 134, 143.

67. This may be one of the unconscious assumptions that inform the raft of studies of the revolution. Certainly for Domingo Sarmiento and a number of nineteenth-century Latin American elites, this was the commonplace assumption regarding the peasantry. For an assessment of nineteenth-century Latin American elites' arrogance toward the peasantry, see E. Bradford Burns, *The Poverty of Progress: Latin American in the Nineteenth Century* (Berkeley: University of California Press, 1980).

68. Although they do not make the argument in these terms, the work of some fine historians of colonial Mexico reveals this with great clarity. See Inga Clendinnen, *Ambivalent Conquests: Maya and Spaniard in Yucatán, 1517–1570* (Cambridge: Cambridge University Press, 1987); Charles Gibson, *The Aztecs under Spanish Rule: A History of the Indians of the Valley of Mexico, 1519–1810* (Stanford: Stanford University Press, 1964); and William B. Taylor, *Drinking, Homicide, and Rebellion in Colonial Mexican Villages* (Stanford: Stanford University Press, 1979).

69. The classic formulation of this approach is Octavio Paz, *The Labyrinth of Solitude: Life and Thought in Mexico,* trans. Lysander Kemp (New York: Grove, 1961).

factors—the sway of the hacendados, the resistance of the church— had influenced the Serratista comeback. It was also because of the inherent difficulty in envisioning what one has not learned to see. Thus when Cárdenas became president in 1934 and again needed men and women who had traveled the terrain of campesino consciousness, he would once more turn to his Michoacán cadre.

CHAPTER FOUR

Call Out a Posse, Gather Up Their Music, Teach Them to Sing

The Reinvention of the Indian in Postrevolutionary Michoacán

Rural teachers would be the ideal collectors, interpreters, and why not the creators, of our vernacular art.

Hugo Conzatti

It will be better not to return to the lost Eden.

Ramón López Velarde

On the eve of his 1934 presidency, a missionary tradition hovered over Lázaro Cárdenas and his former Michoacán cadre.[1] The president-elect and his followers found themselves in a situation akin to that of a Hannah or a John the Baptist. Passionate, troubled individuals, these people had been cast into the desert. Their isolation possessed an incessant quality: their troubles replayed, relentless as winds in the desert. Then suddenly their despair broke, giving way to idealism and hope.

After Cárdenas's Michoacán governorship, his Michoacán followers became part of this tradition. Castigated because of their real or imagined liberalism, they had been tossed out of office. Sometimes they lashed out in response, denouncing a "modern troglodyte" or "useless

1. A version of this chapter was presented at the Yale University Program in Agrarian Studies, New Haven, 7 February 1992. I have benefited from the thoughtful comments of Todd Edelman and James C. Scott. In addition, Diana Wylie's comparative allusions to South Africa and those of Linda Seligmann to Peru have proved most useful.

and jealous rural bosses."[2] But behind their indignation lay a deeper reality. They had been vigorous street fighters, but what had come of it? Whatever they had pieced together about peasant consciousness and behavior had become irrelevant. Because they no longer possessed power, what they knew was futile, stale as old leaves.

Unlike his cadre, Cárdenas possessed the potential power of the president-to-be. Moreover, in hope and desperation, legions of Mexicans ignored by previous postrevolutionary presidents turned to him, magnifying that power.[3] And as an ambulatory president, Cárdenas was not above inflaming the expectations of the campesinos he visited. Alive with projects, he might address Yucatán's henequen workers on a Wednesday and then organize peasants in Guerrero the following Friday.[4]

Yet problems marked the path to the presidency. Of particular concern was the smoldering west, a testimony to Plutarco Elías Calles' give-no-quarters brand of strength. As his war against the Michoacán Cristeros revealed, Cárdenas was a good Calles man in this as in much else. He joined with Calles and the Catholic hierarchy in devising a pact that ignored the popular clamor for a new, cleansed society.

Because of his Callista heritage, Cárdenas found himself thrashing about in his own political desert. Lacking both a ready political solution to a spiritual problem and the sort of cultural understanding that would have allowed him to lay campesinos' religious concerns to rest, he turned to his former followers. Calling them out of solitude, he dubbed them missionaries and told them they were responsible for the "spiritual redemption" of the masses.[5] To establish this mission, Cárdenas invited them to join with national Cardenistas who were sketching campesinos as they had seen them and as they envisioned them. These sketches would serve as a blueprint for Cárdenas's plan to reconstruct the countryside.

Yet missionaries? The term jars. This may be partly because scholarly defenders of popular Catholicism, agog with the buoyancy of feast days

2. "Protesta," *Pueblo Libre: Organo del Comité Radical Pro-Cárdenas,* 2 July 1933, 3.

3. Alicia Hernández Chávez, *La mecánica cardenista,* vol. 16 of *La historia de la revolución mexicana,* ed. Luis González (Mexico City: El Colegio de México, 1979).

4. For his address to henequen workers, see Lázaro Cárdenas, *Palabras y documentos públicos de Lázaro Cárdenas: Mensajes, discursos, declaraciones, entrevistas y otros documentos, 1928–1940,* 3 vols. (Mexico City: Siglo XXI Editores, 1978), 1:119; for his Guerrero speech, see 1:128.

5. Ibid., 169.

and transcendent glory, have derided the Cardenista mission as shallow.[6] At the same time, in their reverential approach toward Cardenismo, scholarly supporters of the revolutionary tradition have missed its spiritual overtones.[7] Most important, some of the most outspoken Cardenistas themselves seem to have viewed their approach to human reconstruction as "natural" rather than as a cultural creation. Nonetheless, in many ways they would follow the distinctly cultural trajectory pioneered by the sixteenth-century friars. It was not simply that their sketches of the rural Mexicans they had encountered reflected images of degeneration reminiscent of the friars' "discovery" of sixteenth-century Mexican idolaters.[8] Nor was it just that the revolutionaries were persuaded that the true campesinos, though hardly the friars' "authentic Christians," shimmered with revolutionary authenticity. It was also that, like the friars constructing Christians out of pagans, it

6. See Jean Meyer, *The Cristero Rebellion: The Mexican People between Church and State, 1926–1929*, trans. Richard Southern (Cambridge: Cambridge University Press, 1976), 189; Enrique Krauze, Jean Meyer, and Cayetano Reyes, *La reconstrucción económica*, vol. 10 of González, *La historia de la revolución mexicana* (1977). Upon occasion, certain emphases in my own older work have conveyed a similar (though erroneous) impression, particularly Marjorie Becker, "Lázaro Cárdenas and the Mexican Counter-Revolution: The Struggle over Culture in Michoacán, 1934–1940" (Ph.D. diss., Yale University, 1988), ch. 5.

7. That is, scholars have neither researched nor fully appreciated the parallels between clerical and anticlerical beliefs in the possibilities of human redemption and reconstruction. And this is true regarding scholars of Cárdenas whose work is interesting and satisfying in other ways. Moreover, it is true of scholars engaged in debate with one another regarding the nature of Cardenismo. See, e.g., Nora Hamilton, *The Limits of State Autonomy: Post-Revolutionary Mexico* (Princeton: Princeton University Press, 1982); Arturo Anguiano, *El estado y la política obrera del cardenismo* (Mexico City: Editorial Era, 1975); Arnaldo Córdova, *La política de masas del cardenismo* (Mexico City: Serie Popular Era, 1974); Adolfo Gilly, *La revolución interrumpida* (Mexico City: El Caballito, 1971). Notwithstanding the "new cultural history," Latin American scholarship remains marked by an analytical blindness to the fact that people much like analysts themselves (in terms of class and aspiration) possess cultures. Indeed, the bare, and barely imagined, truth is that analysts are themselves cultural products. Efforts to untangle this confusion can be found in Immanuel Wallerstein, *The Modern World System: Capitalist Agriculture and the Origins of the European World-Economy in the Sixteenth Century* (New York: Academic Press, 1976); François Furet, *Interpreting the French Revolution,* trans. Elborg Forster (Cambridge: Cambridge University Press, 1981). On the ways cultures become invisible to their participants, see Peter Burke, *The Historical Anthropology of Early Modern Italy* (Cambridge: Cambridge University Press, 1987).

8. See Tzvetan Todorov, *The Conquest of America: The Question of the Other,* trans. Richard Howard (New York: Harper Colophon, 1985), for a deeply humane effort to come to terms with the friars' approaches to the Indians. For Peru, see Sabine MacCormack, "Demons, Imaginations, and the Incas," *Representations* 33 (1991): 121–46.

would be the Cardenistas who seized these wads of clay and fabricated true faces for the campesinos. In other words, Cardenistas made plans to reinvent the campesinos. In the process, as we shall find, Cardenistas would reveal both their knowledge and their innocence of campesino culture.

Inspecting the Damage

As Cárdenas requested, Michoacán revolutionaries began sketching out rural conditions. In letters to the president-elect, in articles for the national education journal *Maestro Rural,* in political plans and platforms, some of the most outspoken Michoacán Cardenistas joined with Cárdenas and national revolutionaries in assessing their experiences and planning a revolutionary future.

Their messages amount to a damage report, as Cardenistas populated the countryside with campesinos reduced to creatures. But how could this be? Please understand that this question does not so much ask how peasants became animals. Rather, it is concerned with how Cardenista thinking regarding rural life came about and how the Cardenistas drew on this thought to construct creatures. What is striking here is the tendency to plunge campesinos into degradation, while remaining optimistic about their possibilities. We shall examine their sunny-minded vision in some detail later, but here it is worth mentioning that for revolutionaries out of a job, it would have been politically and economically expedient to view their potential clientele as redeemable. As for the bleak bestial view of the campesinos with whom they were to work, Cardenistas drew on both the homey, informal lessons in Hispanic personalism provided by family and priests and their breakaway experiments with nineteenth-century liberalism.

In mobilizing the Hispanic tendency to view individuals as the embodiment of problems, Cardenistas refused to fret over the institutional sources of certain rural problems.[9] Instead, they denounced elite representatives of rural landed, political, and clerical institutions. More

9. Richard Morse, "The Heritage of Latin America," in *The Foundation of New Societies: Studies in the History of the U.S., Latin America, Southern Africa, Canada, and Australia,* edited by Louis Hartz (New York: Harcourt, Brace & World, 1964), 123–77.

than that, there was a general, if at times understated, preoccupation with the excesses of elites. Rather than critique rural hierarchy itself, Cardenistas depicted elites as rapacious: a bit creaturely themselves, elites swooped down on the rural landscape and seized its valuables— raw materials, power, people.

In the economic realm, Cardenistas denounced landlords who controlled "subsoil concessions granted against the interests of the country."[10] Handily translating this into undue influence over others, landowners summoned "all the injustices and all the extortions that went hand in hand with large landed estates."[11] As a result, campesinos were economically disfigured, "chained to the hacienda by perpetual, hereditary debt."[12]

With regard to rural politics, Cardenistas singled out caciques and made them into ambulatory power seekers. Upon seizing political control the caciques vanished, denying their constituencies even a glimpse of "the delegate who represented them," let alone a semblance of representative power.[13] Just as suddenly they reappeared, installed in "bars and whorehouses," where they "squandered the money that belonged to honorable hardworking people."[14] While admittedly the metaphor is strained, it seems that Cardenistas, because of their characteristic teetotaler stance and their concern about excesses, hinted that caciques had pushed beyond their limits, consuming more power than was their due. Campesinos, in turn, remained politically ignorant, "unaware of who represents them."[15]

Then there was the Catholic Church. Appropriating the world and its inhabitants, Catholics had fashioned a story about it. Illustrating it with shades of emotion and prestige, they called it the truth. Perhaps because in this case Cardenistas viewed both the institution and its messengers as responsible for campesino inauthenticity, they attacked both the church and its priests. In fact, Cardenistas like teacher Jesús

10. Lázaro Cárdenas, *Obras: I Apuntes 1913–1940* (Mexico City: Universidad Nacional Autónoma de México, 1972), 308.

11. S. Estrada Martínez, "El acaparador de las cosechas ejidales," *Maestro Rural* (Mexico City), 15 July 1933, 39.

12. S. Estrada Martínez, "Emiliano Zapata," *Maestro Rural*, 15 December 1933, 34.

13. Lázaro Cárdenas, "Discurso publicado en la ciudad de Oaxaca," *Maestro Rural*, 15 July 1934, 4.

14. "Los líderes ambiciosos y falsos deben eliminarse," *Brecha: Seminario de Combate e Información* (Morelia, Michoacán), 21 May 1934, 1.

15. Ibid., 4.

Múgica Martínez and journalist Adolfo Velasco charged that Catholicism was founded on falsehood.[16] While science revealed a world in motion, Catholics threw science to the wind, creating a void. Lacking time or movement, this nonspace can be understood as a negation of infinity. For Catholics, this nonarena was mere backdrop, the stage God would play upon when "out of this nothing, God created all that exists."[17] And from that original, troubled premise Catholics developed a number of illusions. There was the "false notion" that Jesus Christ was God. There were the "impossible appearances of Saints like the Guadalupe." There were the "useless" Ten Commandments.[18]

But of most concern to the Cardenistas were the priests, the "social parasites" who disseminated these pious fictions. "Making themselves out to be representatives of divinity, infallible, omnipotent," they effectively exploited "an uneducated, uncivilized" market.[19] For they taught belief in "miraculous images." Then they engaged in brisk transactions in "miracles," the gold and silver images of the Virgin purchased to foster miraculous events. They reproduced "the cult of the saints," then led "processions of the saints to produce rain."[20] Bombarded by landlords, caciques, and priests, campesinos emerged as creatures "almost completely numbed by fanaticism."[21]

While Cardenistas' understanding of personalism led to their encounter with one version of rural bestiality, their liberal heritage led to another. For these Cardenistas, rural life itself produced another type of campesino inauthenticity. For them the countryside—what we might call an unschooled universe—was a "dark and monotonous" area, composed of "region after region lacking roads."[22] This negative vision was based partly on the Cardenista sense that rural life lacked the abstractions associated with the idea of progress. Indeed, as the Cardenistas saw it, time had frozen in the countryside. While they assumed that a timepiece marking linear time simultaneously marked greater human improvement with every passing moment, they were persuaded that

16. See Adolfo Velasco, "Socialización y escuela socialista," *Maestro Rural,* 15 October 1934, 8.

17. Comisión designado al efecto, "Campaña de desfanatización religiosa," uncatalogued, undated documents, Centro de Estudios de la Revolución Mexicana "Lázaro Cárdenas," A.C., Jiquilpan de Juárez, Michoacán.

18. Ibid.

19. Cárdenas, *Palabras,* 169.

20. Comisión, "Campaña," 4–5.

21. Cárdenas, "Discurso publicado," 4.

22. J. B. Durand, "Hacia una civilización campesina," *Maestro Rural,* 1 October 1933. 18.

that clock had broken down in the the countryside. This meant that campesinos were "a nation still being formed . . . centuries behind the times, in a state of abandonment and stagnancy."[23]

In addition, the concrete accessories of linear progress were missing. Joining and jumbling causes and effects, Cardenistas developed a number of whirlwind catalogs of the problems of the poor. For example, they claimed that health and hygiene were notoriously inadequate in the countryside. Peasants were subject to "bad preparation of food, the lack of inspection of foodstuffs, and overuse of frying, of greasy, dry, and irritating foods." Cardenistas also suggested that "work accidents, inadequate and unhealthy housing, the absence of hygienic conditions in clothing, work, and daily habits undermine our rural communities."[24] Then there were the "disastrous conditions of hygiene in our rural homes, the lack of attention to infancy, and the absence of preventative medicine."[25] Yet if this reads like an early rendition of modernization theory,[26] it also implies a literal association between nature and brutishness, suggesting that those who live close to the soil could be nothing but animals. The soil had overwhelmed them, making them its creatures, "covered with dirt, on their faces, their clothing."[27] And they were slow-moving creatures at that. "Lacking a spirit of initiative, they are lazy or indolent, they have no forethought."[28]

The Making of Secular Missionaries

Yet while their vision of the peasantry was disturbingly poor and frayed, Cardenistas saw no ethnic inevitability in that image. Just as prerevolutionary elites had manipulated campesinos into false behavior, revolutionaries could restore campesino authenticity. But there was the rub. In Michoacán Cardenistas were splintered. They shared neither a common economic background, ethnicity, nor politi-

23. Cárdenas, *Palabras,* 132.

24. J. B. Durand, "Equipo indispensable de la futura civilización rural," *Maestro Rural,* 30 November 1933, 18.

25. Urbano Méndez, "Labor social de la escuela," *Maestro Rural,* 1 February 1934, 18.

26. The standard whipping boy is Seymour Martin Lipset, *Political Man: The Social Bases of Politics* (Garden City, N.Y.: Doubleday, 1960). But see also Pablo González Casanova, *Democracy in Mexico* (New York: Oxford University Press, 1970).

27. Erasto Valle, "Los huicholes," *Maestro Rural,* 15 June 1933, 22.

28. Ibid.

cal predilection. Some, like Cárdenas himself, had emerged from comfortable middle-class backgrounds. Some had endured bitter poverty
as children. Though most were mestizos, Cárdenas tapped at least one
Tarascan Indian to a position of local leadership. In addition, a small
minority of Cardenistas were Communists.[29]

The clerical issue, in particular, fostered discord. The Cardenistas
with the greatest access to the president, the Cardenistas who sought
to reshape the peasantry, were the most openly anticlerical. Yet they
were the minority, and a minority at odds with itself regarding tactics.
Cárdenas himself was drawn to the flash, fire, and potential effective-
ness of Tabasco Governor Tomás Garrido Canabal's anticlerical displays. Garrido had followers set the countryside ablaze with saints'
burnings. Cárdenas trundled Jesús Múgica Martínez, a Cardenista
teacher and occasional firebrand, off to inspect.[30] But the revolutionaries determined to wear anticlericalism on their sleeves were no more
than a fraction of the minority. Most of the anticlerical Cardenistas
tended to be more circumspect. As the rural teacher Constantino
Murillo put it, "I told them again and again to go easy on the church.
It was not Catholicism but fanaticism that bothered us."[31]

Moreover, most of their potential cadre splintered in the opposite
direction. As the rural teacher M. Hernández M. put it, "It is public
and notorious that within the corps of rural teachers, and most especially among the women, a large group of professors profess that per-
nicious fanaticism of the apostolic Roman Catholic religion. . . .
Besides, those people, after participating in public processions, confusing the campesinos, are accustomed to making vows and promises to
this or that saint, which, upon being seen by children and neighbors,
similarly confirms false beliefs."[32]

Thus, before they could embark on the work of remaking others,
transformation would have to begin at home. Yet this transformation
would be curious indeed. Rather than seeking any sort of thoroughgoing reconstruction of their colleagues, progressive Cardenistas would
content themselves with behavioral modification. And they would

29. Interviews with Cardenista teacher and ideologue José Corona Núñez, Morelia,
July 1985; Cardenista teacher Jesús Múgica Martínez, Morelia, December 1984; Constantino Murillo, Morelia, July 1985; and Tomás Rico Cano, Morelia, June, August
1990.
30. Interview with Múgica Martínez, December 1984.
31. Interview with Murillo, July 1985.
32. M. Hernández M., "El deporte como medio de desfanátizar al campesino,"
Maestro Rural, 15 November 1934, 14.

develop a two-pronged approach. They urged devout Catholics to keep their devotion under wraps. Resigned to the fact that Catholic teachers would retain their religion, they counseled them to practice Catholicism only in the privacy of their homes. "Once you arrive in the schoolhouse, put your religious dogmas away."[33] "If you're religious, confine it to your house."[34]

At the same time, anticlerical Cardenistas, those seeking the "spiritual liberation" of the peasantry, were to mimic the priests. As Corona Núñez saw it, "The teacher needed to be good and honorable both in public and in private life, so that the people would respect him as much as or more than the village priest. That way the teacher could dominate the people and defend against the religious question."[35] Hilario Reyes enumerated the characteristics that constituted such a "good and honorable" life. Teachers would have to "be careful of our behavior and lead an honest, honorable life, without getting drunk . . . dedicating ourselves to work."[36]

The religious were to mute their fervor, while the anticlerical would play the priests. Awkward, almost comical, it was a pragmatic stance reflecting the anticlerical stalwarts' recognition of their minority status. Yet there is probably also a sociological reason for this cosmetic approach toward Cardenista Catholicism. Revolutionary Cardenistas tended to believe that Catholic Cardenistas could take their religion neat, like whiskey, and not be the worse for wear. Campesinos, however, were another story. In their case, priests had only to say the word, and voilà, fanaticized campesinos joined the Cristero rebellion. Clearly, they would require a total conversion.

Call Out a Posse, Gather Up Their Music, and Teach Them to Sing

The Cardenistas' determination to mimic priestly decorum was not their only resemblance to the missionary friars. On the contrary, upon finding Indians caught in patterns of false behavior,

33. Ireneo Zepeda, "Preparemos el pueblo para el presente y para el futuro," *Maestro Rural,* 1 January 1934, 9.

34. Hernández M., "El deporte," 14.

35. Interview with Corona Núñez, July 1985.

36. Interview with Hilario Reyes, Morelia, July 1985.

Cardenistas echoed the friars in ways they did not acknowledge and probably did not recognize. In coming to America, the friars had found an Indian population engaged in idolatry, human sacrifice, and a host of other practices the priests had been sworn to abhor. But in complicated and at times muddled ways, Las Casas, Sahagún, and the rest believed that Indians possessed a Christian nature buried deep within. Through the simple strategy of converting the Indians, this latent Christianity could be coaxed out. We might say that the friars had needed only to construct altars in front of idols.[37]

The Cardenistas' approach to human rehabilitation was similar. They had seen campesinos lumbering around like animals. Yet as though they—like the missionaries—had been born during the era when belief in ascribed, inborn characteristics was common, the Cardenistas saw true campesino behavior lurking underneath. Blending their preconceptions and their observations from their earlier grassroots work, they developed mental images of the campesinos' true faces.

To a certain extent, Cardenistas rejected racial stereotypes. At times their characterizations of Indian and mestizo campesinos were virtually identical. Indians and mestizos alike had been exploited, their identity miscast. In the absence of such exploitation, uniform campesinos would emerge. In fact Cárdenas stalwartly maintained that Indians constituted an ethnic proletariat. "The program of Indian liberation is essentially that of the emancipation of any country's proletariat."[38]

However, despite the Cardenistas' tendency to deny that destiny could be attributed to biology, such thinking lingered in their view that the true faces of mestizos contrasted with those of the Indians. In the case of the Indians, Cardenistas suspected that they were naturally aesthetic. Indeed, "for all the talk of somnambulism," there was general agreement that Indians "have an intelligence, which they demonstrate in their artistic efforts, their music, dance, songs, handwork, and plastic arts."[39] Cardenistas had encountered fragmentary expressions of such behavior. A contributor to a pro-Cardenista newspaper in

37. The wordplay here, of course, refers to Anita Brenner's *Idols behind Altars* (New York: Harcourt Brace, 1929).
38. Lázaro Cárdenas, cited in Luis González, *Los días del presidente Cárdenas*, vol. 15 of González, *La historia de la revolución mexicana* (1981), 119. Judith Friedlander presents a more recent example of this perspective in *Being Indian in Hueyapan: A Study of Forced Identity in Contemporary Mexico* (New York: St. Martin's, 1975).
39. "El internado indígena en Matlapa," *Maestro Rural,* 1 July 1933.

Zinapécuaro pointed to "a caravan of Indians who generally get together to dance."[40] Cárdenas found that the Mixtecs cultivated "the art of music."[41] *Maestro Rural* celebrated the "plastic arts" in Matlapla, San Luis Potosí.[42]

But how were they to get exploited Indians to act out their aesthetic tendencies? Habitual exploitation promoted false habits. While artistic behavior occasionally flickered through the layers of oppression, Cardenistas could not depend on it. In short, Cardenistas harbored no illusions about natural behavior emerging naturally. Lacking that, they organized a posse. Cárdenas sent his followers out to discover and capture the Indians' essential behavior. The president turned to José Corona and Concha Michel and asked them to "gather a compilation of Indian and popular Mexican music."[43] And there was more. Other rural teachers were instructed to "seek a sampling of our folklore."[44] The goal was to find Indian artistry and bring it back.

Once they had ensnared samples of Indian craftsmanship, Cardenistas would again dip into the missionary repertoire. True, they doubted that exploited Indians would wake up one morning singing. Still, sharing the friars' belief that Indians could learn their own essence, they planned to call them together and teach them to sing. As Hugo Conzatti put it, "The goal of pushing the teachers to collect and invent folklore [is] to instruct the masses in that very folklore."[45]

While these Cardenistas seem to have been touched by an antiquarian sensibility, a will to prove faithful to an exalted past, their project was actually both inventive and destructive.[46] To style an Indian an artist was to streamline Indians' past and present activities. No longer was the reciprocal interchange between ritual accoutrements and concrete tasks relevant; Cardenistas proceeded to deny that religious music had any efficacy in material life. Nor did the specificity of Indian customs much matter. For one thing, Cardenistas often dismissed the

40. "La feria," *La Verdad* (Zinapécuaro), 9 March 1933, 1.

41. Cárdenas, *Apuntes,* 277.

42. "El internado indígena."

43. Expediente 710.1, Lázaro Cárdenas, Fondo Presidentes, Archivo General de la Nación, Mexico City.

44. Hugo Conzatti, "Concepto del arte musical nacionalista," *Maestro Rural,* 15 July 1933, 37.

45. Hugo Conzatti, "La canción mexicana y la educación musical," *Maestro Rural,* 15 August 1933, 34.

46. The widespread refusal to examine the destructiveness must stem from an enthusiastic sense that any revolutionary attention to the Indians must have been beneficial.

fact that in the 1930s Mexico boasted at least fifty distinct Indian tribes.[47] A true, authentic Indian was a singer, a dancer. This artist could sing or dance anything, regardless of the connection to a specific Indian culture. Encouraging Cardenistas to teach students Las Matlachines, a dance that "was taught to the Indians by the Spanish missionaries, taking advantage of elements used by Indians in their theatrical representations," R. A. Saavedra suggested precisely how tenuous the connection to previous Indian life could be.[48]

On the inventive side, there was something equally marvelous going on. For while they never quite acknowledged it, Cardenistas planned to remake human beings. Rural villages were their workshops, and human possibilities their raw materials. And if they were disputing the old efficacies and severing the old connections, they were also creating new ones. Indians were artists, living advertisements of the revolutionary concern for the downtrodden. In this respect, while the idea at first appears ludicrous, teachers' guiding Indians in the art of becoming Indian artists makes sense. Indeed, perhaps Canzatti's notion that "the rural teachers would be the ideal collectors, interpreters, and why not the creators, of our vernacular art" was less distorted than it might appear to be.[49]

Indians without Soul

With the mestizos things would be different. Cardenista definitions of culture precluded them from promoting a restoration of a glorious mestizo past. In fact Cardenista concepts of culture denied mestizos—and their activities—a niche. For Cardenistas saw culture in one of three ways. It was either literacy, the ethnic expression of aesthetic talent and curious behavior, or a high-toned concern for the fine arts. In Mexico only Indians, with their songs and dances; rich people, decorating their homes with borrowed French glitter; and schoolchild-

47. In *La población indígena de México*, 3 vols. (Mexico City: Secretaría de Educación Pública, 1940), Carlos Basauri catalogs and attempts to distinguish the varied Mexican Indian populations.

48. R. A. Saavedra, "Matlachines: Danza, Recopilación," *Maestro Rural*, 1 March 1932, 14.

49. Hugo Conzatti, "Los maestros rurales son los más indicados para recoger nuestro folklore musical," *Maestro Rural*, 1 August 1933, 23.

ren learning to read and write possessed "culture."[50] In other words, blood told for Cardenistas, but it told selectively: only "Indians" had true artistry in them. There would be no plan to restore the glories of the mestizos' artistic past.

Still, Cardenistas suggested that mestizos had drifted into barbarism as deeply as had the Indians. And while mestizos possessed no genetic connection to Indian artistry, as we shall see, Cardenistas proceeded to allot them a portion of the Indian legacy. They designated the ejido, the centerpiece of pre-Conquest Indians' economic arrangements, as the inheritance of the mestizos. This meant that they assigned mestizos the kind of productive role they denied the Indians.

Before the Conquest such ejidal lands had belonged to Indian communities. Although the community owned the land, individual Indians worked it both privately and as members of work teams.[51] After the revolution, various postrevolutionary governments experimented with stylized versions of the ejido.[52] In the Cardenista case, their innovation would be based in part on their vision of mestizos as economic heirs of the pre-Conquest Indians. As with the Indians, Cardenistas determined to deliver mestizos over to their own nature. In concrete terms, this meant that Cardenistas planned to train mestizos to reenact the web of connections surrounding the pre-Conquest ejido. To be sure, this would require reshaping actual peasant behavior. Beginning with campesinos' "divisive" tendencies to "splinter off into isolation,"[53] Cardenistas were to rid campesinos of all "quarreling, all personal bitterness."[54] This would lead to identical campesinos, rural brothers prepared to develop "a genuine cooperation which would enable all workers and consumers to collaborate with each other."[55]

50. For an analysis of these concepts of culture, see Becker, "Lázaro Cárdenas," 163–64.

51. Hamilton, *Limits of State Autonomy,* 68.

52. See Héctor Aguilar Camín, "The Relevant Tradition: Sonoran Leaders in the Revolution," in *Caudillo and Peasant in the Mexican Revolution,* ed. D. A. Brading (Cambridge: Cambridge University Press, 1980); Linda B. Hall, "Alvaro Obregón and the Politics of Mexican Land Reform," *Hispanic American Historical Review* 60:2 (1980): 213–38; and Krauze, Meyer, and Reyes, *La reconstrucción económica.*

53. Cárdenas, *Palabras,* 1:120.

54. Ibid., 123.

55. Ibid., 125. It should be noted that this linguistic sexism follows both the Cardenista usage and the Cardenista intention: for the Cardenistas, the peasants who deserved organizing as productive farmers were almost exclusively men. To a limited extent, they made exceptions for the widows of organized men.

Then Cardenistas would combat the temptation of city lights. True, they had encountered the campesino tendency to "compare the architecture of his small home with the city's palatial mansions, the darkness and monotony of his little hut and the area where he and his family live with the dazzling look of the well-lighted cities, adorned with announcements, bright colors, music, noise, beautiful parks, sumptuous churches, theaters decorated with care."[56] Yet Cardenistas could set peasants aright, bringing them to "appreciate the natural laws,"[57] to "have affection for the land."[58] They would learn to "look from above, from a hill, and see a lovely cornfield where the cornhusks are wide and the little plants strong and happy."[59] Indeed, as proto-Indians, mestizos would become instinctively provincial, naturally bound to specific parts of the world.

Finally, they could learn their true vocation—to make the countryside bloom. All that was called for was adjustments in their habitual tendencies. Herbert Sein, founder of the La Huerta consumer cooperative in Morelia, found that when campesinos were left to their own devices, their behavior was unruly, needlessly generous, ungovernable. He complained that unsupervised campesinos extended credit to friends at the slightest provocation. Their bookkeeping "lacks all formality, because their notations are incomplete and almost all of them note the type and quantity of merchandise without saying where it came from, at what cost."[60]

Nonetheless, with proper training, they would develop an unbounded capacity to turn rural air, water, and soil to profit. Indeed, Cardenista moneymaking schemes sprang up like wildflowers. One eager Cardenista advised campesinos keeping bees to "know them, care for them, imitate them."[61] Another told campesinos how to "select hens that will lay eggs."[62] Still another taught campesinos how to raise and sell the domestic rabbit.[63]

56. Durand, "Hacia una civilización campesina."

57. Belisario Trujillo Rovelo, "La historia natural, la historia patria y de civismo contra el fanatismo," *Maestro Rural,* 1 October 1933, 13.

58. Cárdenas, *Apuntes,* 247.

59. Alfredo Maillefert, "Antena campesina," *Maestro Rural,* 1 September 1933, 33.

60. Expediente x/166.2 (x-5) 723.4–2.1933, Archivo Histórico de la Secretaría de Educación Pública, Mexico City.

61. "Campesino, ¿sabes cuidar tus abejas?" *Maestro Rural,* 1 January 1933, 17.

62. Isidro Foglio, Jr., "Elección de gallinas ponedoras," *Maestro Rural,* 15 October 1933, 12.

63. Manuel A. Echeverra, "Orientaciones sobre la cría y explotación en pequeño del conejo doméstico," *Maestro Rural,* 15 September 1933, 15.

Mestizos, then, lacked Indians' artistic possibilities. Still, Cardenistas saw mestizos as participants in the hopeful but contradictory fantasy of the mixed economy. That notion in itself would lend romance to campesinos devoid of artistry. Put another way, Cardenistas saw mestizos as Indians without soul.

The Reinvention of the Indian

The Cardenista reinventions were streaked with Manichean visions of darkness pitted against light. On the one hand, they deplored the behavior they had encountered. It was all over the map, splattering the landscape with aberration, sloth, hypergenerosity to friends, bouts of drunkenness, Catholic passion. On the other hand, they envisioned dancing Indians and farming campesinos as purehearted. And in this view of behavior defined by ethnic categories, they took the missionary tendency to split off truth from falsehood a step further. By dividing Indian from mestizo, Cardenistas fostered the contradictory and baroque effect of multiplying the number of human categories while limiting the possible activities assigned to each one.

A missionary plan to lead campesinos to the light. Arrogant? Without doubt. Who, after all, is qualified to define the identity of the other? Still, while analysts can deplore all they like,[64] in this case their larger role is to make sense of the extremism in these portraits. What led to such desperation and purity? As we have seen, Michoacán Cardenistas in the main had been lonely liberals in a state encrusted with a deeply reactionary form of Catholicism. They had staked their hopes on Cárdenas's reasonably progressive governorship. With the conservative restoration in 1932 their jobs vanished. Cornered, they couched their plans in overripe terms.

At the same time, it is this all-or-nothing edge that has made the Cardenistas' vision so appealing. For there is a wild and compelling optimism to the Cardenista portraits.[65] From peasants doffing their

64. The tendency to deplore the essentialism of this approach has at times characterized my work. It also characterizes some of the essays in Eric Hobsbawm and Terence Ranger, ed., *The Invention of Tradition* (Cambridge: Cambridge University Press, 1983).

65. The bitterness that has sometimes accompanied scholarly debates seems to reflect the suspicion that in denouncing the arrogance, analysts of Catholic culture have denounced these hopes.

caps upon sighting landlords to people believing in their right to the land they worked. From sharecroppers testifying against their neighbors to people building an agrarian committee together. People whose governing expertise resided in the kind of deferential billing and cooing exacted by the local cacique learning that a national government could be put to work for them.

This is clearly the stuff of religious—and anticlerical—fervor. Still, it would fall heavily on Michoacán campesinos precisely because they had been invented before. Indeed, the sixteenth-century conquerors created the idea of Indians. And for all the moments of passion that punctuate Mexican history, in the main, Mexican rural history has lacked that desperate purity. Sixteenth-century discoverers may have developed the category of Indians, but Indians were not innocents who stopped in their victimized, sixteenth-century tracks. They contested and participated—never as equals, to be sure—in the construction of exploitative colonial and postindependence arrangements.[66] This would mean that when Cardenistas attempted to flesh out their blueprint, establishing revolution in Michoacán, campesinos would plant the fields and sing the songs. But because mestizos were more than brothers in the fields and Indians were more than a chorus singing folkloric favorites, at times campesinos' fields would be overrun with debt. And at times Indians' tunes would be wildly discordant.

66. This is, of course, what hegemony means. For an analysis of one such contest, see Marjorie Becker, "Torching la Purísima, Dancing at the Altar: The Construction of Revolutionary Hegemony in Michoacán, 1934–1940," in *Everyday Forms of State Formation: Revolution and the Negotiation of Rule in Modern Mexico*, ed. Gilbert M. Joseph and Daniel Nugent (Durham, N.C.: Duke University Press, 1994).

CHAPTER FIVE

Revolutionary Lessons, I
Purity up in Smoke

there is nothing before me, but a moment recovered tonight,
standing against a dream that is dreamed of images all
intertwined, sculptured in permanence against the dream:
a moment torn from the zero of this night

Octavio Paz

Formulated from a slender piece of wood and thousands of pious words, La Purísima had been the special confidante of women and the poor. Then rich Ario villagers got wind of the revolutionaries' plans. According to Concepción Méndez, a prominent Ario woman, "They had designs on the saints, so we realized it would be good to protect the images."[1] In a preemptive move, a group of wealthy men entered the church. Gathering up some of her plaster-of-Paris brethren, they secreted them in their homes. Inadvertently, they left the Virgin behind.

Later that night a group of revolutionaries entered the church. Determined to purge the community of its icons, they initially found

1. Series of interviews conducted in Ario de Rayón, Michoacán, with Concepción Méndez, June, November 1990; Mari Elena Verduzco de Peña, May 1990; Esperanza Rocha, May, June, July 1990; and Rafael Ochoa, May 1990. I explore other issues surrounding the torching in Marjorie Becker, "Torching La Purísima, Dancing at the Altar: The Construction of Revolutionary Hegemony in Michoacán, 1934–1940," in *Everyday Forms of State Formation: Revolution and the Negotiation of Rule in Modern Mexico*, ed. Gilbert M. Joseph and Daniel Nugent (Durham, N.C.: Duke University Press, 1994).

only a few remnants, "a precious little Christ, a large picture of Joseph."[2] Then they came upon her. The woman used for metaphoric fences, the Virgin crowned in gold, had been abandoned. Scooping up La Purísima, they hid her overnight. The next afternoon they torched her, reducing her image to ashes.

Why did they turn on La Purísima, the image that provided comfort to the poor? It hardly reflected a sustained interest in what they called *cosas de mujeres*, the business of women. They had come to rehabilitate buried rural possibilities. Some sought to remold the clerical conception of community into an ideology of revolutionary nationalism. Others determined to construct Zapata-style agrarianism out of a male population long immersed in landlessness.

These efforts were contested vigorously by landlords, priests, and some campesinos, and for periods of time La Purísima receded from view. Yet while the torching was limited to one community, La Purísima—and all she stood for—would not relinquish her hold on the revolutionaries. However desperately the poor clung to her image, whatever else she may have been, she posed a political problem for the Cardenistas. Styled by the church as a symbol of abnegation and conformity, she was readily viewed by revolutionaries as an impediment to liberation.

There was also something more troublesome going on. As painful as it was for men to acknowledge the fact, La Purísima represented something furtive. She held women in her grip, leading them to fashion unspoken, perhaps unspeakable, goals. Seemingly submerged in domesticity, women could wander off, uncontrolled, sabotaging their men, sabotaging revolutionary projects. All of the revolutionaries' efforts at rational persuasion were as nothing against them. But perhaps the men could speak through the flames.

From Catholic Dross to Revolutionary Nationalism

Whatever their hopes for reinstatement in Michoacán, upon returning to the villages Cardenistas encountered a mobilized clergy. Frightened by the potential of an activist peasantry, priests

2. Interview with Verduzco de Peña, May 1990.

determined to refurbish the regime of humility and glory. Donning vestments, entering the churches, taking the pulpit, priests engaged more vigorously in what had become for them the habitual suggestion that ordinary matter can be infused with spiritual meaning. Indeed, they prompted what we might call piety by association: in a religion that freely used concrete objects to direct fervor toward God, the objects themselves had long since absorbed holiness.[3]

To reassert their connection to God, priests unfolded a double-edged message. In part it was reprimand. However glittering the revolutionary program, they warned, "It is a grave sin. People who open or go to socialist schools sin deeply. . . . The directors are suspected of heresy . . . and can be excommunicated." Moreover, "parents who send their children to such schools also risk excommunication."[4]

Along with the scolding, priests offered up the consolation of the traditional Catholic community. Far from excluding poor people, the church celebrated them, after a fashion. Despite his dubious parentage, Jesus easily entered the Catholic community to assume his role as "head of the church."[5] The brown-skinned Mary shared a similar fate. In her representation as La Purísima or the Guadalupe, she was hailed "immaculate daughter of God the Father."[6]

It was as though poverty and brownness had dissolved. They were as nothing. This was not because the church had anything tangible to offer in their place. On the contrary, the pope decreed that just as "men are naturally unequal in terms of strength and ingenuity, so they should be unequal in terms of possessions."[7] Because of the Catholic determination to define skin color, rags, and the pain they engendered as beside the ultimate point, social inequity was deemed irrelevant.

Cardenistas responded to this clerical effort to repossess God in at

3. Catholics inherited from the Jews the idea that objects used in a religious ceremony themselves absorb holiness. In recognizing this point Stephen Greenblatt cites the Zohar, but in fact its origins probably stretch much earlier to the Talmudic rabbis. See Greenblatt, *Marvelous Possessions: The Wonder of the New World* (Chicago: University of Chicago Press, 1991), 161.

4. "Normas del Comité Ejecutivo Episcopal a los Sacerdotes y a los Católicos," caja 13, Sacramental y Disciplina, 1901–40, Archivo de la Purísima Corazón (APC), Zamora, Michoacán.

5. Prelados de la provincia de Michoacán, *Carta pastoral colectiva de los prelados de la provincia de Michoacán* (Morelia: Tipografía de Augustín Martínez Mier, 1920).

6. "Edicto de la sexta junta de prelados de la provincia de Michoacán," caja 13, Sacramental y Disciplina, 1901–40, APC.

7. *Carta pastoral colectiva,* 9.

least three ways.[8] There were those who steadfastly refused the ideological battlefield. Angelina Acosta claims that she avoided the religious topic at all costs. "I could see that people had gone too far on both sides, and I just kept quiet. My idea was to watch and find out what the people needed."[9]

Then there was the rambunctious effort to cull out the old. Francisco Elizalde, a Zamora native who attended the Cardenista socialist schools, vividly recounts his teacher's approach:

"I see here that you have an orange. Who made it?"
"The tree," I said.
"Who gave it to you?"
"I bought it with my own money."
"Then God didn't give it to you, because God doesn't give anything to anybody."[10]

Finally, there were the Cardenistas who turned against the sanctification of humility to consciously style themselves alchemists. Purging and reassembling clerical and popular ideological elements, they sought to develop a new ideology establishing the poor in a community. As school superintendent Celso Zamora Flores put it:

We must not forget that the Catholics, to propagate their religion, used elements of fable and symbolism of inexorable beauty . . . that principally take root in the spirits of the young: the birth of Jesus in the stable, the mule, the bull . . . the shepherds with their little sheep adoring the child Jesus. . . . Therefore we can propagate the socialist idea in stories and little animal fables, from which we can always draw a moral lesson. The air, the fire, the house, the cornfield, the school plot: gradually progressing in the later years to propaganda that is clearly revolutionary.[11]

In acts reminiscent of their Catholic rivals (themselves no mean alchemists, if their efforts to use and rechannel pre-Conquest devotion

---

8. Although the Cardenistas' various approaches bore the mark of their cultural backgrounds, the susceptibility of some Cardenistas to popular perspectives on revolution suggests a flexibility distinct from that of the cultural revolutionaries portrayed in Philip Corrigan and Derek Sayer, *The Great Arch: English State Formation as Cultural Revolution* (Oxford: Basil Blackwell, 1985).

9. Interview with Angelina Acosta, Zamora, November 1990.

10. Interview with Francisco Elizalde, Zamora, July 1985.

11. Profesor Celso Flores Zamora, "Circular IV," 7 March 1936, "Colección de circulares giradas por la dirección general de enseñanza en los estados y territorios," caja 557, Archivo Histórico de la Secretaría de Educación Pública (AHSEP), Mexico City.

are remembered),[12] Cardenistas targeted churches in Purépero, Tarejero, Cherán, Pátzcuaro, Uruapan, and Ario Santa Monica for transformation.[13] Throughout the state they entered buildings that had become spiritual through the passive act of hosting religious ceremonies. As though they hoped to siphon off the buildings' potential to compel allegiance, they appropriated them. A sort of exponential piety by association.

Then, they might have been parishioners attending church. Joining together in informal groups, they shuffled toward the altars in Pátzcuaro, Uruapan, Purépero, Tarejero, Jiquilpan, and Ario. Exhibiting what had once been a commonplace gesture of reverence, part of the Catholic body language of affection, they took the images in their hands. They stared at these representations of Jesus and Mary, these scraps of plaster and paint that had come to contain such powers of persuasion. And then, to thwart the image's ability to summon loyalty, they cast the icons aside.[14]

Cardenistas had new plans for Catholic accessories. Once buildings and images had joined with the priests, urging Catholics to disregard their poverty. Now Cardenistas would force these elements to participate in a different message of community. They began by denouncing the old: The poor do not merit membership among fellows through special dispensations rendering their poverty irrelevant. Instead, by enduring conditions that put society to shame, they ensure their place. In a parody of the Catholic creed, José Corona Núñez summarized this perspective. He told a crowd of listeners in Cuitzeo that it was not

12. See, e.g., Inga Clendinnen, *Ambivalent Conquests: Maya and Spaniard in Yucatán, 1517–1570* (Cambridge: Cambridge University Press, 1987). See also Louise M. Burkhart, *The Slippery Earth: Nahua-Christian Moral Dialogue in Sixteenth-Century Mexico* (Tucson: University of Arizona Press, 1989); and the special 1991 issue of *Representations,* an issue devoted to exploring the conquest of America.

13. See the following documents to be found in Lázaro Cárdenas, Fondo Presidentes, Archivo General de la Nación (AGN), Mexico City: on the Ario de Rayón church, 2 May 1940, expediente 547.4/462; on the Purépero church, 18 January 1936, expediente 547.4/220; on the Tarejero church, 30 September 1935, expediente 547.3/85; on the Cherán church, 8 February 1938, expediente 547/36; on a Pátzcuaro church, 18 August 1939, expediente 547.4/133; and on a Uruapan regional church, expediente 547.4/133.

14. On Jiquilpan, interview with Roberto Villaseñor Espinosa, Mexico City, March 1984. On Tarejero, see expediente 547.3/85, Lázaro Cárdenas, Fondo Presidentes, AGN. On Zamora, interview with Maximino Padilla, Zamora, August 1985. And on Ario, interviews with Méndez, June, November 1990; Verduzco de Peña, May 1990; and Esperanza Rocha, May, June, July 1990.

Jesus—"that man who sits up there on his velvet throne, crowned in gold"—who should be revered; rather, it is "you people, whom they call wretched, who are the roots that nourish the soul of the country."[15]

Cardenistas reserved a special place in the new community for campesinos who actively refused humility. Perhaps it is more accurate to acknowledge that Cardenistas recognized that in their revolutionary struggle to regain land, Zapatistas had *claimed* a place in the Mexican community. In gestures at once duplicitous, condescending, and complimentary, Cardenistas replaced the icons with portraits of Zapata, Carranza, and Obregón.[16] The homogenizing effect achieved by uniting Zapata and his battlefield enemies on the schoolroom walls was ahistorical, and Zapata may have posthumously scowled at Cardenistas.[17] Cardenistas, however, were ceding the defeated peasant leader a place beside one of the revolution's military victors.

To make good on the Zapatista claim, Cardenistas led campesino schoolchildren on a voyage of discovery and conquest. In gestures reminiscent of a stripped-down Columbus, teachers invited students to use language and imagination to delineate their new lands. While students did not actually move far from their country schoolrooms, teachers verbally transported them to distant mountain ranges, valleys, the ocean. As José Ventura González put it, he taught students "a clear determination of their nearby communities and those throughout the country, their economic resources, their means of communication."[18] In Villa Victoria, Manuel Godina Horta provided students with the contents of the state—the names of municipalities, towns, villages, rivers, and mountain ranges. He also taught them basic cartography, organizing workshops in mapmaking.[19]

15. Interview with José Corona Núñez, Morelia, Michoacán, July 1985.

16. This was fairly commonplace. On Zamora, interview with Padilla, August 1985; on Jiquilpan, interview with Villaseñor Espinosa, March 1984; on Tarejero, expediente 547.3/85, Lázaro Cárdenas, Fondo Presidentes, AGN.

17. In this regard, Alan Knight's comment that "everybody was a Constitutionalist in 1920" needs to be revised. As Knight himself has shown regarding liberalism, to the extent that this was true, varied factions understood Constitutionalism in radically different ways. Knight made his "Constitutionalists all" comments at the Forty-sixth International Conference of Americanists, Amsterdam, July 1988. See also Alan Knight, "El liberalismo mexicano desde la reforma hasta la revolución (una interpretación)," *Historia Mexicana* 35 (July–September 1985): 59–86.

18. José Ventura González, Profesor inspector federal, Michoacán, caja 412, AHSEP.

19. Manuel Godina Horta, Jr., Profesor inspector federal, Michoacán, caja 412, AHSEP.

Dipping into the same inner storehouse priests had utilized, teachers attempted to cast the new apprehension of lands in benevolent terms.[20] Most frequently, teachers urged students to adorn the notion of nation with song. Despite their bewilderment, Hilario Reyes taught students the national anthem, soothing their fears over the chorus summoning "Mexicans to the cry of war." J. Socorro Vázquez taught revolutionary hymns and regional songs, while José Ventura González organized festivals with revolutionary songs.[21]

In their effort to lodge the rural community in national territory, Cardenistas tailored the clerical image of community to campesino specifications. Granted, gone was the clerical tendency to house campesinos in unfathomable (or at least unverifiable) territories. Yet like the priests, Cardenistas called for loyalty to strangers, and like the priests, they made a home of distant, largely unseen territory. At the same time, like the campesinos who searched the woods and fields for nuts and berries, Cardenistas offered campesinos the use of national territory to meet their personal needs.

Makeshift Zapatismo

For landlords and priests, the prospect was fearful and imminent. The Cardenistas had come into the well-tended lands of northwestern Michoacán to redistribute, and they were surrounded by peons without land. As their landholdings far exceeded the legal limit, landlords clogged the courts with sudden bequests to kin.[22] For their part, priests who threatened recipients of land with damnation styled God a silent partner in Michoacán agrarian capitalist enterprises.[23] Evi-

20. Max Weber attempts to understand appeals to the senses to generate adherence to religion in *The Sociology of Religion,* trans. Ephraim Fischoff (Boston: Beacon, 1964).

21. Interview with Hilario Reyes, Morelia, July 1985; J. Socorro Vázquez, Profesor inspector federal, Michoacán, caja 412, AHSEP; José Ventura González, Profesor inspector federal, Michoacán, ibid.

22. The AGN, the land reform archives in Morelia and Mexico City, and the *Periódico Oficial* (housed in the Colegio de México library) are full of such petitions. See, e.g., "Valencia Madrigal pide no se afecta su propiedad," expediente 404.1/4813, Lázaro Cárdenas, Fondo Presidentes, AGN; and "Carmen Méndez de Méndez pide que sea respetados sus propiedades," expediente 404.1/4999, ibid. An examination of such documents could yield part of the cultural history of the land reform.

23. "Normas del Comité Ejecutivo Episcopal." According to Zamora priest Joaquín Paz, Zamora priests upheld the tenet that "in Christian doctrine, nobody can appropri-

dently, to claim a piece of land was to put a lien on one's eternal future.

While elites at times seemed bound in cell-like unity, campesinos were fragmented and were paid a uniformly bare wage.[24] Moreover, they lacked an ideology of entitlement. In northwestern Michoacán, only nineteenth-century social Catholicism remotely resembled such an ideology, and as priests had disseminated that message in patch-work style, there were campesinos who had not heard of it.[25]

In short, these campesinos were no Zapatistas. In the most glaring sense, this was because of the mestizos' landlessness. But what did that absence of land mean? We have been trained to see the Zapatistas as brimming with benevolent concern for one another because they were smallholders. There they are in Womack's book, plotting revolution together in the most somber and respectful fashion.[26] Because they own land, they are (somehow magically) able to forge a consensus regarding Zapata as their leader.

While there appears to be little doubt that landownership was the key to much about the Zapatistas' movement, this image needs to be readjusted. What the Zapatistas owned was not just land: their landownership enabled them to live out the principle hallowed by both liberalism and Catholicism, namely, that owning a piece of the earth ensured dignity. That, they had learned, made them men. And without that in Michoacán, men were bred to doff their caps to the mayordomos, not to join guerrilla movements seeking the return of their land.[27]

---

ate what belongs to somebody else." Santiago del Río, a member of the Catholic sinar-quista movement, agreed that Zamora's priests maintained this stance throughout the period. Interviews with Father Joaquín Paz, Zamora, August 1985; and Santiago del Rio, Zamora, August 1985.

24. On the uniformity of the pay rates, see "Estudio preliminar de la zona agrícola Zamora," 7 September 1934, Fondo Ramón Fernández y Fernández, Biblioteca, Colegio de Michoacán; interview with Ario peon Carlos Cervantes, Ario de Rayón, June 1990.

25. Moisés González Navarro, *Porfiriato, vida social,* vol. 4 of *Historia moderna de México,* ed. Daniel Cosío Villegas, 13 vols., 3d ed. (Mexico City: Editorial Hermes, 1955–73), 363–64; Luis González, *Zamora,* 2d ed. (Zamora: El Colegio de Michoacán/CONACYT, 1984), 115–16; Interviews with Ochoa, May 1990; Cervantes, June 1990; and Verduzco de Peña, May 1990.

26. John Womack, Jr., *Zapata and the Mexican Revolution* (New York: Vintage Books, 1968), 3–10.

27. While sustenance can be harvested from borrowed land, sustenance was not all that was at stake here.

Nonetheless, in the absence of a homegrown movement, Cárdenas determined to forge Zapatismo. He subcontracted out the work of agrarian organization to men like Ernesto Prado, Once Pueblos political leader, or Juan Gutiérrez, who became president of the ejidal commissariat in Zamora and later muncipal president as well. Men who had come from poverty and perhaps fought in the revolution, they bore long and jagged reputations of fearlessness tinged with opportunism.

Putting up signs, buttonholing his neighbors, alerting the teachers to the project, Gutiérrez collected his proto-Zapatistas. At first glance, they seemed a tumble of disunity. As Zamora natives initially ignored Gutiérrez's efforts to mobilize them, he recruited campesinos from the nearby communities of Atacheo, La Sauceda, and Atecucario.[28] In addition, Gutiérrez awarded ejidal lands to a small group of non-campesinos. These people included merchants, municipal workers, musicians, bricklayers, barbers, and slaughterhouse workers.[29] And in Ario they were a collection of kinfolk, men who like Primo Tapia and his cousins, had spent time in the United States.[30]

These seemingly disparate men shared a sort of backhanded commonality. As elite machinations made the involvement of campesinos most dependent on agriculture unlikely, the potential agraristas shared the paltry advantage of not being the poorest of the poor. In a variety of ways, these men had learned to protect themselves against utter dependency on farming. Some had developed skills as workers in Zamora or in the United States. Some signed up with their kinfolk. In Ario, the early agraristas possessed access to land from the dwindling Indian holdings. Whatever the tendency to divide men like Gutiérrez

28. Interviews with Zamora agrarian leader Ignacio Espitia, Zamora, August 1985; and Francisco Elizalde, Zamora, July 1985, June 1988, November 1990.

29. I determined that perhaps 36 out of the 533 plots in the Zamora ejido went to non-campesinos. My calculation is based on the "Censo para la expedición de certificados de derechos agrarios," housed in the Secretaría de Reforma Agraria in Morelia (SRA-M). To cross-check, I utilized the "Libro de Parcelamiento," to be found in the ejidal office in Zamora. However, the agrarian reform archival documentation does not identify the previous origins and occupations of the recipients of land. It was Ignacio Espitia who generously and painstakingly identified his fellow ejidatarios. My many hours of conversation with Espitia, as well as three interviews with Francisco Elizalde, in July 1985 and June 1988, allowed me to develop a portrait of Zamora ejidatarios.

30. "Acta de Posesión Definitiva, Ario Santa Monica, Michoacán," expediente 135, Fondo Dotación, SRA-M. On agraristas' work history in the United States, interviews with the following agraristas were illuminating: Ochoa, July 1990; Carlos Martínez, Ario de Rayón, September 1985; and Francisco Godínez López, Ario de Rayón, May 1990.

from their fellows, treating the caciques either as vultures swooping down on innocent campesinos or as lonely heroes,[31] Gutiérrez emerged from a world of slight and tenuous democratic gestures and persistent pressure to mistrust neighbors. In this regard, he was very much a man of the people.

In his agrarian organization Gutiérrez embarked on an exercise in democratic authoritarianism. As this awkward term implies, he sought to dominate agrarian politics. This led him to treat agrarian meetings as covens. The agraristas met in appropriated churches, away from the stray glance of outsiders. When Gutiérrez deemed men ineligible for governmental lands, he ejected them from the meetings. Scholars, either because they view land hunger as an almost bodily craving that men will automatically act on or because the notion of organizing in a counterrevolutionary zone has proved depressing, have collaborated in this silence.[32] For this reason, Gutiérrez's democratic streak has proved useful. Inviting campesinos to voice their concerns about his program, he inadvertently provided a window onto his agrarian gyrations.

When he called them together in agrarian meetings, Gutiérrez would unfurl his attempt to tone down humility. It is noteworthy that these meetings were staged in the former churches and that the old seating arrangements—rich women first—were torn asunder. Women were effectively banished, and it was poor men who sat closest to the front. When they looked around, they saw not the Virgin but the makeshift icons of agrarianism, the portraits of Carranza, Calles, and Zapata and the long sheets of cotton emblazoned with caricatures of the priests.[33]

When Gutiérrez entered the room, he seemed distant. He had come from poverty, but he had left the past behind. Now he wore the trappings of power. They were in part economic. He was beginning to award multiple plots to himself and to his mother.[34] In addition, Gutiérrez reveled in his new-found powers of association. When he

31. See the essays in D. A. Brading, ed., *Caudillo and Peasant in the Mexican Revolution* (Cambridge: Cambridge University Press, 1980).

32. There is something of this notion that men almost instinctively rise to redress landed grievances in the work of both the old and the new "populist" historians of the revolution. For an exception to the refusal to study agrarian meetings, see Paul Friedrich, *The Princes of Naranja: An Essay in Anthrohistorical Method* (Austin: University of Texas Press, 1986).

33. Interview with Padilla, August 1985; observation of caricatures in AGN and in Zamora agrarian headquarters.

34. "Censo para la expedición de certificados de derechos agrarios," SRA-M; interview with Espitia, August 1985.

walked into the room, campesinos saw a man who was in continual correspondence with higher-ups in Morelia—Pablo Rangel, the general secretary of the agrarian league, the governor.[35]

Then he began to speak. If the words agraristas flung back at him are any indication, he realized who they had been. He saw that poverty had reduced them "to begging for alms from any passerby before (they would) see (their) children die of hunger." He knew something about their parents, men and women who spent their lives "enriching the reactionaries," only to die "in the most despicable misery."[36]

He also saw that they could become something else. In turning to this he refused to insult their political intelligence. They could be "class brothers" rather than struggling individuals. They could stand up as "Mexicans, not strangers." However, they could not do it alone.[37] If they had been poor and degraded, they had learned the importance of cultivating powerful people to help them.

He spelled out his conditions one by one. First, he was charged with enforcing increasingly stringent governmental agrarian rules, and he basked in it. Over time he fired off instructions about how to use the soil. Campesinos must pay taxes or lose their lands. He insisted that they sell their produce only to the governmental bank, not to the merchants they preferred. And land invasion was taboo.[38]

Second, Gutiérrez was to bring in the vote. He traveled through the countryside, influence in tow, and he told campesinos how to vote. As officers of nine agrarian communities expressed it in a letter to Michoacán gubernatorial candidate Felix Ireta, "when the elections for the governor who oversees the destinies of the state approach, it happens that citizen Juan Gutiérrez, currently the municipal president of Zamora, capital of this district, is the only person who orients us." Gutiérrez, they duly reported, "has filled our ears with your name."[39]

Finally, demanding tolerance of the government's anticlerical policies, Gutiérrez forged a loose collection of villagers to monitor their

35. Juan Gutiérrez to Pablo Rangel, 6 September 1938; Juan Gutiérrez to governor of Michoacán, 3 January 1930, Archivo Juan Gutiérrez (AJG), Zamora.

36. "Relativo al desparcelamiento de ejidatarios del poblado de Zamora, año 1937," Fomento y Agricultura, 1936–40, Archivo Municipal de Zamora (AMZ).

37. Ibid.

38. On paying taxes, Antonio Valencia, chief of ejidal zone, to president of ejidal commissariat, 17 February 1935, AJG; on trading exclusively with the government, zone chief Simon Guzmán to Manuel Rangel, ejidal officer of Zamora ejidal credit local, 4 April 1938, AJG; on land invasions, "Circulares dirigidas a esta presidencia municipal por la secretaría general del gobierno," expediente 6, Fondo Gobernación, 1935, AMZ.

39. Loose documents, n.d., AMZ.

neighbors' behavior. One of their tasks was to pinpoint overt Catholic activities. Gutiérrez led them in using terms such as *fanatic* and *agitator* to describe and denounce practicing Catholics, for example, when he wrote to a Morelia official to denounce the "fanatic agitation" in Tangancícuaro. Or again, he referred to priests leading underground worship as "agitators, stirring up the population."[40]

Washing Away Fanaticism

Moving away from the more formal realm of the former churches, some Cardenistas encountered their own stereotype of an abandoned peasantry. J. Socorro Vázquez, the school inspector in Villa Victoria, reported that 90 percent of the campesinos in the region lived so poorly that "various families during the period of most scarcity are reduced to eating quelites and mezquites and other products of scanty nutritional value, and these campesinos' discolored faces reveal the sad truth of their chronic hunger." Moreover, "it is very common to see men, women, and children wearing one set of clothing until it drops from their bodies."[41] To still their pain, another Cardenista added, they turned to "the fictitious happiness inspired by alcohol."[42]

In a series of activities destined to enrage certain Catholics, revolutionaries made rural bodies objects of attention. Indignant, school inspector J. Socorro Vázquez claimed that fanatics circulated lurid rumors. "The priests advised them to say that the teachers force students to strip and to engage in CARNAL ACTS with one another."[43] The blasphemy, if such it was, was more intellectual, less physical, as revolutionaries determined to transfer purity to the hygienic realm.

In piecemeal ways Cardenistas attempted to create campesinos anew. The approach drew heavily on substitutions. Dirt and the habits "devoid of the most elementary routines of hygiene"[44] were to give

40. The first instance is found in Juan Gutiérrez to Lázaro Cárdenas, 13 September 1935, and the second in Juan Gutiérrez to Secretary General of the Morelia Liga, 6 September 1938, both in AJG.
41. José Ventura González, Profesor inspector federal, Michoacán, caja 412, AHSEP.
42. Manuel Godina Horta, Jr., Profesor inspector federal, Michoacán, caja 412, AHSEP.
43. J. Socorro Vázquez, Profesor inspector federal, Michoacán, caja 412, AHSEP.
44. Ibid.

way to cleanliness. In place of campesino routines they determined to eradicate dirt. Drawing back the curtain of privacy surrounding personal habit, Cardenistas surrounded cleanliness with an aura of sociability. In several communities cultural festivals celebrated "the habit of personal cleanliness," as it was called in Ario.[45] In Yurécuaro, they referred to latrine building as a "fiesta of cleanliness."[46] In Villa Victoria, teachers organized campesinos into a sanitary brigade. The brigadiers dropped in on neighbors, spruced up their homes, and encouraged them to bathe. They paid follow-up visits to determine how many people had followed their advice.[47]

Occasionally, Cardenistas treated more serious diseases. In Puruándiro, Cardenista teachers vaccinated three thousand campesinos with antismallpox vaccine.[48] Finding that children were dying of whooping cough, teachers in Aquililla vaccinated the population.[49] Far more frequently they battled behavior they deemed escapist or even vicious. If Cardenistas had their way, traditional campesino pastimes like card playing and cockfighting would become things of the past. When both activities were outlawed throughout the state in 1934, governmental agents received instructions to enter establishments that permitted card playing and close them down.[50]

More than any other campesino habit, alcoholism incited Cardenista concern. However, Cardenistas wavered between the punitive approach that alcoholism at times inspires among teetotalers and a sense that campesinos' weariness and helplessness drove them to drink. Cárdenas himself established a series of laws meant to generate sobriety. Distribution and sales of alcoholic beverages were regulated during his administration.[51] In Zamora, saloons serving alcoholic beverages were ordered closed.[52]

45. Ibid.

46. Pablo Silva, Profesor inspector federal, Michoacán, caja 412, AHSEP.

47. Manuel Godina Horta, Jr., Profesor inspector federal, Michoacán, caja 412, AHSEP.

48. Pablo Silva, Profesor inspector federal, Michoacán, caja 412, AHSEP.

49. J. Socorro Vázquez, Profesor inspector federal, Michoacán, caja 412, AHSEP.

50. "Actas celebradas por el H. Ayuntamiento de Zamora, Michoacán, 1934–1938," Libro de Cabildo, AMZ; "Expediente relativo a juegos prohibidos por la ley," expediente 25, Fondo Gobernación, AMZ.

51. Luis González, Los días del presidente Cárdenas, vol. 15 of La historia de la revolución mexicana, ed. Luis González (Mexico City: El Colegio de México, 1981), 276.

52. "Actas celebradas por el H. Ayuntamiento de Zamora, Michoacán, 1934–1938," Libro de Cabildo, AMZ.

Following Cárdenas's lead, national educational officials began to stalk "the fictitious happiness inspired by alcohol" with a vengeance.[53] National directives on this issue could be quite brusque. Upon learning that children were singing drinking songs like "La Valentina" and "La Borrachita," the national director of public education, Celso Zamora Flores, exploded. Firing off a memo, he claimed that "these things are a tribute to alcoholism." He demanded that more wholesome songs replace them immediately.[54]

On the other hand, local school inspector Teodoro Mendoza believed that rural life itself induced alcoholism. If campesinos were furious over the closing of a cantina, it was because alcohol granted them temporary reprieve from the tedium of rural life. "Rural life has none of the beauty suggested in the neatly rhymed lines of the poets. Living for a while in a village brings on boredom." Lacking a "healthy means of recreation," campesinos turned to drink.[55]

Perhaps, some of the Cardenistas thought, sports would arrest the tedium. Bent on developing alternatives for campesinos, Jesús Múgica Martínez managed to "link the anti-alcoholism campaign with sports." He also contrived ways to schedule sports events "at the same time the priests were holding Sunday Mass."[56] Teachers in Yurécuaro, Los Reyes, and the Aguilla regions also established sports programs.[57]

In a world where governmental dictums regarding the poor and quasi-religious faith in hygiene have become commonplace, it is easy to view the Cardenista attempt to replace godliness with cleanliness as a sort of natural, if open-hearted, approach to the poor. Nonetheless, the Cardenista efforts were scarcely neutral. They revealed a touching yet intemperate belief in science's latest offerings regarding health, hygiene, and sobriety. They displayed little concern for peasant modesty, less still for the efficacy of peasant ways. At the same time, they placed themselves, and the government of the revolution, squarely on the side of peasant health and well-being. Peasants were not to be reduced to eating quelites without a whimper.

53. Teodoro Mendoza, Profesor inspector federal, Michoacán, caja 412, AHSEP.

54. Manuel Godina Horta, Jr., Profesor inspector federal, Michoacán, caja 412, AHSEP.

55. Teodoro Mendoza, Profesor inspector federal, Michoacán, caja 412, AHSEP.

56. Interview with Jesús Múgica Martínez, Morelia, December 1984.

57. Reports from Camerino Lara T., Teodoro Mendoza, and José Ventura González, Profesores inspectores federales, Michoacán, all in caja 412, AHSEP.

Revolutionary Women's Auxiliaries

The revolutionary lessons for women, and the motivations behind them, were especially tangled. A number of revolutionaries suspected that women acted as clerical puppets. As such, "women tried to make men follow the priests," according to Zamora agrarian leader Vicente Pérez. "And the priests were on the landlords' side. They said agraristas would go to hell."[58] Maximino Padilla, another Zamora agrarian leader, found women "more religious, too religious really. They would do what the priests said."[59]

Believing that women stood in the way of a program that would shower revolutionary largess on men, caciques like Gutiérrez organized women's leagues *(las ligas de mujeres)*. He allowed agrarian leaders' wives, including Matilde Anguiano, María Loreto Pacheco, and María Trinidad Ríos, to assume leadership of the ligas. While the leaders were no longer compelled to direct political energies toward private life, if Gutiérrez had his way, their principal goal would be to discourage Catholic religiosity from hampering revolutionary goals. He seemed determined to make revolutionary use of women's traditional awareness of village activities. Moreover, in the light of the Cardenista refusal to extend equal land rights to married women, the protofeminism of the ligas was limited. In fact, since liga leaders devoted themselves to generating enthusiasm for revolutionary programs, these groups can be likened to women's auxiliaries.

At the same time, liga leadership offered women a strenuous intellectual challenge. The ligas provided a forum for people who had been publicly silenced to experiment with an alternative model of womanhood. The ligas enabled women to flex their intellectual muscles against Catholicism, a tradition of proven depth and power. Furthermore, they could tackle the more mundane problem of male alcoholism, a real women's issue as long as women were responsible for stretching the family budget to feed their families.

To a large extent, liga leaders sought to pry women away from the church. This process could be adorned with prohibitions and substitutions. As Esperanza Rocha explained, "In the liga we couldn't baptize

58. Interview with Vicente Pérez, Zamora, August 1985.
59. Interview with Padilla, August 1985.

our children. It was forbidden. We had to baptize them with honey," in a pseudospiritual ritual the Cardenistas developed.[60] Liga women also forbade women to attend church, receive the sacraments, or wear Catholic medallions.

In letters to agrarian officials, liga leaders occasionally denounced political leaders who protected Catholic culture. Sometimes, as in Atecucario, liga leaders targeted local political leaders. Writing to Gutiérrez, they asked him to use his power to remove the supervisors of public order there because they were "in cahoots with reactionaries to destroy the work of the revolutionaries."[61] Occasionally, liga leaders confronted priestly power head-on. In this, the liga women recognized something about their neighbors' Catholic loyalties. Overtly severing their own ties with Catholicism, they acknowledged the priests' potential sway over their neighbors. "This federation has learned that on the twenty-ninth of last month, a priest of the CATHOLIC RELIGION came from the village of Atecucario to practice his ministry and provoke agitation among fanatic and revolutionary elements here."[62]

Most commonly, liga leaders used their homegrown knowledge of villagers, their movements, and their activities to identify backsliders. There was a certain search-and-destroy sensibility here, as liga leaders displayed their findings in a series of political reports to superiors. Then they turned on their neighbors, pinpointing the overt practitioners of the old-time religion. María Loreto Pacheco and a group of liga women in Atecucario denounced Mrs. Josefa García for her "house-to-house campaign soliciting alms for the Zamora parish."[63] They found three agraristas "engaged in deviation and fanaticism" because "they have asked for a priest."[64] Pacheco recommended that the gov-

60. Interview with Rocha, June 1990. The origins of this concoction are disputed in Ario and Zamora, with anti-Cardenistas sustaining Rocha's contention. They attribute the honeyed baptisms to Salvador Sotelo, a Cardenista teacher who spent many years in Ario. But according to Jesús Tapia Santamaría, Sotelo denied involvement with this sticky issue, throwing it back into the lap of the ligas. See Tapia Santamaría, *Campo religioso y evolución política en el Bajio zamorano* (Zamora: El Colegio de Michoacán/Gobierno del Estado de Michoacán, 1986), 215–16.

61. Juan Gutiérrez to Zamora municipal president, 15 July 1936, expediente 4.1936, Fondo Gobernación, AMZ.

62. Series of letters to Zamora municipal president, 2 December 1937, Loose documents, 1937, AMZ.

63. Matilde Anguiano to Juan Gutiérrez, 6 July 1937, Loose documents, 1937, AMZ.

64. Matilde Anguiano to Ing. Gustavo Martínez Baca, 9 August 1937, Loose documents, 1937, AMZ.

ernment repossess their plots of land. Then there were Margarita Méndez and Concepción Gutiérrez, women engaged in "agitation, agitation that is inspired by religious leanings." According to María Loreto Pacheco, president of the women's liga in La Ladera, Méndez and Gutiérrez deserved to be thrown out of town.[65]

Despite the emphasis on the anticlerical aspect of Cardenismo, village leaders pursued other deviations from the revolutionary program found among their fellow citizens. For María Guadalupe Barosa, president of the Liga Femenil Anti-Religiosa, the culprit was ejidatario Eraclio Torres, who had visited her house while drunk to inform her that his wife could not belong to the liga. An argument ensued, in which Guadalupe told the ejidatario that because she was a member of a revolutionary organization, "it would be illogical to speak to an imbecile." She called on Gutiérrez to punish the man.[66]

María Trinidad Ríos, secretary-general of the Liga Femenil de Lucha Social of Ojo de Agua, also embarked on revolutionary vigilance. In her view, the trail led to card playing. She reported to the Zamora municipal president that various ejidatarios met daily in the home of ejidatario David Martínez to play cards. Viewing such recreation as noxious for the ejidal organization, she asked Gutiérrez to prohibit Martínez from holding card games in his home.[67]

Dancing at the Altar

After the Ario bonfire, men and women entered the church. The building once dominated by priests and attentive female parishioners would have looked different. The priest was gone. The icons had been destroyed. Then, in an invitation to experience their surroundings differently, men approached their wives and girlfriends and invited them to dance before the altar.[68]

65. María Loreto Pacheco to Zamora municipal president, 19 October 1937, Loose documents, 1937, AMZ.
66. Juan Gutiérrez to Zamora municipal president, 26 August 1936, expediente 4.1936, Fondo Gobernación, AMZ.
67. María Trinidad Ríos to Zamora municipal president, 21 November 1937, Loose documents, 1937, AMZ.
68. Interviews with Rocha, Verduzco de Peña, and Ochoa, May 1990; and Méndez, November 1990.

The particular revolutionaries involved are dead.[69] In partial compensation, I have collected thousands of words regarding the torching and the dance. I have conducted interviews with women young and old, with rich and poor villagers, and with a probable participant in the dance. None of these people, however, initiated either the torching or the dance. The revolutionary men left traces of their activities, but these traces consist only of details regarding the men's concrete participation in the bonfire and the dance. They left no record of their ruminations or their efforts to transform spiritual life.

While a number of villagers were troubled by the men's activities, they demonstrated little curiosity about the men's motivation. A certain tautology—that anticlerical behavior proves the existence of a blasphemous soul—lingered over their pronouncements. As Concepción Méndez put it, "They were bad people. They did it to deny the existence of God." Even Esperanza Rocha, a serious Catholic who frequently tempered her remarks regarding anticlerical behavior, claimed that "they were trying to mock Catholicism. They were saying it was worthless."[70] La Purísima. The image designed to encourage humility and forgiveness. What was happening here? Why was La Purísima exciting male interest? Why did this interest have a sexual cast? Did she somehow threaten the men?

When priests animated La Purísima, the Virgin-returned-to-life encouraged women to direct their energy toward forgiving transgressions, toward prayer, toward decorating the church with flowers, toward accepting a hierarchical social order as God's design. And toward venerating the priests.

What could the revolutionaries have been thinking? Some of them had repeatedly demonstrated an edgy distaste for the priests.[71] And if much of their wives' routines and virtually everything about their devotion to the church remained obscure to the revolutionaries, one man witnessed the women's activities. Worse still, one man witnessed their daily lives. While the husbands worked in the fields, the priest remained in the village. What is more, in the confessional he was privy

---

69. Interviews with Ochoa, Verduzco de Peña, and Godínez López, May 1990.

70. There were times, for example, when Rocha refused to condemn the dancers, pointing out that "they were only young girls. Perhaps they did not realize what they did." Interviews with Rocha, May 1990; and Méndez, November 1990.

71. The portraits of Jesús Múgica Martínez, José Corona Núñez, and Tomás Rico Cano developed in chapter 2 reveal much of this ambivalence, as did the August 1985 interview with Padilla.

to some version of the women's private lives. Is it too fanciful to believe the men acted on some version of male rivalry?

Speculative? Definitely. Fanciful? Perhaps not. For that night it was different: the church became a dance hall. The granddaughter of one of the dancers, Carmela Valadéz, suggested that the church was entirely altered. Men and women milled about, filling the room with street noise and everyday talk. "They had gotten a band," Valadéz said. "And they got up on the pulpit and danced."[72]

As awkward as it may seem, it is time to interrupt the narrative. More than interrupt, in order to enable readers to explore with me the men's and women's motivations for engaging in what many villagers pointedly condemned as blasphemy, it is necessary to break, if only briefly, with the traditional form of historical narrative. But why? After all, the prevalent form of historical writing enables its practitioners—which includes most of us—to disseminate the idea that historical actors act while scholarly outsiders observe.[73] Clearly, a case can be made for allowing campesinos' varying versions of the torching and the dance to fill these pages. After all, Michoacanos set fire to the icons. They danced before the altar. They developed thoughtful and theologically rich perspectives on what occurred. What they did not do, however, was to commit their interpretations to prose. Rather,

---

72. Interview with Carmela Valadéz, Ario de Rayón, June 1990.

73. As Hayden White pointed out in *Tropics of Discourse* (Baltimore: Johns Hopkins University Press, 1978), this linear narrative formula, based on a combination of nineteenth-century positivist science and romantic novels, does not reflect twentieth-century experience. Nor, as White demonstrates, does it reflect sweeping twentieth-century scientific and artistic discoveries. Although for some time White went virtually unheeded, recently scholars have engaged in various experiments with forms of representation. See, e.g., Natalie Zemon Davis, *The Return of Martin Guerre* (Cambridge: Harvard University Press, 1983); Robert A. Rosenstone, *The Mirror in the Shrine: American Encounters with Meiji Japan* (Cambridge: Harvard University Press, 1988); and John Demos, *The Unredeemed Captive: A Family Story* (New York: Knopf, 1994). Such experiments have proved particularly appropriate for scholars engaged in anthropological fieldwork. See, e.g., James C. Scott, *Weapons of the Weak: Everyday Forms of Peasant Resistance* (New Haven: Yale University Press, 1985); Clifford Geertz, *The Interpretation of Cultures* (New York: Basic Books, 1973); Theodore Rosengarten, *All God's Dangers: The Life of Nate Shaw* (New York: Knopf, 1974); Ruth Behar, "Rage and Redemption: Reading the Life Story of a Mexican Market Woman," *Feminist Studies* 16 (summer 1990): 223–58; and Marjorie Becker, "When I Was a Child, I Danced as a Child, but Now That I Am Old, I Think about Salvation: Soledád Barragán and a Past That Would Not Stay Put" (paper presented at "Narrating Histories: A Workshop," Division of the Humanities and Social Sciences, California Institute of Technology, Pasadena, April 1994).

their perspectives emerge from the interviews I conducted in this region from 1985 to 1990. And whereas the historian's task in confronting written documents is to interpret them, in this case I also participated in their creation. It seems only fair, then, to share something of my encounters with the villagers.

Let me invite you, then, to Ario. Actually, let me encourage you, just once, to be me in Ario. Your strategy will be to appear personally uninteresting, while acting on a genuine interest in the history of others. In an atmosphere charged with messages demanding women's modesty, you might exaggerate your reticence. You will definitely wear respectable but lackluster clothing—a long, dark blue skirt will do. Upon encountering villagers, you will follow the rules of oral history, explaining that you are not exactly a stranger to the region: you have lived here for some time, you have engaged in systematic archival research. Yet because you are an intellectual woman in a society that has virtually no such category, that never seems to register. Somehow, though, you manage to communicate an interest in these villagers' stories, which elicits various renditions of the torching and of the dance.

If there is some implication that revolutionary men, along with the priests, distilled women's possibilities down into some sort of carnal—or conversely, asexual—concentrate, there were villagers who shared that conviction. Among the villagers I interviewed, the tendency to identify women with their sexuality seemed widespread. In a region where even the revolutionaries shared this sensibility, this was not surprising. Who would have suspected, though, that the revolutionaries offered women possibilities that they themselves did not seem to understand? In different ways, a woman born to prominence and an impoverished daughter of one of the first agraristas led me to this perspective.[74]

Concepción Méndez was the daughter of what villagers described as "one of Ario's first families."[75] She lived in one of the houses on the plaza, the area long inhabited by the village's prominent families. What struck me immediately was the glass windows: Though they were hardly a curiosity in Mexico in the late 1980s,[76] Méndez assured me that during the 1930s almost no one could see what their neigh-

74. The following section is based on my interviews with Méndez, June, November 1990; Valadéz, June 1990; and Martínez, September 1985.
75. Interviews with Valadéz, June 1990; and Verduzco de Peña, May 1990.
76. The homes I visited in Jarácuaro in 1985 generally did not have windowpanes. Similarly, the barnlike homes that continue to be constructed across the Tarascan sierra

bors were up to from within their homes. Méndez, however, rose from her siesta and opened her curtains onto the spectacle of the torching.

One of the promises of two-way glass in a society filled with Michoacán's gregarious potential is the windows' hint of conviviality. People can peer at each other from opposing sides of the glass. As I spoke with Méndez, however, I found that her house and the habits she had cultivated there had served as a barrier against the lives of poor people like Carmen Barragán.

Very early in our meetings, I asked Méndez to tell me about her daily routine. It became clear that, notwithstanding her wealth and prominence, poor people had been part of her life. Her father owned a dry goods store, and campesinos shopped there. Poor women worked in her kitchen. It is probably fair to say that a few poor people mattered to her. Still, she minimized their importance. "My sisters and I took turns preparing the noonday meal. There would also be the housekeeping. We were lucky enough to have servants, but we, of course, were in charge."

As for the hacienda peons, it was true that in this region rimmed by large estates they were located nearby. She could have seen what happened there, but to do so would have been to create a disturbance. Who would have supervised the cooking and cleaning? Besides, out of deference to the preoccupation with women's modesty, was she to ask her male relatives to stop their work and accompany her as she observed the work lives of the poor?

When I asked her to tell me about her religious life, I learned that her days had been filled with activities that excluded the poor. She was aware of a Catholic's obligation to relieve the suffering of poor people, and she said that "we tried to help out as best we could." Generally, though, she spent her time with her cousins, the daughters of the sprinkling of wealthy people in the village. It was a quiet, pious life she had come to relish. When they went to church, they took the best seats, close to the image of La Purísima, away from the occasional Indian who wandered in to worship. In the evening they walked in the plaza arm in arm.

She spent some afternoons singing with her cousins. "We divided up. Each of us went to a different street corner. And from our corner, we would each sing a stanza of the hymn, first one, then another, then the last two. It gave us such joy."

---

appear to lack windowpanes. See Ricardo Barthelmy and Jean Meyer, *La casa en el bosque: Las "trojes" de Michoacán* (Zamora: El Colegio de Michoacán, 1987).

But when I asked how the revolution had affected that life, her tenor changed. I was to understand that before the rise of Cardenismo things had been different. "The pueblo was so beautiful, so peaceful. They tried to change things." The revolutionaries had begun to redistribute land, to outlaw priests. The women's ligas "[spied] on us, hovering, listening to find out if we had sneaked a priest into our homes."

Then the girl had come by her house. She did not know her. All kinds of people passed by. The Indian men who had sold the remaining pieces of their property to the agraristas. The blind man, cane in tow. Sometimes a few poor girls, noisy and uncouth. She knew none of them, only her own friends. Until that afternoon when Carmen Barragán dropped by. "She knocked on my door, and then—can you believe it Señorita? She spat in my face."

Méndez would not allow her to leave. The girl was edging away, but she would not have it. She could hardly get her to take it back, but she would force her to own up to her actions.

I said, "Listen Carmen, why did you spit at me?"
"They told me to."
"No, this is your own thing, your own rudeness. How would you feel if I spat at you? Why did you do it?"
"Because I wanted to very much."

There was more. If poor women had once struck her as nondescript and shadowy, identifiable only by their shabby clothing, now Méndez found it difficult to contain herself. Revolutionaries had helped to forge an unforeseen but rancorous connection. Carmen Barragán died years before I met Méndez, but when I asked Méndez who had danced in the church, she attempted to reestablish Barragán's presence. The dancers, she said, were "Carmen Barragán. Carmen Bueno. Soledad Barragán. But Carmen was shameless. She was a little piece of trash, absolutely worthless. They all were. The whole pueblo knows it."

This kind of condemnation invites rebuttal. So too did the kind of rumor that seemed to surround the torching. As one-time revolutionary Carlos Martínez expressed it, "They danced in the church. Then they claimed they repented, but it did no good. Before they died their legs shriveled up. Fell off. I'm not one to say it, but they say it was God's will—the legs falling off. There is no escape."[77]

---

77. Interview with Martínez, September 1985.

Although that rejoinder would have to come from the last surviving dancer, Soledad Barragán almost refused to discuss it. In fact, while numerous villagers identified her as one of the dancers, she never directly acknowledged her presence in the church that night. Perhaps this was partly because her daughter, a fervent Catholic, accompanied me. This undermined the oral historian's standard strategy of affecting respect for the informant's biases no matter how personally distasteful. I could sympathize with La Pasionara, I could even sympathize with the pope, but to do both simultaneously? The awkwardness may have contributed to Barragán's reticence. Perhaps her neighbors' taunts had affected her. Or perhaps she had embraced a more pious version of Catholicism since the dance.

I initially asked a series of mild informational questions regarding her mother. "When was your mother born? Where? What kind of work did she do?" Intent on developing a religious image, Barragán told me that "she was very Catholic, miss. Of course she was. She took us to Mass. It's just that she also knew what justice was. She knew people were hurt there on the haciendas."

Eventually I attempted to steer her to more controversial territory. Nobody I had spoken to about the women's ligas had suggested that they were anything but iconoclastic and flashy.[78] I told Barragán that I wanted to talk with her "about something delicate, the women's liga. Tell me what the women in the liga did."

If it had been left to Barragán, the women's controversies would have remained a thing of the past, so she focused on their patriotism. "They had these civic festivals. They had parades and speeches. Each one would commemorate a revolutionary—this one Zapata, this one Villa." But her daughter cut in. "No, Mamá. There was more than that. Everybody says they went into the church and had a dance. I know because my husband, José, lived on that street. He said that the people went into the church and they had a dance. I also heard they danced with horses. They danced with the icons. They got up on the pulpit and danced."

If villagers such as Méndez were to be believed, Barragán was part of this blasphemous hubbub.[79] However, through hours of conversa-

78. Interviews with Pérez, August 1985; Elizalde, June 1988; Padilla, August 1985; and Rocha, May 1990.
79. Verduzco de Peña and Rocha also identified Barragán as one of the dancers. Interviews with Verduzco de Peña and Rocha, May 1990.

tion with me, Barragán refused to admit her participation in the dance. If the dancers had once determined to resist priestly efforts to define them, that was long ago. Better to leave it there. Then I said, "You know, I would think it would have been exciting to see the dance. This did not happen every day. To see what people were wearing."

Something changed. She seemed to feel the misunderstanding had gone too far. Villagers had whispered about them. Priests had preached against it. Revolutionaries found the issue troublesome. She refused. In her sweet, quiet voice, she denied it all. "I don't want you to think they were like the girls today. I don't want you to think they wore fancy clothes. They just wore what they had on from working." Even if this amounted to some kind of tacit acknowledgment on her part, she would not allow the dancers to be seen as sluts.

Revolutionary Lessons in Smoke

When they entered the classrooms or the agrarian halls, Cardenistas confronted more than their students. In an important sense they were looking behind them. What had caused the Cristero rising? What lessons could they bring to still that violence? This uncertainty, coupled with the Cardenistas' personal variations, gave the lessons a porous, negotiable quality.

For the more progressive revolutionaries, the problem was more clearly etched. When they turned around they saw a rendition of clerical ideology enacted on the battlefields and in the homes. Clerical and civil authorities demanded that men construct the social order and women protect and nurture the status quo. Cristero men dynamiting towns, then returning to their women for comfort, reflected this clerical will to assign behavioral characteristics on the basis of gender.

The Cardenista response was to construct neo-Zapatismo and to put the torch to the Virgin. In other words, they developed a political refabrication of clerical imagery. Like the priests, they developed one message for men, quite another for women. Organizing, cajoling, redistributing land, they responded directly to the men who had risen in rebellion.

The message to the most disempowered—poor, mestiza women— was more ambiguous. The revolutionaries treated women both in accordance with historical treatments of women in Mexico and as political metaphors. They saw them as bearers of children, compañeras to men, cooks—the whole litany. They also subjected them to the same revolutionary measurements to which they subjected others. They meted out revolutionary largess in proportion to overt popular dissidence. As we have seen, the revolutionaries did little to directly improve the economic and political position of women. Rather, their central lesson was that the kind of abnegation and underground power women had possessed in this region dotted with churches was to be no longer. Women were invited to develop in its place public roles as helpmeets of revolutionary men.

This suggests that revolutionaries read women as powerful obstructionists but not necessarily as powerful in their own behalf. As women had been trained over the generations to devote their energies to the well-being of others and to foster their own interests only in an off-hand, after-the-fact manner, this revolutionary reading of women's potential resistance was both precise and suggestive. Peasants clamoring for their own benefit, backing that clamor with the power of the gun, had caught the attention of the victorious revolutionaries. While such behavior called for recognition, abnegation, humility, and poverty in themselves would not be sufficient certification for full entrance into the new revolutionary alliance.

CHAPTER SIX

Revolutionary Lessons, II

The Compensations of Indianism

Whoever thinks of Ilhuicamina, Axayácatl, Cuauhtémoc,
Morelos, Juárez, Altamirano, Cajeme, and so many others will
admit that our Indians are made of iron with an interior of silk
and that they constantly shame us to our souls, for all of us, up
to now, have only contributed to embitter their lives with our
incomprehension, our mockery, and even our disdain.

Roberto Quiróz Martínez

Returning to the Tarascan meseta, Cardenistas stumbled
onto villagers in conflict. Since at least the nineteenth century the battles had been joined.[1] On one side were members of the Indian communities forged in colonialism, communities determined to preserve
hierarchies based on possessions, gender, and age. Within these communities, popular Catholic rituals and land tenure played complemen-
tary roles. Indians turned profits from communally owned lands to
support ritual expenditures. Conversely, Tarascans drew the saints into

1. Gerardo Sánchez Díaz and José Napoleón Guzmán Avila provide nuts-and-bolts
descriptions of this process in Michoacán in Gerardo Sánchez Díaz, "Movimientos campesinos en la tierra caliente de Michoacán, 1869–1900," in *Jornadas de historia de occidente: Movimientos populares en el occidente de México, siglos XIX y XX* (Jiquilpan de
Juárez: Centro de Estudios de la Revolución Mexicana "Lázaro Cárdenas," A.C., 1981),
31–45; and José Napoleón Guzmán Avila, *Michoacán y la inversión extranjera,
1880–1911* (Morelia: Universidad Michoacana de San Nicolás de Hidalgo, 1982).

their daily lives, expecting devotion to result in more bountiful harvests.

On the other side stood the liberals. In a countryside choked with tired old patterns—economic stagnation, the priests' persistent request for sustenance—liberals found the idea of motion entrancing. Seeking to free up men and their possessions, to establish a republic of rural smallholders, they outlawed corporate property—Rome's vast holdings and the Tarascan community fields alike.[2] Confronting the legal necessity of styling their communal holdings private property, Indians characteristically turned to their more prosperous, Spanish-speaking neighbors, making them mediators with the government. Frequently, they found their trust misplaced, as these men appropriated their property.[3]

The Cardenistas' overwrought sympathies took over. Oblivious to the fact that Indians had long assimilated imposed ideologies and put them to many uses, Cardenistas saw only literal testaments to suffering. Out of deepest shame—they too were white, they too had "only embittered Indian life through incomprehension"—they saw little more than the degradation of the Indian.[4] Mexican Indians had once been absolutely elemental creatures, the sort of earthbound beings outsiders characteristically look to for the redemption of civilization.[5]

2. At a time when the Reform Laws' effects on Indian communities were widely viewed as unintended consequences of liberals' necessary attack on the clerical monopoly of economic life, T. G. Powell's work provided an important antidote. See, e.g., T. G. Powell, "Los liberales, el campesinado indígena, y los problemas agrarios durante la Reforma," *Historia Mexicana* 21 (April–June 1972): 653–75; and idem, "Priests and Peasants in Central Mexico: Social Conflict during La Reforma," *Hispanic American Historical Review* 57:2 (1977): 296–313.

3. For vivid examples, see César Moheno, *Las historias y los hombres de San Juan* (Zamora: El Colegio de Michoacán/CONACYT, 1985); Carlos García Mora, "Tierra y movimiento agrarista en la sierra purépecha," in *Jornadas de historia de occidente*, 47–101; and Pedro Carrasco, *Tarascan Folk Religion: An Analysis of Economic, Social, and Religious Interactions* (New Orleans: Middle American Research Institute, Tulane University of Louisiana, 1952).

4. Roberto Quiróz Martínez, "El indio como factor social," *Maestro Rural* (Mexico City), 1 August 1934, 26.

5. The parallels with non-blacks' images of the black are very suggestive. For an evocative treatment of white teachers' efforts to teach and remake black ex-slaves, see Willie Lee Rose, *Rehearsal for Reconstruction: The Port Royal Experiment* (New York: Oxford University Press, 1964). For later literary reflections on this issue, see Toni Morrison, *Playing in the Dark: Whiteness and the Literary Imagination* (Cambridge: Harvard University Press, 1992).

Turning clay into cooking pots, feathers into ornaments, the sun into "a God more responsive than the Catholic saints," they had once fashioned civilization from unvarnished natural materials.[6] Yet as Cardenista school inspector Policarpo Sánchez expressed it, one "lovely tradition" after another "had been relegated to oblivion by fanaticism."[7]

It did not have to be. To a certain extent the Cardenistas rejected the Enlightenment notion that each life is an open book, to be written in at will. Rather, drawing on the sort of genetic determinism they shared with the priests, they set out to liberate Indians' artistic potential.[8] Though land was scarce on the meseta, farming would not be the only option. Determined to portray governmental concern for the poor in a graphic fashion, they called on Indians to deck themselves out in aesthetic garb. Though the revolutionaries would never have said it (at least partly because of their ambivalence toward women), they were proposing that Indians, particularly Indian men, usurp the symbolic role women had played for the church. Like the revolutionaries, the priests had developed a double-edged approach to liberation. After all, promoting humble behavior for women and the poor corresponded to the Catholic hierarchical understanding of God's will. At the same time, women (and others driven to modesty and silence) played a role for the church. If there had been no one to redeem, whatever would priests have done? In a similar sense, Cardenistas sincerely promoted Indian liberation as they understood it. At the same time, their view of Indians as downtrodden enabled Cárdenas and his government to adopt the role of saviors.

Still, Cardenistas were more than priestly impersonators; they were also liberals. As such, they determined to free Tarascans from what they viewed as spiritual bondage. Central to this liberation would be

6. "Campaña de desfanatización religiosa, Centro de Estudios de la Revolución Mexicana, "Lázaro Cárdenas," A.C. [CERMLC], Jiquilpan de Juárez, Michoacán.

7. Policarpo T. Sánchez, Profesor inspector federal, Michoacán, caja 412, Archivo de la Secretaría de Educación Pública (AHSEP), Mexico City.

8. According to Anthony Pagden, the sixteenth-century Spanish friars pondered the issue of Indians' biological status—what manner of being were these creatures?—with great intensity. Of particular concern was the issue whether Christians were barbarians, which the Christians' heritage from the Greeks suggested. This would seem to imply that while the missionaries' framework was flexible, the categories themselves—savage, barbarian, child of nature—were definitive. See Anthony Pagden, *The Fall of Natural Man: The American Indian and the Origins of Comparative Ethnography* (Cambridge: Cambridge University Press, 1982), esp. 15–26.

the notion that, stripped to their ethnic essence, Indians were inherently glorious. The company of Jesus, Mary, and the saints was both unnecessary and harmful.

It was this combination, this liberal proto-Catholicism, that led Cardenistas to seek a peculiar Indian renaissance. It was as though ethnicity and its accompanying aestheticism could be enough. The new Indians would be both grander than their predecessors and lonely as only moderns can be.

Uprooting Ritual

In the Once Pueblos, headquarters for Tarascan political activity after Tapia's death, Cárdenas placed Ernesto Prado in charge of the land reform.[9] Prado was a man who inspired deep ambivalence. Moisés Sáenz knew him in Carapan and found him barely tolerable, a man "bent on satisfying that desire to command so vehement in people who have been subjugated for much time." He considered him at once full of "machinations and intrigues" and "the revolution and of the government."[10]

Ironically, it was Prado's unwitting rejection of the Cardenista image of aesthetic victimization that provoked this ambivalence. As a man of individual initiative, Prado embodied liberal ideals. In this monolingual desert, he spoke Spanish as well as Tarascan. He fought in the revolution as a Zapatista,[11] then waited for the other Once Pueblo leaders to die off before he assumed leadership.[12] With Cárde-

---

9. That the Once Pueblos became revolutionary headquarters emerged with clarity in my research at the Archivo General de la Nación (AGN), Mexico City, in 1985, 1986, 1988, and 1989. I proceeded by analyzing the archival categories, themselves a version of official history. From those categories I developed a series of counterrevolutionary categories (*atropellos, asesinatos, fanáticos,* and *la educación socialista,* to name a few), then selected and analyzed those documents. On the Cardenistas' use of caciques, interviews with José Corona Núñez (Morelia, Michoacán, July 1985) and Jesús Múgica Martínez (Morelia, December 1984) proved important.

10. Moisés Sáenz, *Carapan: Bosquejo de una experiencia* (Lima: Librería e Imprenta Gil, 1936), 257, 259, 269.

11. José Zamora Martínez. . .certifica que el C. Ernesto Prado. . .," 5 July 1931, Loose documents, Archivo Municipal de Zamora (AMZ).

12. Luis Alfonso Ramírez, *Chilchota: Un pueblo al pie de la sierra* (Zamora: El Colegio de Michoacán, 1986), 86.

nas's assistance, he placed his brothers Isaac, Eliseo, and Alberto in control of three of the eleven pueblos.[13]

Whereas the northern estates serve as monuments to Indian land losses stretching back for generations,[14] in the Tarascan areas conflict over land endured well into the twentieth century. In these Indian areas where liberal laws encouraged villagers to devise fictions treating communal lands as private property, villagers suffered widespread land loss. In addition, impoverished Indians at times were forced to sell lands to wealthier neighbors.

Despite this sharpened land hunger, the Cardenista government refused to redistribute non-hacienda properties. Moreover, it made little effort to make meseta lands more profitable through improvement. Though they occasionally donated shovels and rakes for working Tarascan school plots, the Cardenistas awarded Tarascans neither credit nor significant infrastructural aid, such as fertilizer and machinery.[15]

As a consequence, campesinos repeatedly petitioned for land, only to be turned away empty-handed. The government rejected nineteen campesinos in Colonia Revolución and eleven in La Tinaja. The enumeration continues with seventy-one denials in Santa Ana Chapitiro, forty-nine in Santa Juana, thirty-seven in San Miguel Charahuen. All of these campesinos were deemed eligible for lands, and in some of the communities, such as La Tinaja and Colonia Revolución, they watched neighbors no poorer than they were actually receive lands. In San Miguel Charahuen, governmental officials found that the campesinos received only .37 pesos daily for their agricultural labor but that the available lands had been promised to other villagers.[16]

13. Sáenz, *Carapan*, 23.

14. This fact emerged with some clarity as I read documents in the AMZ and the Archivo Municipal de Ario (AMA) referring to "extinguished Indian communities" in the precise areas where Zamora and Ario haciendas stood. See, e.g., "Expediente relativo a la reclamación que hacen varios vecinos de Sta. Monica Ario de varios títulos de la extinguida comunidad que les fueron recogidos por la Prefectura del Distrito," expediente 16, ramo gobernación, AMZ; Ignacio Ceja et al. to Zamora municipal president, 25 March 1918, in "Comunidad Ario," expediente 35, AMZ; interim municipal president to secretary-general, 17 June 1919, sección civil, prefectura juzgado del districto, Loose documents, AMZ.

15. This information is found in a series of five reports submitted by Policarpo T. Sánchez, school inspector for the Pátzcuaro region, on 2 January, 13 March, 26 March, 24 June, and 17 September 1936, Policarpo T. Sánchez, Profesor inspector federal, Michoacán, caja 412, AHSEP.

16. On Colonia Revolución, see Resoluciones Presidenciales, October 1937, Colonia Revolución; on La Tinaja, Resolución Presidencial, Fondo Dotación de Tierra; on

Cardenista teachers responded to this demand by promoting numerous small craft industries to revitalize what they understood as the Indians' ancestral talents. These included carpentry, ceramics, toy making, and furniture construction.[17] Prado, however, fostered a different understanding of Indianism, an understanding that avoided any association of Indians with handicrafts.

He had developed his vision in the persistent battles over land and political domination that raged in the meseta area beginning in 1917. While he almost never set his understanding of Indianism to paper, when he did he framed it within a military idiom of friends and foes.[18]

Something of Prado's sensibility emerged in 1934. Serrato was governor and Cárdenas was president-elect, and campesinos belonged to either the conservative agrarian groups sponsored by Serrato or the revolutionary group loyal to Prado. In a letter defending his followers to the head of the CRMDT, Prado described them as reduced to would-be farmers, thwarted in their efforts to farm:

As always, the rural workers of the Agrarian Community of Chilchota, members of this Federation, continue to be victims of the most brutal assaults by the municipal authorities of Chilchota, for yesterday at one P.M., when a group of agraristas engaged in cleaning the drainage ditches to water their lands, which remain unplanted due to the opposition of the

---

Santa Ana Chapitiro, Resolución Presidencial, Santa Ana Chapitiro, 20 July 1938; on Santa Juana, Resolución Presidencial, Santa Juana, 8 March 1939; on San Miguel Charahuen, Report of Carlos García de Leon, 23 April 1935, expediente 665, Fondo Dotación; on the lopsided redistribution, Resolución Gubernatorial, 4 April 1938, Expediente Dotación de Tierras 1404, and Resolución Presidencial, October 1937; on the governmental engineers' findings, Miguel Charahuen, expediente 665, all housed in Secretaría de Reforma Agraria, Morelia.

17. Policarpo T. Sánchez, Profesor inspector federal, Michoacán, caja 412, AHSEP.

18. Although I have uncovered numerous denunciations of Prado, his own writings are sparse. Still, in testimony at the subversion trial of Ignacio Ixta and Reynaldo Torres, the military idiom predominated. Characterizing Ixta and Torres as cattlemen, Prado claimed that they traveled to Zamora, Coalcomán, and Chila "advising the residents there of subversive tactics against the federal government, that Ixta was a Cristero who turned the Michoacán government on its head for so long that he armed the Cristeros and was personally involved in aggression against the government."

It is also true that in a 1940 letter asking Cárdenas to release his followers from jail Prado portrays them as "victims of various assaults." For the testimony against Ixta and Torres, see J. Espinosa, Agente Federal de Hacienda, to Zamora municipal president, 25 October 1939, Loose documents, AMZ. For the effort to free his followers, see Ernesto Prado to Lázaro Cárdenas, 19 February 1940, expediente 542.1/2644, Lázaro Cárdenas, Fondo Presidentes, AGN.

authorities and clerical reactionaries who keep trying to take their land away from them . . . they were assaulted in a villainous, cowardly way by a group of forty armed men.[19]

The unplanted land. The loss of the harvest. The assault. According to Prado, all these events were unnecessary, resulting directly from campesino frictions. "It is lamentable and very sad that class brothers of one and the other group have confused each other with this hatred of one another, going to the extreme of trying to murder one another," Prado wrote.[20] Without the "opposition of the authorities and clerical reactionaries," none of these events would have occurred.

Whether Prado's distress was actual, rhetorical, or a bit of both, his land reform depended on "clerical" campesinos. Without them, he would have been unable to make anticlerical behavior a requirement for his agraristas. Confronting the intense land hunger prevalent on the meseta, Prado adapted Callista criteria for land redistribution to the meseta. Mobilizing followers with the lure of the land, he directed them in a series of anticlerical acts. In Chilchota agraristas insisted that the church be turned into a school. In Paracho and Tangancícuaro they petitioned to expel priests. In Tangancícuaro they also planned to burn images of the saints. Throughout the region they mounted anti-clerical demonstrations.[21]

This anticlerical agrarianism produced two significant results. First, there was the fairly common perception among Tarascans that Prado and other caciques fostered continuing inequality in some of the villages. In Chilchota itself Prado encountered claims of unfairness as early as 1934. According to Reynaldo Torres, head of a Chilchota workers' association, Prado was all bluster and fraud. He hid behind a false front by "saying that he is a compadre of General Lázaro Cárdenas and making himself out to be a colonel in the army, a title we know nothing about considering that we have never known what ser-

19. Ernesto Prado to secretary-general, CRMDT, 11 January 1934, expediente 525.3/72, Abelardo Rodríguez, Fondo Presidentes, AGN.

20. Ibid.

21. On making a church into a school, see Margarita Sosa et al. to Lázaro Cárdenas, 16 January 1935, expediente 547.4/36O, Lázaro Cárdenas, Fondo Presidentes, AGN. On the efforts to expel the priests, see Francisco Pérez et al. to Lázaro Cárdenas, 30 April 1935, expediente 547.351, ibid., for Tangancícuaro; and G. Gómez et al. to Lázaro Cárdenas, 4 November 1935, expediente 547.3/79, ibid., for Paracho. On the attempted burning of the icons, see expediente 547.1/6, ibid. On the demonstrations, see García Mora, "Tierra y movimiento agrarista en la sierra purépecha," 84.

vices to the government enabled him to claim that position."²² Emilio Torres, of the Chilchota Indian community, viewed Prado's followers in the same light when they "started trying to help themselves to cultivable lands that belong to the Indian community in this town, lands that have never been treated as plots that can be redistributed because they cannot be, because they are legitimate community property."²³

In Jarácuaro, Naranja, and Tiríndaro agrarista groups seized former communal lands and redistributed them among themselves. In Jarácuaro, the most populous of the Lake Pátzcuaro islands, campesino landholdings were insufficient before the revolution. To supplement their meager incomes and to support their ritual life, the nine hundred campesinos living on the island depended on the communal reed lands. In the name of the revolution, a group of eight local Cardenistas seized the reed lands for themselves, closed the church, and insulted campesinos who sought its reopening.²⁴

In Tiríndaro 105 families out of a population of 2,500 monopolized the redistribution of land. The agraristas brandished anticlericalism as a weapon against those who did not receive land. Many were murdered. Others were thrown out of town.²⁵ Nearby Naranja's agraristas had banished the village's Catholic majority and monopolized the redistributed landholdings since the twenties. Nonetheless, social peace remained elusive in the 1930s, as agraristas united with Cárdenas murdered non-agraristas and seized their lands. They also put a stop to village rituals.²⁶

The burnings of saints and anticlerical gatherings caused the second transformation. While similar events occurred elsewhere, here as every-

22. Reynaldo Torres to governor of Michoacán, 8 August 1934, expediente 525.3/72, Abelardo Rodríguez, Fondo Presidentes, AGN.

23. Emilio Torres et al. to governor of Michoacán, 5 September 1934, expediente 525.3/72, Abelardo Rodríguez, Fondo Presidentes, AGN.

24. Interviews with Jervacio López, Jarácuaro, Michoacán, August 1985; Eulario Capilla, Jarácuaro, September 1985; and Celerino Ramírez, Jarácuaro, September 1985. Carrasco, *Tarascan Folk Religion*, 21. For a historical reconstruction unearthing Tarascan ideology and comparing its flexibility with the relative woodenness of Cardenista ideology, see Marjorie Becker, "Black and White and Color: *Cardenismo* and the Search for a *Campesino* Ideology," *Comparative Studies in Society and History* 29 (1987): 453–65.

25. Paul Friedrich, "Revolutionary Politics and Communal Ritual," in *Political Anthropology*, ed. Marc J. Swartz, Victor W. Turner, and Arthur Tuden (Chicago: Aldine, 1966), 211.

26. Expediente 542.1/20, Lázaro Cárdenas, Fondo Presidentes, AGN.

where context shapes meaning. In Tarascan villages anticlerical activities assaulted a world in which Indians had been rewarded for their acceptance of hierarchy. For Tarascan men this meant accepting a place lower than God, Jesus, saints, landlords, lower than anyone, in fact, except Tarascan women. For women it meant a sort of double (and doubly ambivalent) celebration of their role of extreme modesty, the modesty of Indians coupled with the modesty of women. At the same time, the Cardenista anticlerical activities cast doubt on the old reciprocities binding land and ritual. Traditionally summoned into the clerical universe, clay figurines and ponderous buildings had evoked desire for reward. To bring flowers into the buildings, to place offerings before the figurines, might have yielded more bountiful harvests. By burning the icons and mounting anticlerical demonstrations, some Tarascans treated the figurines as wood and paint, unaltered by Catholic meaning. At the same time, they unleashed spiritual energy for other uses. In this respect, they set the old meanings adrift.

Compensatory Rhythms

The rituals would not lack meaning for long. Persuaded that through ritual life Indians expressed their most basic truths, Cardenistas developed two new ritual forms. The first was born of a certain resigned sensitivity to Tarascan Catholicism. Cardenistas refused to attack it or suppress it. They would tolerate Catholic practices, only encouraging Indians to dabble in revolutionary activities on the side.

Combining pragmatism with a concern for Indian culture, it was just the approach for a man of Corona Núñez's perception and complexity. Turning to the Tarascans he worked with in Panindícuaro, he insisted, "It's not true that we oppose religion. The proof is that you should organize your dramatic performances, your fiestas, consult with the Virgin of Guadalupe. Why not?"[27]

Similarly, Constantino Murillo adopted a gradualist approach. He lent the Tarascans he taught his "complete support to help them celebrate their saints' days fiestas." At the same time, he attempted to lead the Tarascans toward governmental projects. He encouraged his stu-

27. Interview with Corona Núñez, July 1985.

dents to celebrate only Friday and Saturday of Holy Week in traditional style. The boys were to "dedicate the remaining days to sports, while the girls would spend their time sewing." By sponsoring such activities Murillo hoped to "dispel the intensity of Catholicism little by little."[28]

These stopgap measures, rooted in an expedient form of sensitivity, did not deter Cardenistas' pursuit of their deeper vision. It was a vision in which Indians, particularly Indian men, belonged to nature in two ways. They had a natural, or genetic, destiny. But then, the meaning of nature slipped into something else, as Indian identity was engaged with nature in the sense of the unspoiled products of the universe. Thus, Cardenistas believed that Indians exhibited their true nature (or biological destiny) by beautifying fragments of nature. These fragments, in turn, included clay, wood, feathers, and the flesh of Indians themselves.

Nature, in these intertwined senses, came together in the fantasy of the Indian clamoring for release. An expressive clamor, it was one part visual enchantment, one part plea for liberation. To still the clamor, Cardenistas would promote a program of Indian aestheticism designed to compensate for both prerevolutionary elite abuse and the inadequacies of the Indian land redistribution.

As forecast in their lesson plans, teachers displayed only the most diffuse concern for historical authenticity. In general, this stretched only to the ethnic similarities between pre-Conquest and postrevolutionary Indians, and even that was vague, as Cardenistas tended to view all Indians as descendants of the same genetic pool of artistic talent.

When it came to crafting objects of clay, the link between twentieth-century Tarascans and their ancestors was vague. Rather than reestablishing an earlier way of life, Cardenistas would evoke a sensibility. The effort of a group of Cardenistas associated with the Michoacán University of San Nicolás de Hidalgo to reestablish fabrication of "artistic work in antique styles" provides a telling example. While they adopted a hopeful tone toward the proposition that they were restoring pre-Cortesian artisanal styles, the Cardenistas remained cautious. Although the teachers had promoted a "pre-Cortesian renaissance," they made no claims for authenticity.

28. Interview with Constantino Murillo, Morelia, July 1985.

During the past two years the secretary of public assistance, in collaboration with the Michoacán University of San Nicolás de Hidalgo and the secretary of the economy, has undertaken a special effort to assist the poorest indigenous groups in the regions of Lake Pátzcuaro, the Cañada of the Once Pueblos, Paracho, and Tirepetío, an effort that consists in giving facilities to the Indians that live there to produce artistic works in antique styles that have qualities of endurance and utility, guaranteeing their rapid sales.

. . .[These groups] have gotten the Indians to return to making some objects that practically were no longer being produced and that now are in demand. Thus, there has been a rebirth in the production of trunks, candelabras, small pieces of furniture, small barns in Paracho, feather embroideries in Tirepetío, and ceramics of form and finish similar to the pre-Cortesian in Huansito and Tzintzuntzan.[29]

Then too, when Indians themselves were to serve as the natural objects to be refurbished, Cardenistas refused to fret over historical accuracy. In such cases, Indians were targeted for restoration as natural performing artists. As they had planned, teachers themselves sometimes wrote the songs. Corona Núñez boasted that he "invented a song, a dance of the tierra caliente," and went from house to house in Panindícuaro, teaching the Tarascans "to sing the song, dance the dance." In Uruapan teachers trained students in composition. They taught students to recite "El Fresno" (The Ash Tree) and to sing "La Primavera" (Springtime).[30]

More commonly, Cardenistas interspersed Indian artistic activities with revolutionary propaganda. In five Domingo Cultural (Cultural Sunday) programs held in Uruapan in February and March 1935, Cardenistas constructed a revolutionary framework for Indian artistry. On March 2 the Cardenista teacher began the program by calling for the emancipation of women. Then schoolchildren stepped forward to sing a corrido dedicated to the agrarista. Pichátaro residents brought the program to a close with their performance of the Tarascans' traditional Danza de los Viejitos (Dance of the Little Old Men).[31]

Finally, Cardenistas refurbished the traditional Tarascan capital of

29. Secretaría de la Asistencia Pública, Arte Indígena Michoacano, Mexico City, 10 November 1940, Fondo Ramón Fernández y Fernández, El Colegio de Michoacán, Zamora, Michoacán.

30. Interview with Corona Núñez, July 1985; expediente 533.3/61, Lázaro Cárdenas, Fondo Presidentes, AGN.

31. Expediente 533.3/61, Lázaro Cárdenas, Fondo Presidentes, AGN.

Pátzcuaro into a stage backdrop for Indians. Commissioning architect Alberto Le Duc, Cárdenas charged him with making Pátzcuaro into "an official colonial city." Cultural eclecticism became the unconscious order of the day. In the construction Le Duc intentionally included "all the possible elements from the existing buildings, such as arches from the patio of the former convent of San Nicolás." He also used regional materials, along with "typical decorative elements of the state of Michoacán for the ornamentation."[32] Then Cárdenas ordered a statue of Morelos to be built there. In addition Cárdenas ordered a market and a theater of the people to be built in the Plaza of San Augustín alongside the church and former Augustinian convent.

Against this mosaic setting of popular elements, Cardenista teachers and agrarian agents staged the Congreso Femenil Socialista (Feminine Socialist Congress) in late 1934. While national and local Cardenistas seldom emphasized the specific revolutionary role of women, just this once they did so with a vengeance.[33] Antonio G. Bautista and Consuelo M., widow of Bolaños, congress delegates reporting the event for *Maestro Rural*, focused on a revolutionary identified only as Pérez H.[34] According to Bautista and the widow Bolaños, Pérez H. demanded "schools, not churches, workshops, and not seminaries, cooperatives, and not saints." With these few words Pérez H. asked women to reject the main public space where their modesty and humility had been celebrated. Then again, those same words invited the women to abandon buildings that had functioned as physical representations of the clerical constraints surrounding them. As long as those walls served as barriers to women's other possibilities, they were to avoid them.

32. Alberto Le Duc, architect, to Luis I. Rodríguez, private secretary of Cárdenas, 3 December 1935, CERMLC, carpeta 10, caja 13.

33. Many writers for *Maestro Rural* reproduced the cultural commonplace that *Indian* signified "Indian man." See, e.g., José D. González Velasco, "Solo el amo a los hermanos indios puede transformarlos en sus medios en todos los órdenes," *Maestro Rural*, 15 February 1934, 11–12; "El niño proletariado," ibid., 1 April 1935, 3; and "Como se entrena y organizen un equipo atlético," ibid., 15 February 1935, 16. To be sure, *Maestro Rural* writers occasionally devoted attention to women and men, yet when they did, the tendency was to portray women as a subset of men. See, e.g., "Programa de enseñanza doméstica," ibid., 15 July 1934, 9–12, dedicated to teaching young people housekeeping techniques. Girls were instructed to devote themselves to tasks such as "work in the kitchen, preparing the soup, cleaning and serving the plates with the dishes they themselves prepared," while boys were to engage in "construction tasks, whitewashing walls, cleaning the patio."

34. The following analysis is based on "Las mujeres rojas de Michoacán," *Maestro Rural*, December 15, 1934, 22.

The Cardenistas invited women to act naturally rather than fester in what the journalists referred to as the clerical "cauldron of lies." Or did they? The evidence for this contention is the Cardenistas' literal understanding of the women's nature, which was based on women's biological abilities to accept sperm and bear children. The implication, then, was that this return to nature depended on women's adopting a role as receptacle. Just as women could be impregnated by men and emerge as mothers, so their natural behavior would depend on their ability to absorb. This wanders far from the equally literal biological association for men, that as they become fathers by making babies, they become artists by making pots. But how were Tarascan women to absorb revolutionary meaning, as it were?

The Cardenista writers offered two suggestions. First, they extolled women's mannequinlike qualities. "We saw a gathering of genuine Indians," they wrote, "with their children on their backs, wrapped up in their traditional blue rebozos, carrying their red and black banners."

Live women asked to impersonate plaster figurines, themselves impersonations of women? But doesn't it follow? For with mannequins, the body is in fact relatively insignificant. It is intended to be viewed as the foundation for garments. And in this case the women vanish alongside their revolutionary role as scaffolding for symbols.

Focusing on the women "with their children on their backs," the Cardenistas singled out the ways their involvements with men transformed them into mothers. Then the Cardenistas shifted their gaze to the women's outfits. Dressed in "their traditional blue rebozos," almost uniforms for women who had accepted the Catholic notion that women should embody humility and modesty, they struck the Cardenistas as "genuine Indians." Finally, the writers singled out the revolutionaries' ability to persuade women to "[carry] their red and white banners," thus becoming advertisements for the revolution.

Then the Cardenistas seemed to move away from the liberating potential in their notion of women-as-vessels. For the *Maestro Rural* journalists, a long list of Tarascan demands represented "feminine gallantry." The Indian women, the Cardenistas reported, called for "land for all adult women, liberty for all their imprisoned menfolk, cooperatives made out of churches, workshops/schools for their children, and arms to defend the revolutionary government."

Without doubt, the demand for land represented a radical departure from a governmental land policy that denied land titles to married women. Yet the Cardenista enthusiasm for this innovation was tempered by their endorsement of the women's more traditional demands. With each of those demands, the Indian women vigorously championed their husbands' and children's needs. And there can be no question that as long as the Tarascans' family-based economies remained unaltered, the women too would have profited. Still, though the Cardenistas did not openly acknowledge it, their operative assumption seemed to be that women's interests and activities stemmed from their reproductive abilities, abilities binding women and their destinies to the needs of men and children.

To attempt to do justice to Cardenista Indianism is particularly painful, for idealism, enthusiasm, and affection for the Indians marked the project. However, it was a cramped idealism. It was hampered by—can this be said?—a sense of Indian potential that was simultaneously exaggerated and limited.

This was true of the land reform, an effort resembling nothing so much as nineteenth-century liberal agrarian economics in the area. To be sure, this contention demands explanation, as the liberals promoted individual landholding and the Cardenistas favored communal land tenure. In a superficial sense, the resemblance is to be found in the fact that both Cardenistas and liberals promoted land policies that resulted in widespread landed inequity, whether in the form of the "extinguished" communities of the liberals or the revolutionary cliques of the Cardenistas. Yet the resemblance emerges more clearly if we consider that both groups of ideologues seem to have believed that Indians would approach land programs in a uniformly honest fashion, that poverty and community contentiousness would not at times temper the Indians' own senses of equity and justice. Neither group seems to have recognized that Indians themselves might be partially responsible for the resulting inequities.

Cardenista aesthetics proved equally troublesome. This is not to deny that they functioned as an economic alternative. They did. It is because, once again, the revolutionary understanding of the Indians was too highly colored, too loosely romantic, too glossy. To suggest that all Indians, or at least those Indians lacking adequate lands, possessed artistic instincts was to offer up an inverted scapegoat. It was to make the Indians both more and less than what they were.

CHAPTER SEVEN

Some Lessons of Their Own

We want you once and for all to tell us if liberty is a gift reserved for the wicked and if we don't have the right to breathe the air shaped by the Revolution.

Ario villagers

When the revolutionaries entered their lives with revolutionary lessons, mestizo campesinos and elites were attentive. All over the state they seized on what they had been told and concocted an image of a revolutionary. He was a man concerned about the poor and their well-being. He had developed a curious interest in historical buildings and statues. He possessed a fervent—some might say religious—disdain for the Catholic realm.

Most importantly, he was malleable. Campesinos were trained in recasting symbolism, coaxing benevolence from symbols of self-denial. Elites, on the other hand, were determined to protect their socioeconomic preeminence. And in nooks and crannies throughout the mestizo sections of the state sundry campesinos—men, women, agraristas, and non-agraristas—attempted to remold the revolutionary image. They gathered in the villages and towns nestled in Michoacán's northwestern corner near Jalisco—places like Yurécuaro, Tinquindín, Los Reyes, Pamatácuaro, Atacapan, Zacán. They could be found in the towns of Zitácuaro in the northeast, Queréndaro and Zinapécuaro east of Morelia, in the Michoacán Bajio towns of Sahuayo and Zamora.

Occasionally, they were neither manipulative nor soft-spoken. The bare-bones assaults on teachers come to mind. Then too, we shall find that some Tarascan communities exploded into fratricidal violence. In general, however, campesino tools were linguistic. Drawing on the new revolutionary language, the old Catholic idiom, a combination, they molded the phrases to express their needs.

In the stricter terms of power relations, the revolutionaries brought campesinos lessons, lessons forged in the hope of alliance. With their long experience of reading the practices of outsiders, eyes trained to ferret out discrepancies, campesinos did not dismiss those lessons summarily. Rather, they called for a revolution that simultaneously restored Catholic ritual and fulfilled the government's own liberating promises. In short, Michoacán campesinos could teach some lessons of their own.

Salvaging Agrarian Dreams

When news of Cardenista agrarianism first filtered into Michoacán, it seemed that the mestizos' years of hopeless yearning for land they worked but did not own might be over. Suddenly the Cardenistas claimed that the fields were there for the taking. Indeed, as we have seen, in some mestizo communities agrarian leaders practically begged campesinos to become agraristas. "Don't you want a piece of land?" Zamora agrarian leader Juan Gutiérrez reportedly beckoned.[1]

Mestizo campesinos soon learned that the truth was more complex. Outright possession of Michoacán's green and fertile pastures seemed as elusive as ever, as the Cardenistas had awarded no titles to ejidal lands.[2] Moreover, the land redistribution was mired in a welter of contradictory rules and administered by caciques bound by dual loyalties—to administer governmental rules, to mobilize campesinos.

While this was scarcely the agrarian utopia the campesinos had longed for, an offer of land was still the stuff of dreams. After all, mestizos came from rugged agrarian landscapes. In a world where people were trained to believe that land ownership made the man, their par-

1. Interviews with Zamora resident Francisco Elizalde, Zamora, Michoacán, July 1985; and Cardenista agrarian leaders Ignacio Espitia and Maximino Padilla, Zamora, August 1985.
2. Interviews with Padilla, Espitia, and Padre Joaquín Paz, Zamora, August 1985.

ents had been landless, forced to work long hours on the landowners' estates. Burdened by harsh landlords, they spent their time surreptitiously coveting the fields—and the more comfortable lives—denied them. As though recognizing that the Cardenistas were no landlords plucking the fruits of campesino labor, the mestizos refused to renounce their agrarian dreams. The initial land redistribution would serve as a first round in negotiations as they set about to salvage their dreams as best they could.

Where insufficient lands jeopardized their goal, the campesinos clamored for more. Ramón Zaragoza, president of the agrarian community of Sauz de Abajo, charged that a governmental official had awarded half of the village's water to a neighboring pueblo.[3] José González of Ario claimed that despite being assigned a plot of land in the agrarian census, he never received it.[4] Martín Herrera, one of the representatives of the agrarian community of Sauz de Abajo, protested that cacique Juan Gutiérrez had deprived thirty-two responsible ejidatarios of their land.[5]

Where no plots were awarded, many campesinos helped themselves to land. Ejidatarios of El Espíritu in the Zamora municipality who had been awarded 119 hectares of governmental land found the land grant insufficient. To rectify the situation, they invaded neighboring property and claimed an additional thirty-one hectares.[6] They were hardly alone. In 1935 Michoacán's governor reported that the state government was "receiving repeated complaints from various places in the state saying that campesinos continue to take over lands to farm without authorization and without fulfilling the prerequisites established by the agrarian laws."[7] Two years later Cárdenas received letters from landowners in Yurécuaro complaining that the campesinos had illegally invaded their land.[8]

Where Cardenistas attempted to define agrarian relations through

3. Expediente 404.1/8939, Lázaro Cárdenas, Fondo Presidentes, Archivo General de la Nación (AGN), Mexico City.

4. José González to Luis Vega, president of the ejidal commissariat, 9 April 1940, Juan Gutiérrez private archive (AJG), Zamora.

5. Expediente 404.1/8939, Lázaro Cárdenas, Fondo Presidentes, AGN.

6. Expediente 404.1/4192, Lázaro Cárdenas, Fondo Presidentes, AGN; *Libro de Cabildo,* 53, Archivo Municipal de Zamora (AMZ), Zamora; *Diario Oficial,* 16 February 1936.

7. Expediente 6, Fondo Gobernación, 1935, AMZ.

8. Expediente 404.1/287, Lázaro Cárdenas, Fondo Presidentes, AGN.

the ejidal bank, many campesinos simply ignored state agencies and eluded their control. Their defiance was particularly notable in the Zamora area, where campesinos refused to pay either their taxes or their debts to the bank despite repeated warnings.[9] And to the chagrin of governmental agents who attempted to control land use, campesinos saw ejidal plots and ejidal crops as their own, to dispose of as they pleased. Although he was chastised by Cardenista officials, ejidatario Augustín Ramírez insisted on selling his garbanzo beans to a local merchant rather than to the bank.[10] On the nearby La Rinconada ejido, ejidatario José Ramírez persisted in allowing his son to feed a horse garbanzo grown on his ejidal plot even though governmental officials intended it as ejidal produce to be marketed.[11] And against all governmental regulations, campesinos in the Zamora area continued to pasture their animals on their ejidal lands.[12]

A Portrait Gallery of Caciques

A number of campesinos turned to Cárdenas with comments and denunciations of revolutionary caciques. Playing on Cárdenas's quest for rural allegiance, the campesinos developed two linguistic ploys to alert him to their needs. Rural autodidacts, they instructed themselves in the Cardenista idiom, which portrayed the revolution as popular, just, and free, then cloaked their anti-Cardenista complaints in Cardenista language. At times they would also use the older discourse, the Catholic idiom, which rooted justice in Christianity. Throughout the state campesinos expressed their grievances against caciques in these languages.

These idioms lent themselves to sketching verbal portraits of caciques' effects on rural life. When placed side by side, these portraits fill a gallery with abuses. Again and again, groups and individuals style

9. On taxes, see "Pacto de honor de las sociedades de la zona XXXI-F," July 10, 1935, AJG; on the debts, see "Acuerdo de sociedad del crédito ejidal," 28 November 1937, AJG.

10. Simon Guzmán, zone chief of national ejidal bank, to Manuel Rangel, delegate of ejidal credit local of Zamora, 4 April 1938, AJG.

11. Francisco Vega R., president of ejidal commissariat, to Juan Gallegos, 3 February 1938, AJG.

12. Juan Gutiérrez to Antonio Guerrero, 22 July 1935, AJG.

themselves campesinos wronged by oppressive rural bosses. Again and again, the reality is more complex.

Notice, for example, one of the most apparently popular deployments of this idiom, the denunciation of cacique Ramón Cuevas by 105 Ario residents. In their complaint, the campesinos create a vivid image of revolutionary hope undermined by arbitrary bossism. Once they had expected an end to tyranny, the "right to breathe the air shaped by the revolution." More than a turn of phrase, an idle linguistic flourish, this remark led to a plea for liberation, a liberation that campesinos couched in democratic terms. They saw themselves as a "free and sovereign people," possessing "the right to elect our leaders." Those leaders were obligated to "be aware of the rights that belong to everyone as citizens."[13]

Betraying these goals, Cuevas reduced them to "eternal victims of the village scourge." Without provocation, Cuevas began tossing innocent campesinos in jail. On January 14, 1935, it was Emilia del Río. In April he imprisoned Vicente García Verduzco for eight days, denying his family the rights "to visit or to bring even one meal a day." On June 12 the cacique "grabbed María Refugio Martínez by her hair" and jailed her for a week. Later in the summer he illegally entered the house of the Río García sisters and "for three hours scolded them and rebuked them in language only fit for people of his class." In short, he suggested that "liberty is a gift reserved for the evil."[14]

Who were the campesinos who devised this heated outburst? Verduzco was one of the town's most prominent men, and María Refugio, Emilia del Río, and the Río García sisters were his relatives. They were all engaged in furtive efforts to restore Catholicism to the village. One of their relatives, Concepción Méndez, remembers their outrage at the imprisonment. As Méndez put it, "They were so angry that Verduzco and some of the other men trained in the seminary applied what they knew about rhetoric to write that letter."[15] Verduzco's large, floppy signature appears across the top. Those of the women appear below.

That accounts for only five of the signatures. The rest belonged to

13. Group of villagers from Ario Santa Monica to Lázaro Cárdenas, 11 November 1936, Fondo Gobernación, 1935, AMZ.

14. Ibid.

15. Interviews with Concepción Méndez, Ario de Rayón, Michoacán, June and November 1990.

poor Ario campesinos.[16] As Verduzco's employees, men and women who lived from his credit, they were bound up in networks of enforced obligation. As agrarista Rafael Ochoa put it, "They were too cowardly to stand up to him."[17] Perhaps they were, but Catholic practice was not an exclusive concern of the rich. It seems more precise to understand the multiple signatures as the result of a fairly subtle form of coerced voluntarism.

Six men from different villages developed the next image of cacique abuse, an image that took on a somber, millenarian cast. They had believed that exploitation was to be relegated to the prerevolutionary past, as campesinos received the right to "land and work." They had also come to accept the fact that the revolution could tolerate "the opening of the church." However, the Once Pueblos cacique Ernesto Prado, "a false messiah, a wolf in sheep's clothing," had scarcely ushered in this dominion of freedom. Rather, by reducing the villagers to victims "tyrannized by an evil master," he had turned back the clock, placing around the villagers "A HEAVIER YOKE THAN THAT OF THE RICH, WHICH WE JUST THREW OFF."[18]

Notwithstanding the indignation and self-righteousness, these men—who call themselves only José of Purépero, Antonio of Tlazazalca, Luis of Patamban, José of Jacona, Ramón of Chilchota, and Juan of Zamora—had once been Prado's allies. Themselves village bosses, at least some of them had initiated showy anticlerical displays. When their own followers had made up inadequate crowds, they had turned to Prado for anticlerical reinforcement. Now, however, popular and elite protest suggested that Prado had become politically undesirable, and so they had abandoned him to his fate.

A number of villagers themselves drew on the revolutionary idiom to condemn cacique behavior. Unfinished sketches, each one draws on an idiom of revolutionary justice, and each one would benefit from greater detail regarding motivation. Even in the absence of that detail, however, these portraits reflect a widespread sense of grievance and the equally widespread conviction that the government should not tolerate

16. Interviews with Méndez, November 1990; and Rafael Ochoa, Ario de Rayón, July 1990, enabled me to identify these campesinos' occupations and their relationship with Ario elites.

17. Interview with Ochoa, July 1990.

18. José of Purépero et al. to Gustavo Izazaga Cárdenas, Zamora municipal president, 13 April 1937, expediente 11, Fondo Gobernación, 1937, AMZ.

injustices committed in its name. These are portraits of men intoxicated with revolutionary power. According to La Piedad agrarista Felipe Estrada, Congressman Brígido Alatorre had gone on an anti-agrarista rampage. Hiring "ruffians to kill ejidatarios," he jailed men without cause and "assassinated members of the agrarian community."[19] In Ario Santa Monica forty-seven campesinos charged that two supervisors of public order, Margarito Morado and Melchor Ramos, had fostered an anti-agrarista riot.[20] In La Rinconada agraristas depicted a supervisor of public order who insulted them and threatened to kill them. They came to believe themselves "in constant jeopardy, for we have no security."[21] Such portraits could have filled the gallery. According to Conrado Arreola, the secretary-general of the Michoacán League of Agrarian Communities and Campesino Syndicates, agrarian committees' descriptions of caciques assaulting campesinos and stealing lands arrived daily at the league office.[22]

Another section of the gallery was dedicated to linguistic snapshots of revolutionary caciques grown fat off the spoils of land redistribution and powerful through manipulating ejidal elections. Several campesinos accused Cardenista congressman Abraham Martínez of manipulating agrarian elections. Rafael García, president of the ejidal commissariat of San José Rabago, La Piedad, charged Martínez with seeking to depose members of the commissariat and replace them with his own men. To further these goals, Martínez "substituted signatures and threatened ejidatarios."[23] According to ejidatario Salvador Lorenzo of Santa Fe del Río, Martínez was "a stranger to the movement" intent on "trafficking in the campesinos' suffering."[24] Two other groups of

19. Felipe Estrada to Lázaro Cárdenas, 2 September 1936, expediente 542.1/820, Lázaro Cárdenas, Fondo Presidentes, AGN.

20. Forty-seven Ario campesinos to Zamora municipal president, 3 July 1934, expediente 12, Fondo Gobernación, 1934, AMZ.

21. Emilio Sánchez and Luis Herrera to members of Zamora municipal government, 20 January 1934, expediente 12, Fondo Gobernación, 1934, AMZ.

22. Conrado Arreola, secretary-general of Michoacán League of Agrarian Communities and Campesino Syndicates, to Lázaro Cárdenas, 12 June 1939, carpeta 11, caja 13, Fondo CERMLC, Archivo Histórico del Centro de la Revolución Mexicana "Lázaro Cárdenas," A.C. (CERMLC), Jiquilpan de Juárez, Michoacán.

23. Rafael García, president of ejidal commissariat of San José Rabago, La Piedad, and Pablo Piñon, president of ejidal commissariat of Cañada de Ramírez, La Piedad, to Lázaro Cárdenas, 7 June 1937, expediente 402.2/408, Lázaro Cárdenas, Fondo Presidentes, AGN.

24. Salvador Lorenzo to Lázaro Cárdenas, 1 November 1938, expediente 404.1/682, Lázaro Cárdenas, Fondo Presidentes, AGN.

campesinos also sent Cárdenas telegrams of protest against Martínez.[25]

Other caciques were shown using the land redistribution for personal profit. A group of thirty-two campesinos from the Zamora area characterized cacique Juan Gutiérrez as an ejidal thief who seized their governmental lands. "Even if it costs our lives," they threatened, "we refuse to tolerate this theft simply to satisfy the whim of a single individual."[26] Flanking Gutiérrez's portrait were pictures of other caciques greedy for land. Agraristas from Aquiles Serdán claimed that the municipal president there had "framed [agrarista Marcelino Sánchez] by falsely accusing [him] of robbery and tossing [him] into prison." Fellow Aquiles Serdán villagers Fermín Apolinar, Simon García, and Abel Torres also denounced the municipal president's lust for land and claimed that he had "persecuted" them.[27]

The Schoolhouse Rebellion

For campesinos, elite control of agrarian relations and of national politics was not new. A staple of rural life, villagers had been forced to endure such control for generations. Moreover, with priests stationed on haciendas, enforcing the old order, there was a clear link between work and belief. With the revolutionary government's entrance into the arena, however, campesino choices became contingent and tantalizing in new ways. Now state officials informed the campesinos that only those campesinos willing to forgo Catholicism would be eligible for plots of land,[28] and the church reversed the injunction. Only those campesinos who refused governmental land and kept their children home from the socialist schools could consider themselves upright Catholics.

The mestizos found the situation intolerable and refused to accept

25. M. de Orozco et al. to Lázaro Cárdenas, 3 July 1939, and Pablo Rangel Reyes to Lázaro Cárdenas, 27 June 1939, expediente 404.1/682, Lázaro Cárdenas, Fondo Presidentes, AGN.

26. "Zamora ejido, October, 1935–January 1939," AJG.

27. Expediente 542.1/2411, Lázaro Cárdenas, Fondo Presidentes, AGN.

28. See chapter 5; Francisco Frías to director of the agrarian department, 10 March 1936, caja 412, Archivo Histórico de la Secretaría de Educación Pública (AHSEP), Mexico City; René Enrique Villar, school director, Chaparaco, to Zamora municipal president, 21 August 1935, expediente 2, Fondo Gobernación, 1935, AMZ.

either elite agenda in its totality. Ignoring the priests' prediction that eternal damnation awaited ejidatarios, many campesinos accepted governmental lands. At the same time, they decisively rejected the Cardenista politicization of belief. More than any other Cardenista initiative, the government's effort to recast their system of beliefs, values, and rituals provoked dissidence.

In no case would the mestizos' rejection of the Cardenista demand for ideological conformity be more widespread than in their schoolhouse rebellion. In general this resistance was marked by the nonviolence and reticence characteristic of the past. Yet if most campesinos developed nonviolent weapons, small groups of diehard Cristeros refused to abandon their guerrilla tactics. Ragtag Cristero bands swept through the state, assaulting teachers in a swath of villages and towns. They seemed to be everywhere. In Michoacán's northeastern corner they descended on Irimbo, Ciudad Hidalgo, Zitácuaro, Paquisihuato, Maravatío, and Contepec.[29] In Contepec municipality they attacked the villages of Salitrillo, La Margarite, San Antonio Molinos, Molinos de Caballero, El Tecolote, Mogotes, and La Estanzuela.[30] Cristero bands were sighted in the municipality of La Piedad near the state of Guanajuato.[31] Bands also attacked La Huerta near Morelia and Coro, in the municipality of Zinapécuaro, northeast of Morelia.[32] Finally, Cristeros threatened Cardenistas in the hot land towns of Ario de Rosales and La Huacana, in Coire in the municipality of Aquililla, in Manzanillo and Apatzingán.[33]

29. On Irimbo, see Davila Morín to Lázaro Cárdenas, 24 December 1934, expediente 703.1/23, Lázaro Cárdenas, Fondo Presidentes, AGN; on Hidalgo and Zitácuaro, Luis Mora to Lázaro Cárdenas, 20 January 1935, expediente 551.3/14, ibid.; on Paquisihuato, Esteban García to Lázaro Cárdenas, n.d., expediente 559.1/46, ibid.; on Maravatío, ibid.; and on Contepec, Tiburcio García to attorney general, 24 August 1938, ibid.

30. Expediente 559.1/46, Lázaro Cárdenas, Fondo Presidentes, AGN.

31. J. Socorro Márquez and Juan Murillo to Lázaro Cárdenas, 26 September 1935, expediente 542.2/314, Lázaro Cárdenas, Fondo Presidentes, AGN.

32. On La Huerta, see Macario Villa to Lázaro Cárdenas, 15 October 1936, expediente 534.6/95, Lázaro Cárdenas, Fondo Presidentes, AGN; and on Coro, J. Sacramento Sánchez et al. to Lázaro Cárdenas, 15 December 1934, expediente 559.1/46, ibid.

33. On Ario de Rosales and La Huacana, see Gildardo Magaña to Lázaro Cárdenas, 11 October 1938, expediente 559.1/76, Lázaro Cárdenas, Fondo Presidentes, AGN; on Coire, Lt. Colonel Cristobal Guzmán Cárdenas to Lázaro Cárdenas, 8 November 1937, expediente 559.1/46, ibid.; on Manzanillo, Roberto Lara to Lázaro Cárdenas, 8 April 1937, ibid.; and on Apatzingán, Arturo Chávez to Lázaro Cárdenas, 10 April 1935, expediente 541/343, Lázaro Cárdenas, Fondo Presidentes, AGN.

The Cristeros made teachers the principal targets of their vengeance. Among the most dramatic assaults was the May 1935 lynching of Professor J. Trinidad Ramírez in Contepec. One month before the lynching, Ramírez had demanded that the local priest and two teachers who continued to celebrate Holy Week be thrown out of town. According to municipal president Felix García Villalpando, this incited the lynching. After the murder, between three hundred and four hundred Cristeros apparently "dragged García Villalpando through the streets, kicking him, spitting on him, insulting him, with the fury of rabid beasts."[34]

While the Contepec lynching was distinguished by the cruelty of the assailants and the size of the lynching party, it was by no means an isolated attack. Professor Pedro García was killed in Apatzingán, Juan González Valdespino in Huajúmbaro, José Rivera Romero in Ciudad Hidalgo, María Salud Morales in Tacámbaro.[35] And the list goes on. In all at least forty-two teachers were killed.[36]

For these Cristeros, it was as though the 1929 truce ending the civil war did not exist. Perhaps Cristeros understood their attacks on teach-

34. Expediente 541/366, Lázaro Cárdenas, Fondo Presidentes, AGN.

35. Arturo Chávez to Lázaro Cárdenas, 10 April 1935, expediente 541/343, Lázaro Cárdenas, Fondo Presidentes, AGN; Ignacio Mucino Pérez to Lázaro Cárdenas, expediente 553.3/18, ibid.

36. These figures are based on David Raby's "Los maestros rurales y los conflictos sociales en México (1931–1940)," *Historia Mexicana* 18 (October–December 1968): 190–226, and the following archival documentation, which I discovered. On threats against teachers in Ario, see J. Socorro Vázquez, Profesor inspector federal, Michoacán, caja 412, AHSEP; expedientes 541/366, 541/343, Lázaro Cárdenas, Fondo Presidentes, AGN; and expediente 3, Fondo Gobernación, AMZ. On the Apatzingán killing of Pedro García, see expediente 541/343, Lázaro Cárdenas, Fondo Presidentes, AGN; on the Contepec lynching, expediente 541/366, ibid.; on the killing of the teacher in Tafolla, expediente 541/703, ibid.; on the assault on Profesor Carlos F. López of Arteaga, expediente 533.3/18, ibid.; on the killing of Profesor Juan González Valdespino in Huajumbaro, ibid.; on the killing of Profesor José Rivera Romero in Ciudad Hidalgo, ibid.; on the attempted lynching of Profesor Encarnación Castillo in Santa Ana Maya, ibid.; on the killing of teachers José Rivera R. and Juan González V. in Angangueo, expediente 559.1/16, Lázaro Cárdenas, Fondo Presidentes, AGN; on the armed threat against Profesor Paz Maya in Ciudad Hidalgo, expediente 542.2/967, ibid.; on the attack on Profesor María Piedad Flores in Villa Escalante, expediente 534.6/48, ibid.; on the killing of Profesor Marciano Sánchez and campesino Pedro Espinosa in Tirio, expediente 534.6/95, ibid.; on the peons set on Profesor Duran Lira in Zinapécuaro, Francisco Frías, Profesor inspector federal, Michoacán, caja 412 AHSEP; on priests threatening teachers with hanging unless they left Arteaga, expediente 547.3/29, Lázaro Cárdenas, Fondo Presidentes, AGN. Unfortunately, the information to be found in these documents is minimal, usually nothing more than the name of the alleged victim and the location of the assault.

ers as an attempt to mete out rough justice. After all, the Cardenista state had assigned teachers the task of eradicating the Catholic roots of the original Cristero rebellion. Although church officials recommended that campesinos demonstrate their disaffection with the schools through peaceful means, the Cristeros would not relinquish their military option. Most Michoacán mestizos, however, recognized that guerrilla warfare was useless against teachers transforming churches into schools and substituting portraits of revolutionary heroes for icons. The campesinos' time-worn practice of manipulating elites for their own purposes seemed to be a more serviceable stratagem.

Throughout the state priests and citizens' groups began to organize a school boycott. Speakers entered pueblos and buttonholed peasants. In addition, speakers at secret village meetings criticized the teachers. As Zamora resident Francisco Elizalde remembers, the speakers effectively evoked campesino resentment of the teachers' activities. When a campesino decried the teachers' anticlericalism, images came forth of "the Saturday before Easter when the teachers were so bold as to have had a great many firework replicas of Judas constructed, and every single one of those Judases was a figure of a monk or a nun, and they mocked them and made fun of them as they burned them in front of the Army prison."[37] When priests claimed that the teachers "forced the schoolchildren to strip and to engage in carnal acts with one another,"[38] other campesinos remembered that the teachers "taught notions of sexual education, but with all the malice in the world."[39] In village after village, such exhortations served to ignite a statewide movement.

What emerges is a portrait of widespread school desertion, as Cardenista school inspectors throughout the mestizo sections of the state reported that the schoolhouses were abandoned. In Tacámbaro the "work of the teachers was obstructed by verbal and written propaganda."[40] The Queréndaro and Zinapécuaro teachers acknowledged that "we haven't been able to convince the parents to send their children to the schools."[41] In Arteaga and Pamatácuaro, with "few chil-

---

37. Interview with Elizalde, July 1985.
38. J. Socorro Vázquez, Profesor inspector federal, Michoacán, caja 412, AHSEP.
39. Interview with Elizalde, July 1985.
40. "Tacámbaro plan de trabajo para 1936," Leocadio Rodríguez, Profesor inspector federal, Michoacán, caja 412, AHSEP.
41. Profesor Francisco Frías to chief of agrarian department, 10 March 1936, caja 412, AHSEP.

dren in attendance," the story was the same.[42] The desertion led Yurécuaro inspector José Ventura González to reflect that "the main problem in Michoacán is the division between teachers and campesinos."[43]

In 1935 Zamora municipal president Guillermo Vargas pointed out that of the 5,000 children in the municipality, only 391 were attending the schools within the town of Zamora.[44] However, in general the Cardenistas refrained from tallying up the extent of the boycott with any regularity.[45] And in any event, statistics would be an imprecise index of campesino sentiment. Yet there is no doubt that school desertion was widespread. Cárdenas himself repeatedly commented on the persistence of the problem. During a September 1934 speech to the national press, a July 1935 address to a campesino assembly in Guadalajara, and a February 1936 speech in Ciudad Guerrero, Tamaulipas, he deplored the school boycott and blamed it on campesino ignorance.[46]

Perhaps most revealing of the degree of hostility to the schools is the fact that even those campesinos with the most at stake also refrained from sending their children to the schools. While school desertion was illegal for all campesinos, the governmental officials had attempted to establish a special sense of obligation among the ejidatarios. The Cardenistas expected the ejidatarios to send their children to the schools in return for their plots of land.

Although they risked losing their lands, many ejidatarios proved to be as determined in their resistance as were the non-ejidatarios.

42. On Arteaga, Camerino Lara T., Profesor inspector federal, Michoacán, caja 412, AHSEP; on Pamatácuaro, Teodoro Mendoza, Profesor inspector federal, Michoacán, ibid.

43. José Ventura González, Profesor inspector federal, Michoacán, caja 412, AHSEP.

44. Expediente 17, Fondo Gobernación, 1935, AMZ.

45. Or at least this appears to have been the case, as governmental statistics on the boycott do not currently exist in the AHSEP archives. However, they may have once existed, for in 1985 an AHSEP archivist informed me that in a periodic "purging of documents," age was the criterion for destroying them. The older the documents, the greater the chance for destruction. For the period 1934–40, relatively complete AHSEP documentation for Michoacán exists only for 1936.

46. Cárdenas's national press speech is found in Lázaro Cárdenas, *Palabras y documentos públicos de Lázaro Cárdenas: Mensajes, discursos, declaraciones, entrevistas y otros documentos, 1928–1940*, 3 vols. (Mexico City: Siglo XXI Editores, 1978), 1:135; the speech in Guadalajara, 1:169; the speech in Ciudad Guerrero, 1:193.

Indeed, in Queréndaro, school inspector Francisco Frías found his threats to seize ejidal plots useless. He reported that "it is not possible to come to an understanding because they won't listen to reason and they see the teacher as something noxious. They claim that they are prepared to renounce their agrarian rights, to abandon their plots, but under no circumstances will they enroll their children in the schools."[47]

Elsewhere the situation was similar. In Chaparaco, Professor René Enrique Villar held a series of meetings with the ejidatarios in which he pointed out that as the agraristas "benefit more than anyone else from the governmental aid," they should "be the first to support the revolutionary ideals." Yet his admonitions were useless. Though "I have repeatedly told them that they are making a mistake, they tell me that they prefer to pay the fine rather than send their children to the schools."[48] Despite threats by the government to evict them from their lands, ejidatarios from Santa Ana Maya, Zinapécuaro, and Curimeo also refused to send their children to the schools.[49]

Within this volatile setting, individual teachers sometimes gained peasant loyalty. This was particularly true of teachers who set aside the anticlerical lesson plans and attended concrete peasant concerns. When Aquililla revolutionaries cured sick children of whooping cough, campesinos applauded. In fact, inspectors saw the medicines as a remedy for the school boycott, for teachers managed to "create much sympathy toward the teachers and the schools." Similarly, the teacher in Los Reyes who built a pharmacy and a hospital gained peasant approval. In Ario de Rosales the teacher built a canal, leading "previously hostile" peasants to send their children to the schools. And of course staples like the sports festivals were "widely attended by the villagers" in Jiquilpan.[50]

47. Francisco Frías, Profesor inspector federal, Michoacán, caja 412, AHSEP.
48. Expediente 17, Fondo Gobernación, 1935, AMZ.
49. On Santa Ana Maya, see J. H. Pedrero to Lázaro Cárdenas, 1 July 1937, expediente 533.3/18, Lázaro Cárdenas, Fondo Presidentes, AGN; on Zinapécuaro, J. Natividad García to Lázaro Cárdenas, 4 July 1936, ibid.; on Curimeo, Salvador Valencia to Lázaro Cárdenas, 8 February 1935, expediente 533.3/20, Lázaro Cárdenas, Fondo Presidentes, AGN.
50. On Aguillila, see Camerino Lara T., Profesor inspector federal, Michoacán, caja 412, AHSEP; on Los Reyes, Teodoro Mendozo, Profesor inspector federal, Michoacán, ibid.; on Ario de Rosales, J. Socorro Vázquez, Profesor inspector federal, Michoacán, ibid.; on Jiquilpan, Ramón Reynosa G., Profesor inspector federal, Michoacán, ibid.

From Rebellion to Reclamation of Belief

For the mestizos, the repudiation of anticlericalism was a half-measure, and they would only be satisfied with the restoration of Catholic worship. However, many obstacles stood in their way. Public worship had been banned, and the state had appropriated many of the church buildings and turned them into governmental offices or schools.

To resolve the problem, the campesinos again depended on their past experiences of resisting the elites. Practiced in the art of dissimulation, some campesinos attempted to re-create a Catholic order underground. Expressions of Catholic observance, whether routine or festive, suddenly became invisible. Priests were smuggled into villages to perform baptisms and to administer communion in secret. José Ochoa began to celebrate Mass illegally in the Zamora area. Another outlawed priest led the worship in nearby Atecucário. Frequently, campesinos like the Pérez sisters in a village near Zamora harbored priests in their homes.[51]

Campesinos concealed both religious objects and church ornaments from public view. Behind a partition in the church, villagers in Ario Santa Monica hid candelabras, prayer stools, a decorated saint on a throne.[52] In the same village Ignacio Cuadra protected a saint within his home, while Miguel Martínez guarded the candelabras and the artificial flower arrangement.[53] In Yurécuaro the campesinos surreptitiously placed images of the Virgin in the public spaces.[54] Campesinos also established secret schools throughout the state.[55] In Ario Santa Monica, María Escolástica and María del Río opened such a school, in which they taught the catechism and "aroused hatred against the gov-

51. On José Ochoa, see expediente 547.3/72, Lázaro Cárdenas, Fondo Presidentes, AGN; on Atecucário, Loose documents, 1937, AMZ; on the Pérez sisters, Raquel M. de Mendoza to Juan Gutiérrez, August 1939, Loose documents, 1939, ibid.

52. Expediente 2, Fondo Gobernación, 1935, AMZ.

53. Ramón Cuevas, village chief, Ario Santa Monica, to Zamora municipal president, 4 July 1935, expediente 17, Fondo Gobernación 1935, AMZ.

54. Expediente 547.5/23, Lázaro Cárdenas, Fondo Presidentes, AGN. Other, less specific reports of the violation of the anticlerical legislation are found in expedientes 11 and 24, Fondo Gobernación, 1935, AMZ; expediente 547.1/20, Lázaro Cárdenas, Fondo Presidentes, AGN.

55. Loose documents, Fondo Gobernación, 1939, AMZ.

ernmental school and teachers."[56] Similar schools were opened in Zamora.[57]

Other campesinos chose a more public method to reinstate Catholicism. Like the villagers protesting revolutionary caciques, they seized on the portrayal of Cárdenas as a president responsive to campesino needs. While it is likely that in some cases outsiders assisted them, this enabled campesinos to unsheathe a double-edged weapon designed both to indicate that they accepted the Cardenistas' claim that the peasants and the Cardenistas shared identical interests and to persuade Cárdenas to accept their interests as his own.

In Zinapécuaro Francisco Nieto and the eight other men who represented the villagers implied that they accepted the government's self-portrayal as custodian of Mexico's aesthetic and historical legacy. They consequently found puzzling the national government's transformation of the Zinapécuaro church annex into a military outpost. Invoking Cárdenas's role in historical preservation, they pointed out that his "love for archeological monuments" should have made military use of the building inconceivable. Indeed, the campesinos suggested, it was inconsistent with Cárdenas's own policies. They were sure that had he been aware of the significance of the annex, he would never have allowed such a thing to occur. Only because he was "so busy" had he "forgotten that we are talking about a true national monument . . . for it is a former convent from the sixteenth century and a true gem of colonial art." To promote his own objectives, Cárdenas should "reconsider the accord and not destine it for any use that will either destroy it or cause it to deteriorate."[58]

Hoping to summon revolutionary notions of legality to their cause, 216 campesinos in Ario denounced the 1935 closing of the church as illegal. Citing the national constitution, they pointed out that "closing it is a violation of our constitutional rights, as stated in article XXIV of the national constitution, which states that all acts of religious worship

56. The quote is found in expediente 6, p. 11, Fondo Gobernación, 1938, AMZ. In addition, loose documents found in the AMZ indicate the existence of the secret schools. Señora Crespin Méndez, Concepción Méndez, and Mari Elena Verduzco discussed these schools in interviews. Interviews with Señora Crespin Méndez, Ario de Rayón, August 1985; Concepción Méndez, November 1990; and Mari Elena Verduzco de Peña, Ario de Rayón, May 1990.

57. Interviews with Paz, August 1985; and Elizalde, July 1985.

58. Francisco Nieto et al. to Lázaro Cárdenas, 11 July 1935, expediente 547.4/157, Lázaro Cárdenas, Fondo Presidentes, AGN.

must take place within the church and that all men are free to worship as they please."[59] Numerous campesinos from Ixtlán relied on a similar stratagem. While the municipal president had closed the church in the name of the government, they asked Cárdenas to reopen it in the name of six thousand Catholics.[60]

Most campesino requests were simpler, lacking the embroidered explanations equating Cardenista interests with those of the writers. Still, numerous mestizos attempted to manipulate Cárdenas's professed responsiveness to campesino demands. A group of twenty villagers from Purépero hoped to persuade Cárdenas to reopen the church to celebrate the pueblo's patron saint's day "in consideration of the fact that numerous villages have asked that their church be reopened and that you in your characteristic generosity have allowed it."[61] Campesinos in Chavinda used a similar tactic, pointing out that Cárdenas had even permitted the church in his hometown of Jiquilpan to be reopened.[62] The flood of citizens' letters asking for church openings in Tlazazalca, Panindícuaro, Jungapeo, Atacheo, La Ladera, San Simón, Ario, and Jiquilpan[63] and for priests in Taretan, Zirahuato, Zitácuaro, Atacheo, San Juan Tumbio, and Purépero were variations on this theme.[64]

There is a carefully guarded, almost hazy quality to the campesino responses to the government. Previously landless campesinos proved

---

59. Two hundred sixteen residents of Ario Santa Monica to Zamora municipal president, 8 July 1935, expediente 17, Fondo Gobernación, 1935, AMZ.

60. Francisco Martínez to Lázaro Cárdenas, 15 April 1936; Alejandro Guillen to Lázaro Cárdenas, 28 May 1936; and Martínez Verduzco, president of citizen committee, to Lázaro Cárdenas, 28 May 1938, expediente 547.4/250, Lázaro Cárdenas, Fondo Presidentes, AGN.

61. Mucio Sepulveda et al. to Lázaro Cárdenas, 9 June 1937, expediente 547.4/220, Lázaro Cárdenas, Fondo Presidentes, AGN.

62. Expediente 547.4/248, Lázaro Cárdenas, Fondo Presidentes, AGN.

63. From Tlazazalca, María Carrillo and Elpidia Cano to Lázaro Cárdenas, 1 June 1938, expediente 547.4/334, Lázaro Cárdenas, Fondo Presidentes, AGN; from Panindícuaro, expediente 547.4/106, ibid.; from Jungapeo, Wenceslao Silva to Lázaro Cárdenas, 16 August 1936, expediente 547.3/137, ibid.; from Atacheo, Ignacio Villa to Lázaro Cárdenas, 29 December 1935, expediente 547.4/31, ibid.; from Chavinda, expediente 547.4/248, ibid.; from La Ladera, Ismael López to Lázaro Cárdenas, 20 January 1939, expediente 547.4/409, ibid.; from San Simón, Francisca Rodilles to Lázaro Cárdenas, 27 May 1939, expediente 547.4/427, ibid.; from Jiquilpan, Abundio García to Lázaro Cárdenas, 9 January 1938, expediente 547.4/330, ibid.

64. On Ixtlan, see Francisco Martínez and Alejandro Guillen to Lázaro Cárdenas, 15 April 1936, expediente 547.4/250, Lázaro Cárdenas, Fondo Presidentes, AGN; on

willing to accept governmental lands, but they resisted the government's efforts to tell them how to farm. Other men and women sought the reformation, but not the abolition, of cacique rule. Even in their politics of spirituality, the arena that engendered the most persistent disagreement with governmental policies, campesinos couched their demands in governmental terms. When they bargained with Cárdenas over the role of Catholicism in their lives, they ceded to the state the right to pontificate over spiritual matters. And when they constructed underground churches, they resigned themselves to governmental domination of public discourse. Indeed, campesinos behaved more like people determined to forge an alliance with the government than a people intent on undermining Cárdenas's revolutionary government.

Taretan, María de la Cruz and Gómez de Raya to Lázaro Cárdenas, 8 February 1939, expediente 547.3/81, ibid.; on Zirahuato, Guillermo Sebastian and José María Norbelo to Lázaro Cárdenas, 13 August 1936, expediente 547.4/873, ibid.; on Zitácuaro, Conrado Campos to Lázaro Cárdenas, 29 February 1940, expediente 547.3/178, ibid.; on San Juan Tumbio, Agapita Sosa to Lázaro Cárdenas, 12 April 1935, expediente 547.4/101, ibid.; on Purépero, Josefina Magaña et al. to Lázaro Cárdenas, 21 May 1937, expediente 547.4/220, ibid.

CHAPTER EIGHT

An End to the Innocence

Ernesto Prado has surrounded himself with malicious people who pretend to be inoffensive campesinos, and with these people he has terrorized most of the villages.

Antonio Gómez Velasco

If you like me, think the way I do.

John Dollard

Approaching Chilchota, a group of Ernesto Prado's followers encountered the anti-Pradista mayor of the village, General Enrique Morfín Figueroa. According to Prado's spokesman, though the group protested its innocence, Morfín refused them entrance. Instead, relentless, he turned to his men and unleashed an order: "Kill four or five sons of their fucked mothers! Seize the bandits and assassins!"[1]

They complied without argument. Most of Prado's men escaped before Morfín's pistolero discharged, but the women were thrown against the highway embankment. They fell to their knees, clutching their children. Three men died. Once again, the meseta was littered with bodies reduced to silence. Survivors fled to the hills, abandoning home and property.[2]

1. Gustavo Gallardo González to Lázaro Cárdenas, 26 January 1940, expediente 542.1/2644, Lázaro Cárdenas, Fondo Presidentes, Archivo General de la Nación (AGN), Mexico City.
2. Ibid.

There was nothing impersonal here. The mangled bodies once belonged to neighbors. The killers could recount where their victims lived, whether they lived alone or with women and children. They knew which families Prado could count as loyal and which people were "counter-revolutionaries." They could recount the details of the land deals—the seizures of land or crops, the strategies to defraud neighbors.[3]

They may well have been closer still. If activities were to be divided into strictly delineated ideological camps, Tarascans had indulged in considerable ideological and practical promiscuity. They went to Mass, they petitioned for land, they embraced new anticlerical heroes.[4]

As the demand that they choose church or state became more insistent, some of them tried to conform. One way to lessen their discomfort over the choice was to treat their own desires as alien. Those who expressed those discarded desires in turn would become somehow less than human. As Tarascans began to behave as though their own desires were foreign, their responses to one another began to betray an aura of claustrophobia and falsehood.

The sources for this long habit of refusing a neighbor's humanity come readily. Members of the church hierarchy, some of the Cardenistas, and the Tarascans themselves had nurtured this hope of restricted community. As for the church, the hierarchy portrayed Catholic largess as plentiful, indeed infinite. Nonetheless, Catholic redemption would be available only to those who renounced the governmental land program. Then there had been governmental disdain and sometimes outright fury against practicing Catholics. The Taras-

---

3. Between 1933 and 1940, participants in the political conflicts engulfing the region wrote a series of denunciations of their enemies. While in each case the writers portrayed their enemies as aggressors and themselves as victims of inequities, the authors left evidence that enabled me to develop this portrait of their intimacy. Examples include documents focusing on inequities surrounding land and crops, such as Rafael Morfín to Lázaro Cárdenas, 30 December 1939, expediente 542.1/2644, Lázaro Cárdenas, Fondo Presidentes, AGN; Wenceslao González to Lázaro Cárdenas, 30 December 1939, ibid.; Conrado Arreola and Eliseo Prado to Lázaro Cárdenas, 28 December 1939, ibid.; Juan Lázaro, Jefe de Tenencia, Urén, to C. Gral., División General Benigno Serrato, governor of the state, 27 February 1933, expediente 525.3/72, Abelardo Rodríguez, Fondo Presidentes, AGN; and Miguel Herrera et al. to the state government, 27 February 1933, ibid.

4. Primo Tapia's ability to appear in Catholic pageants yet hoodwink priests and manipulate village religious sentiment provides an early example of Tarascan ideological flexibility. See Paul Friedrich, *Agrarian Revolt in a Mexican Village* (1970; reprint, Chicago: University of Chicago Press, 1977), 62–63, 121–23.

cans weighed in with their own long tradition of styling themselves victims of their neighbors' greed.

That said, it would be well to set aside any sense of a natural Tarascan predilection to violence. In fact it had not always been this way. Or, expressed more fully, this was not the only way it had always been. For many years Tarascans had written to Cárdenas revealing the discomfort the demand to adhere rigidly either to governmental or to clerical demands caused them. For years these letters had gone unheeded. Discarded, perhaps, or collecting mold, these messages seemed destined to be forgotten.

Then in 1937 the government began to turn on its former allies. Responding to pressures from church and the national bourgeoisie, Cárdenas abandoned Ernesto Prado and his followers in the Once Pueblos. Once again elites aligned with the church unleashed antigovernmental rhetoric. Meanwhile, Tarascans turned on one another. Was the Mexican west destined to endure violence without end?

Slowly, perhaps, Cárdenas turned—as we must—to the moldering papers on his desk. As he read them, the Indians' lessons began to sink in. There could be another way to forge a government.

Of Schoolrooms and Indian Shawls

It is possible to view the revolutionary and corresponding clerical challenges to the Indians in clear, rather rigid terms. I could say the church demanded that Indians live within the hierarchical but gregarious company of the icons, that the government asked Indians to *impersonate* icons. And if we consider Constantino Murillo's efforts to "dispel the intensity of the saints" or Ernesto Prado's 1935 efforts to terrorize worshipers, that would be partially true.[5]

At the same time, the Cardenistas in the villages not dominated by Prado had promoted an idiosyncratic, flexible version of revolutionary Indianism. This began with their clear affection for things Indian, even when the objects and artifacts might be called fanciful representations of an Indian past. Besides, the Cardenistas had used a clerical formula to promote revolutionary modernism. This formula depended upon

5. Interview with Constantino Murillo, Morelia, Michoacán, July 1985; expedientes 547.1/6, 547.3/79, 547.351, Lázaro Cárdenas, Fondo Presidentes, AGN.

gathering the Indians inside specific buildings, in fact the very buildings used by priests. Both groups utilized a leader (priest, teacher) to
minister to the Indians. Whether in processions or open-air plays,
enacting a sort of rough-hewn theater was an important tool for both
priests and Cardenistas in fostering the view that their particular perspective was the norm.

The Indians themselves would draw on the wavering political sensi-
bilities we have come to recognize. For while Tarascans shared much
with one another, there was a tenuous quality to all of their common-
alities. They shared a neighborhood, but what is sharing when your
neighbor's land produces twice the corn that yours does? All Indians
spoke Tarascan, yet a handful of men—and virtually no women—also
spoke Spanish. They shared a Catholic background, but women, and
not men, wore the marks of humility.

These conflicting emphases and contradictory hopes force a cautious analysis of Indian responses to Cardenista modernism. For the
lines keep blurring. To some extent, the Indians refused to be categorized by a single allegiance. Playing on some of the Cardenistas' own
flexibilities and insecurities, resisting rigid demands either to possess
icons or to be them, Indians demanded the birthright of modernism,
participation in a range of experiences.

Nonetheless, many Indians forged rather loose alliances with church
or state. And because the government had summoned men both to
relinquish their own humility and to appropriate the symbolic mantle
the church had awarded women, it would be largely men who endorsed
the schools. If the men did not overtly revel in their new status as icons
or deplore the loss of Catholic conviviality, this may well have been
because women's symbolic attachment to Catholicism had been greater.

While Indian men found the governmental schoolhouses attractive
for varying reasons, chief among them was the government's promise
to ensure their livelihood. Indeed, Odilon López, president of the
regional campesino committee in Pátzcuaro, embraced governmental
notions of material liberation. At the same time, he pointed out that
"the Indians in the communities of Gehuanhuachen, Las Palmitas,
Coenembo, Cuanajo, Buena Vista, La Tirimicua, Santa Fe de la
Laguna, and San Andrés Zirondaro find themselves without any land
grants; having made their requests to the appropriate Department,
they find themselves in a desperate situation."[6]

---

6. Odilon López et al. to Lázaro Cárdenas, 6 October 1939, expediente 734/67,
Lázaro Cárdenas, Fondo Presidentes, AGN.

The least the government could do in compensation was provide work tools, medicines, a library. Most importantly, López continued, "we beg you, Mr. General Cárdenas, that so the education of the rural and urban workers will be more efficient, schools be established for the children who live in San Miguel Charahuen, La Tinaja, former hacienda of Charahuen, Las Palmitas, Chapultepec, Buena Vista, Gehuanhuachen, and Colonia Plutarco Elías Calles."[7]

Others accepted and even endorsed the government's anticlerical approach. This acceptance could include church bashing, a response to priests' continuing insistence that peasants boycott the schools. Indeed, in February 1936 José Calderón, the president of the municipal National Revolutionary Party (PNR) in Pátzcuaro, demanded that the church be closed because "children attending religious schools stoned the federation offices and the teacher's house." Policarpo Sánchez added that the Catholic Sagrario Church "has become a center for subversive propaganda assaulting the social conquests."[8]

Still, the rationale behind anticlericalism was also at times a relatively passive desire to use church buildings for secular studies. Consider, for instance, the Indians in Uruapan who reminded Cárdenas that church buildings could be remade into schools. Hipólito Rodríguez, a representative of the Indians of the neighborhood of the Uruapan barrio of La Trinidad, pointed out that the government had appropriated the barrio's old church building. The building was empty, and it could be transformed into a "coeducational school for girls and boys for our children to attend." And the Bonifacio Moreno plaza, located in front of the church, could become a garden for their children's recreation. The Indians would even be willing to "take on the work of restoration ourselves and pay for it."[9]

In at least one case, a group of women seized on modernity's promise of alternatives. These were the women featured in the pages of *Maestro Rural* as the "red women of Michoacán." In fact, the women's response to the revolutionaries revealed the ambiguity characteristic of models determined to pursue their own goals even though they wore clothing chosen by others.

7. Ibid.
8. José Calderón to Lázaro Cárdenas, 16 January 1936, expediente 547.4/133, Lázaro Cárdenas, Fondo Presidentes, AGN; Policarpo Sánchez to Lázaro Cárdenas, 17 February 1936, ibid.
9. Hipólito Rodríguez to Lázaro Cárdenas, 3 November 1937, expediente 547.4/133, Lázaro Cárdenas, Fondo Presidentes, AGN.

Or did they? Wearing shawls and long skirts that outsiders viewed as heirlooms celebrating a once-proud pre-Conquest tradition, they called for "cooperatives, for workshops, for schools for their children, and for arms to defend the revolutionary government."[10] Perhaps they had come to view the outfits as relics of their pre-Conquest legacy? Or did they wear the traditional long skirts and rebozos to protect themselves from clerical accusations of whorishness? Then again, perhaps the revolutionaries' program had won the allegiance that their demands implied. The possibilities multiply with an alacrity demonstrating that, if nothing else, campesinos of many ideological persuasions could have found common ground with Michoacán's red women.

"We don't do it out of fanaticism."

Cardenista politics also unleashed a significant Tarascan demand for the reopening of the churches, a demand sometimes linked to a boycott of governmental schools. Many of these protesters were women, and some were wealthy. Those facts, combined with the Indians' clamor for the restoration of prerevolutionary clerical culture, lent an aura of reaction to their pleas.

Yet there was something different here, something self-conscious and distinctly modern. After all, it was one thing to stumble into a prerevolutionary church after a night of drunkenness, sure that confession would yield forgiveness. To use a revolutionary idiom to call for the reinstatement of the church was quite different. This choice was strategic, yet in adopting it these Tarascans demonstrated a certain refusal of dogma.

It is also true that revolutionary participants in the contest over the schools might have wondered at that judgment. In particular, Policarpo Sánchez, school inspector for the Pátzcuaro region, found little evidence for this spirit of compromise. A school boycott in Pátzcuaro represented a setback for his revolutionary hopes. Disappointed, he reacted as though stung and—was it because the women refused to act like men? Or was it because they rejected their position as revolution-

10. "Las mujeres rojas de Michoacán," *Maestro Rural* (Mexico City), 15 December 1934, 22.

ary adjuncts, instead persisting in their affection for the priests?—he lashed out. In a tone betraying his sense of injustice (at least men could be called out to a shooting match), he proclaimed,

The men play nothing more than secondary roles in this battle full of ignominy and wickedness. It is the women who work the invisible strings of all the propaganda against the educational work. It is women who unite an infinite number of children in the annexes of El Sagrario to teach them the catechism. It was women who spoke with the president to solicit continuing lodging for the nuns at the Colegio Josefino, thus tacitly ensuring that they will continue private schooling for the children of the fanatics and the bourgeoisie. . . . It is women who have gone from house to house to persuade the students of the Centro Proletariado (Proletarian Center) to quit attending classes. The priests always make use of the discipline and efficiency of fanaticized women to promote their ominous work.[11]

To Sánchez, the bourgeois women represented a will to maintain an outmoded, unjust system, and there is something to be said for his perspective. In letters to Cárdenas asking that the Josefino convent and women's school remain in the nuns' possession, women, including Virginia Muribe, revealed the class nature of their concern for the poor. In return for the convent, they wrote the president, they would be willing "to collaborate with you in your effort to improve the proletarian class by founding an Industrial Academy that will provide its services free to all the women in Pátzcuaro."[12]

In the women's assumption that the poor inhabited not only barrios but also categories unlike their own there is something reminiscent of the Catholic hierarchy's perspective that God himself orchestrated different roles for rich and poor. Still, upon recognizing the Cardenista threat to privilege and promise of material liberation, these women, whether they liked it or not, found themselves seeking a new association with the poor. Previously they may have attempted to alleviate the poverty of the poor, but now when they went to the women's homes, they attempted to find common political ground.

It would be villagers from the Lake Pátzcuaro island of Jarácuaro who crafted one of the more poignant efforts at conciliation. In 1937 these villagers confronted the fact that Cardenistas had appropriated

11. Policarpo Sánchez to Pátzcuaro municipal president, 12 February 1936, caja 412, Archivo Histórico de la Secretaría de Educación Pública (AHSEP), Mexico City.
12. Virginia Muribe et al. to Lázaro Cárdenas, expediente 547.4/133, Lázaro Cárdenas, Fondo Presidentes, AGN.

their communal lands and closed the church. It was an assault on the longstanding connections between material and spiritual life, the use of land to support religious ritual, the corresponding dependence on religion to ensure bountiful harvests. In response nineteen villagers repeatedly went to officials "opposing the church closing."[13]

Again and again, the villagers' efforts had been thwarted. As though inviting Cárdenas to relive their frustrated journey through the labyrinth of revolutionary bureaucracy, they wrote a letter reproducing the steps they took. There was the encounter with the doctor, who assured them that he acted to control epidemics of the measles, whooping cough, and the flu, "that the closure was temporary . . . that as soon as the epidemics were controlled, the church would reopen." When the church remained closed, the campesinos went to the municipal authorities in nearby Erongarícuaro. There they met another refusal to reopen the church. When they returned to the doctor, "demanding that he make good on his word," he "sent us back to the municipal president of Erongarícuaro."[14]

Then, as though lowering their voices, their tone became more intimate. Suddenly the issue was betrayal. First, their neighbors and the Jarácuaro municipal authorities had maintained the church "closed, threatening us all they wanted, committing many injustices."[15] As for Cárdenas himself, the villagers reminded him, "You said you would not close the church if we would send our children to the schools." As their children's school attendance demonstrated, they had fulfilled their end of the bargain. The church, however, remained locked. Had Cárdenas reneged? Forgotten them? Defiant, they threatened:

Don't wait, Mr. President, for blood will run, much blood, because of bad authorities. If they continue to bother us, and if they put us in prison because of this bargain we have made with you, you have to understand that although we are impoverished and forsaken, we will defend ourselves so that they do not make a mockery of us.[16]

Notwithstanding the threat, the Jarácuaro villagers included a conciliatory note. In return for the restoration of church worship, they

13. Simon Valdéz et al. to Lázaro Cárdenas, 7 May 1936, expediente 547.4/257, Lázaro Cárdenas, Fondo Presidentes, AGN.
14. Ibid.
15. Ibid.
16. Ibid.

promised their children's continuing school attendance. And then, in a display of fervor, they offered Cárdenas something intangible. A sentimental gift, its importance to a man of Cárdenas's studied silence would have been unclear. Yet they persisted, claiming that "if you will keep your end of the bargain, our children will remember you always, always, with veneration and [they will] respect you after you die."[17]

In Uruapan, Dolores F. V. de Perza and Josefina C. de Cuevas envisioned a similar compromise. If the president permitted a priest to officiate and if he denied governmental teachers the use of the inner court of the parish, a use they considered "a serious hardship for believers," their children would attend the schools.[18]

For other Tarascans, the most varied aspects of revolutionary rhetoric proved serviceable in their insistence that Catholic restoration be a revolutionary aim. Rosendo Ortega in Pátzcuaro told Cárdenas that he shared in the president's concern for historical preservation. According to Ortega, the campesinos sought the opening of the La Companía church in Pátzcuaro simply because it was built in 1546 "by the most illustrious Sr. Don. Vasco de Quiroga." Opening the church would serve as a "memorial to its founder, who was a true benefactor of the Indians, who still venerate him."[19] In Erongarícuaro the campesinos placed their petition for the church opening under the rubric of respect for family and tradition. They wrote to Cárdenas, "We don't ask that you keep the church open out of religious fanaticism. We only want it in commemoration of our ancestors."[20] In Tangancícuaro, Benjamin Maciel and twenty other Tarascans deplored the burning of the statues in the church as an assault on "government property."[21]

Still other Tarascans drew on the concept of the revolutionary state as guardian of legality. Denouncing inadequate enforcement of the government's legal code, Paracho campesinos G. Gómez, Esteban Escobeda, and Genaro Talpa told Cárdenas that "according to the law of worship of May 1932 a Catholic priest is authorized to officiate in

17. Ibid.
18. Dolores Viuda de Perza et al. to Lázaro Cárdenas, 28 August 1935, expediente 547.4/133, Lázaro Cárdenas, Fondo Presidentes, AGN.
19. Rosendo Ortega to Lázaro Cárdenas, expediente 547.4/133, Lázaro Cárdenas, Fondo Presidentes, AGN.
20. Erongarícuaro villagers to Lázaro Cárdenas, 29 September 1937, expediente 547.4/133, Lázaro Cárdenas, Fondo Presidentes, AGN.
21. Benjamin Maciel et al. to Lázaro Cárdenas, 4 January 1935, expediente 547.1/6, Lázaro Cárdenas, Fondo Presidentes, AGN.

the villages of Paracho, Cherán, Nahuatzen, Charapan, and Parangari-cutiro." However, the Paracho municipal president had denied the priest the right to officiate beginning on November 4, 1935.[22]

By far the majority of the Tarascans who requested that Catholicism be reinstated publicly relied on less elaborate ploys. Relying on Cárde-nas's concern for ordinary people, campesinos from Pátzcuaro, Chara-pan, Chilchota, Parangaricutiro, and Tangancícuaro did not embellish their requests; they simply asked the president to reopen the churches.[23]

Death without End?

Outside of the Once Pueblos area dominated by Ernesto Prado, then, the Tarascans had asked for adjustments to the revolu-tionary political culture. They had differed with one another about the terms of everyday life. Frequently they had refused to see eye to eye. Still, the differences between a Tarascan woman maintaining the per-sona of the traditional Indian while fighting for more equitable land redistribution and the Tarascans willing to send their children to socialist schools in order to retain access to the church were barely per-ceptible. While there were rifts, they were narrow enough to bridge.

In Prado territory things had been different. Cárdenas had allowed him considerable latitude, and Prado had administered revolution with a vividness and a thoroughness people were unlikely to forget. It had been too personal. One Indian received land, perhaps community land at that, while his neighbor was forced to make hats.[24]

Then in 1936 the political climate began to change. Revolutionary

22. G. Gómez et al. to Lázaro Cárdenas, 4 November 1935, expediente 547.3/79, Lázaro Cárdenas, Fondo Presidentes, AGN.
23. These requests included the following: on Pátzcuaro, Esperanza S. de Silvia et al. to Lázaro Cárdenas, 18 August 1939, expediente 547.4/133, Lázaro Cárdenas, Fondo Presidentes, AGN; on Charapan, Amparo M. de Gómez and Victoria Galván to Lázaro Cárdenas, 6 January 1939, expediente 547.4/407, ibid.; on Chilchota, Mar-garita Sosa et al. to Lázaro Cárdenas, 16 January 1935, expediente 547.4/36, ibid.; on Parangaricutiro, Toribio Sandoval to Lázaro Cárdenas, 16 August 1935, expediente 547.4/184, ibid.; and on Tangancícuaro, Bartolito Valdéz and Gabriel Amaya to Lázaro Cárdenas, 12 July 1938, expediente 547.4/272, ibid.
24. On campesinos' claims that Prado erroneously redistributed community land, see chapter 6.

reconstruction, its egalitarian promises as much as the excesses, incited fear throughout the country. For landowners, what Corona Núñez referred to as Cárdenas's attempt to "open the nation's pocketbook and throw the wealth to the people" proved intolerable.[25] And members of the Catholic hierarchy and laypeople alike found socialist education alarming, as much because of its possibilities of social equality as because of its rumors of boys and girls bathing together in the nude.

This anxiety prompted numerous, often contradictory efforts either to alter or to undermine the revolutionaries' work in the nation at large and in the Tarascan meseta. Events that occurred at times simultaneously, at times sequentially, their reconstruction calls for a certain modesty. Most importantly, political and personal motivations cannot be ascertained with any finality. Guesswork is involved even regarding the extent of Cárdenas's involvement in his followers' activities.

Still, it is reasonably clear that four responses to revolution intertwined, leading first to bloodshed and ultimately to a transformation of postrevolutionary political culture. These responses included Cárdenas's efforts to salvage what he could of his cadre's efforts to remake the countryside. Then in 1937 members of the national bourgeoisie founded the Unión Nacional Sinarquista, a counterrevolutionary movement that recruited Michoacán peasants with considerable success. The same year, various Michoacán Cardenistas voiced their discomfort with Ernesto Prado, targeting him as a political liability. Finally, Prado himself marshaled a defense. If he had been designated the sacrificial lamb, Prado had no intention of going without a bleat.

More than elite machinations, these events would feed a certain Cain-and-Abel sensibility apparent among Once Pueblo peasants. If it remains impossible to reconstruct a step-by-step psychological account of the ways the fratricidal approach affected Michoacán campesinos, their activities began to reveal a fear that only one son would be favored by the revolutionary government. Portraying themselves as heroes, bleached into innocence, their enemies emerge as shady and double-dealing. Finally, as though language had proved insufficient, they shot each other up.

How did these factors converge? Perhaps the simplest approach will be to begin with Cárdenas's efforts to refurbish the revolution and then to proceed chronologically. In response to peasants' murdering and

25. Interview with José Corona Núñez, Morelia, July 1985.

decapitating teachers, Cárdenas asked teachers to shoulder a portion of the blame. Although he had lent his prestige to socialist educators, in a series of speeches delivered in 1936 Cárdenas distanced himself from their most dramatic efforts to affect change. Displaying his characteristic subtlety, Cárdenas's speeches appeared to reflect a will to defend unarmed teachers and to placate religious concern over unbridled anticlericalism.

On February 16 in Ciudad Guerrero, Tampico, he claimed that "it is not the intention of the government to fight against the beliefs of any religion. It has been said that socialist education wars against religion. That's a lie." In Ciudad González, Guanajuato, the next month he responded to an assault on the teachers. There Cárdenas maintained that it was

a lie that socialist education would result in the breakup of homes. It is also a lie that it perverts children, separating them from their parents. . . . The socialist school will make stronger men, men more aware of their responsibilities and more capable of acting within an organization promoting social justice and [participating] in an accelerated economic climate. Otherwise, neither the government nor the socialist educators engage in attacking religious beliefs.[26]

Probably because Cárdenas considered him loyal, reliable, and legalistic, Gildardo Magaña assumed the Michoacán governorship in 1936.[27] While Magaña's stance toward his job remains somewhat enigmatic,[28] his close collaboration with Zapata led Michoacán Cardenistas such as Jesús Múgica Martínez to harbor false expectations of the man. "We expected him to embody the spirit of Zapata, to give out land

26. For the Ciudad Guerrero speech, see Lázaro Cárdenas, *Palabras y documentos públicos de Lázaro Cárdenas: Mensajes, discursos, declaraciones, entrevistas y otros documentos, 1928–1940*, 3 vols. (Mexico City: Siglo XXI Editores, 1978), 1:193; for the Guanajuato speech, 1:206–8. He made the same point in a Guadalajara speech in late March 1936; see 1:199–200.

27. Alicia Hernández Chávez, *La mecánica cardenista*, vol. 16 of *La historia de la revolución mexicana*, ed. Luis González (Mexico City: El Colegio de México, 1979), 100.

28. That is, he appears to have left no written traces describing his approach to the Michoacán governorship. I researched this issue in the AGN, Fondo Presidentes, Lázaro Cárdenas; the Archivo General del Poder Ejecutivo; and the Archivo Histórico del Poder Ejecutivo de Michoacán. In addition, I explored Magaña's political stance in Michoacán in interviews with Corona Núñez, July 1989; Ignacio Espitia, Zamora, Michoacán, August 1985; Tomás Rico Cano, Morelia, June, August 1990; and Jesús Múgica Martínez, Morelia, June, August 1990.

quickly and easily." "Who would have thought it?" mused Nacho Espitia. "He became our enemy."[29]

In fact, the pleasure Magaña took in forging compromise distinguished him from Zapata. When Zapata died, Magaña became the architect of the pact with Obregón that led Zapatistas—at last—to lay down their arms and participate in the reconstruction of postrevolutionary Mexico. Perhaps Cárdenas determined that a revolutionary with Magaña's legalistic credentials would prove helpful in Michoacán's frayed political atmosphere.

There would be an increasing need for such a person in the state. In 1937 members of the national bourgeoisie established the Unión Nacional Sinarquista. Suddenly strangers dressed in dark, respectable clothing were entering Michoacán *pueblitos,* setting up meetings, mobilizing campesinos with their rhetoric. Engineered by middle- and upper-class men fearful of the revolution and its egalitarian promises, this rhetoric was fascistic in many ways. Intent on liberating themselves from foreign ideological influence, sinarquistas denounced "foreign symbols holding sway over Mexico: foreign flags, hammers and sickles, communist or fascist emblems."[30] They shared fascists' respect for capitalism, proclaiming themselves "defenders of private property."[31] Sinarquistas also feared allegiances based on class, demanding "subordination of particular class interests against the supreme interest of the *patria.*" It was chiefly their overt refusal to engage in institutional politics that distinguished them from fascists.[32]

In addition, sinarquistas tailored a message that mobilized Michoacán peasants. Campesinos trudged from villages to major cities, forg-

29. Interviews with Múgica Martínez, August 1990; and Espitia, August 1985.

30. "Pentálago sinarquista," private archive of José Lomelí (AJL), Zamora. The same sense of nationalism appears in "Bases del sinarquismo," a key sinarquista document, in the Archivo Municipal de Ario (AMA), and in "Diez normas de vida para los sinarquistas," AJL.

31. "Pentálago sinarquista."

32. For Albert Michaels, however, what distinguished sinarquism from fascism most clearly was sinarquism's uniquely Mexican identity, the fact that "middle class leaders of Sinarquismo looked to neither Italy, Germany, Spain or Rome for their ideal." See Michaels, "Fascism and Sinarquismo: Popular Nationalisms against the Mexican Revolution," *Journal of Church and State* 8 (spring 1966): 234–50. Jean Meyer's perspective, that sinarquista leaders manipulated what was genuine about the Mexican peasantry, "the importance of custom and religion, the opposition to power based on wealth and to the democracy of the masses, a concrete concept of liberty," is more complex. See Meyer, *El sinarquismo, ¿un fascismo mexicano?* (Mexico City: Editorial Joaquín Mortiz, 1979), 150.

ing sinarquista flanks behind the Mexican flag.[33] But why? How did sinarquistas manage to so deeply affect a people who had developed marked if wayward connections to revolutionary efforts to alter rural life? Is it too far-fetched to consider the appeal of sinarquistas' idiosyncratic efforts to bind a traditional sense of family with a quasi-egalitarian approach to property?

Sinarquismo derived much of its energy and appeal from a concern for family, but the movement's leaders understood family in a specific way. The source of the kinship was not born of the kind of camaraderie that emerges from shared tasks or experiences, the quasi-communities forged on the haciendas, the women washing together at the stream. Rather, sinarquistas saw family as an inclusive but embattled unit. For sinarquistas the fact that Mexicans shared national physical boundaries and a belief in the Catholic God was enough. This led to the "true union of the Mexican family" and "the permanent union of all its sons." There was, nonetheless, a problem of recognition. Mexicans tended to splinter off, leading sinarquistas to "repudiate the antipatriotic tendency that divides Mexicans into 'leftists' and 'rightists,' 'revolutionaries' and 'reactionaries.' Mexico, to save yourself, take back the permanent union of all your sons and establish only one division: Mexicans and anti-Mexicans."[34]

Cognition would not be the only requirement for absorption into the sinarquista family. All Mexicans could become family members only if they accepted a principle of inequality. As in traditional Catholic families, sacrifices would be required. Most importantly, sinarquistas were to assume a meek demeanor. They were instructed to "never complain to your bosses. Treat your work companions like brothers. Don't look for quarrels with your enemies."[35]

If inequality was a requirement for sinarquista peasants, landlessness was not. Deserting the traditional Catholic insistence on an inequitable social order, sinarquistas developed an openhanded approach to Mex-

33. Meyer, *El sinarquismo,* 144–68; César Moheno, *Las historias y los hombres de San Juan* (Zamora: El Colegio de Michoacán/CONACYT, 1985), 156–61; interviews with sinarquistas Eulario Capilla, Jarácuaro, Michoacán, September 1985; Jervacio López, Jarácuaro, August 1985; and Celerino Ramírez, Jarácuaro, September 1985. In fact, sinarquista fervor persisted in northwestern Michoacán until at least the mid-1980s, as revealed in interviews with sinarquistas José Lomelí, Santiago del Río, Luis Garibay, and Enrique Losornio, all conducted in Zamora, August 1985.

34. "Bases del sinarquismo."

35. "Diez normas."

ico's widespread land hunger. Without acknowledging it, sinarquistas appear to have relied on the revolutionaries' extensive land reform for inspiration. Their platform, however, promoted individuality rather than communal solutions to problems. As a sinarquista ideologue put it, "We affirm the right to private property and demand the creation of social conditions that make easy access to it possible for all who work. Against the cry 'all proletarians,' we oppose ours, 'all owners.'"[36]

Campesinos were to behave deferentially, confident in the eventual recognition of their merit. While the diverse motivations behind campesinos' engagement with sinarquismo have only begun to be plumbed,[37] these sinarquista emphases were at least consistent with concerns emerging from the culture of purity and redemption in Michoacán. If Michoacán mestizo men had adopted a respectful, if inwardly sullen, demeanor toward the force surrounding their hacienda labor, the sinarquista demand that workers refrain from complaining about their bosses would have been a commonplace in a world where peasants customarily weighed and measured—and sometimes manipulated—elite efforts to silence them. When combined with the sinarquista rhetorical insistence that all peasants become landowners, its appeal among these people becomes more convincing.

In 1937 Michoacán Cardenista leaders initiated efforts to scuttle Ernesto Prado. Were they prompted by restive sinarquistas? By Cárdenas's seeming apprehension? Was it something else, hidden? One of the frustrations of this work is the recognition that human motivation remains at least partly unclear. Analytical caution is required at the very moment when Michoacán Cardenistas leaders, including Prado himself, appear to have been most agitated.

A number of Michoacán Cardenistas pinpointed Prado as the source of peasant discontent with the revolution. The six agrarian leaders who branded him a "wolf in sheep's clothing"—José of Purépero, Antonio of Tlazazalca, Luis of Patamban, José of Jacona, Ramón of Chilchota, Juan of Zamora—come to mind, forcing an uncomfortable memory of their readiness to make use of Prado's organized followers when it suited their purposes, their readiness to denounce him at will.[38]

36. "Bases del sinarquismo."

37. For interesting efforts to understand sinarquismo's popular appeal in the village of San Juan Parangaricutiro, see Moheno, *Las historias.*

38. José of Purépero et al. to Gustavo Izazaga Cárdenas, 13 April 1937, expediente 20, Fondo Gobernación, 1937, Archivo Municipal de Zamora, Zamora.

The agrarian leaders did not act alone. In 1937 socialist school-teacher Salvador Sotelo composed a letter to Juan Gutiérrez describing an agrarian conference held in Tangancícuaro that June. A jumpy letter, it was punctuated by numerous denunciations, counterdenunciations, comings, goings:

There had been a meeting in Tierras Blancas that left us in liberty to form a plan to integrate the federation in Tangancícuaro.

After that Tierras Blancas agreement, the [municipal] president gathered the delegates in his house with the members of the central committee and Don Eliseo Prado, and there they discussed the fact that the municipal president had been maneuvering against Don Mauricio, claiming he is Cristero and manipulated the election of Prado, with these details and in agreement in the house of the president. Determined to obstruct the congress, they did what they could, but it was clear to see that what [the enemies] sought was to undermine the control of the Prados in Tangancícuaro.

Before the congress got underway, Vicente Pérez showed up, claiming that the governor had ordered the suspension of the congress, but that was rumored to be an intrigue. Rangel [the secretary of agrarian communities for the state CRMDT] arrived from Zamora, bringing the news that the governor had not given that order.[39]

Attempting to decipher this series of events for Gutiérrez, Sotelo made it plain that he saw Prado as a political liability. He viewed "Prado's domination in Tangancícuaro" as the source of the confusion. Adopting a protective, if paternalistic, stance toward the rural workers, Sotelo suggested that Prado's political machinations ran roughshod over unsuspecting workers. "It is a crime what is committed with the workers, in this case what Ernesto Prado does, we shouldn't be surprised what elements like him do, because of his political ambition. . . . It has been proved that for such elements, their ambition overtakes them and it does not matter what disaster is created for the workers or for the rural teachers."[40]

His domination challenged, Prado's final opportunity to forge unity in the Once Pueblos would come in 1939 under much harsher political conditions. Because the stability of Cárdenas's government was at stake, the peasants and their tendencies to attack each other return to documentary view.

---

39. Salvador Sotelo to Juan Gutiérrez, 6 November 1937, Juan Gutiérrez private archive (AJG), Zamora.
40. Ibid.

But not at first. At first the issue of political purpose, of what role leaders were to play, proved confusing. Trouncing him as a presidential hopeful, Cárdenas made Francisco J. Múgica head of federal military operations in Michoacán.[41] But which Múgica? If questions regarding his complex political personality have pursued him for years, Múgica's stance toward Cardenista revolution took on a particular urgency for Prado in 1939. Would it be the legalistic Múgica, author of the 1917 constitution? The radical Múgica who helped Trotsky gain asylum in Mexico? More to the point, how would he respond to Prado? In short, would the connection between Prado and revolution persist, or would some version of the prerevolutionary order be restored?

In 1939 and 1940 these seemingly disparate issues—Cárdenas's apparent flexibility, the rise of sinarquismo, Magaña and Múgica's establishment in Michoacán, the brittleness of Prado's position—came together. Hardly abstract concerns, they led Tarascans to vie for domination of the Once Pueblos. On one side, Prado and his allies implicitly wondered if their past loyalty to Cárdenas still mattered. On the other, anti-Pradistas demanded inclusion in the postrevolutionary reconstruction.

Anti-agraristas first challenged Prado's domination in the village of Charapan. As Ernesto Ruíz Prado described it, the anti-Pradistas indulged in a facsimile of Prado-style political theater. Like the Prados themselves, the Catholic leaders chose men from various villages, thus minimizing the possibility of easy neighborhood vengeance. Then, according to Prado, these "forty campesinos from Corupo, San Felipe, Sicuicho, Zacán, Coicucho, and Charapan attacked Charapan, screaming, 'Long live Magaña! Long live small property! Death to agrarianism!'"[42]

The next year, another Pradista complained that "the governor of the state dismantled the local government guaranteed by the constitution," replacing its members with anti-agraristas.[43] This seems a bit

41. On Múgica's loss of the presidency, see Hernández Chávez, *La mecánica cardenista*, 199–208; and Javier Romero, "Múgica en 1939–1940: La frustrada candidatura a la presidencia," in *VII Jornadas de historia de occidente: Francisco J. Múgica* (Jiquilpan de Juárez: Centro de Estudios de la Revolución Mexicana "Lázaro Cárdenas," A.C., 1985), 195–208.

42. Expediente 559.1/83, Lázaro Cárdenas, Fondo Presidentes, AGN.

43. Expedientes 559.1/83, 542.1/1890, Lázaro Cárdenas, Fondo Presidentes, AGN.

disingenuous, cranky, unless we feel Aguilar's real anxiety: Do the old allegiances stand? Can we conjure with them?

From the perspective of the agraristas, the situation would worsen. But let them tell it. They had seen themselves as the revolution's favored sons. As Cárdenas had once been "a humble worker in the Zinapécuaro office of rents," they considered him "a brother of the workers." His revolutionary strategy had guaranteed them economic and personal security. Then something changed. Anti-Cardenistas, they learned, threatened to seize control. Charapan was to be occupied by federal forces. They were to be "arrested in our own homes, subjects of a tremendous butchery." Terrified, they left: "all dispersed, in flight, pursued by bullets." In their absence, the anti-agraristas "harvested our crops, robbing us of our products, leaving us in the saddest personal and familial misery." Finally, the agraristas claimed, their enemies "took advantage of our absence to threaten our defenseless families."[44]

In Chilchota, the government's abandonment of its former allies proved even more jarring. According to Eliseo Prado and Conrado Arreola, "the forces of the state government, the military zone, and the reactionary group in Chilchota had deposed the constitutional municipal council, had jailed and tortured many agraristas."[45] The anti-Cardenistas countered with the complaint that the agraristas were "razing the land already sown, challenging the verification of the corn harvests and the preparations for planting wheat."[46] Juan Santos, the Chilchota municipal president, claimed that Ernesto Prado was harboring criminals in his house in Tangancícuaro.[47]

Neither side gave up hope of dominating the Once Pueblos. While they met to iron out their differences, it is reasonably clear that both sides saw conciliation as a means to establish—or reestablish—the control of their particular cadre. The breaking point came on January 25, 1940, when a shootout punctuated the peacemaking attempts.

But what happened? The participants' versions cannot be recon-

---

44. Eutimio Aguilar and Rubén Martínez to Lázaro Cárdenas, 15 April 1940, expediente 542.1/2644, Lázaro Cárdenas, Fondo Presidentes, AGN.

45. Conrado Arreola and Eliseo Prado to Lázaro Cárdenas, 28 December 1939, expediente 542.1/2644, Lázaro Cárdenas, Fondo Presidentes, AGN.

46. Rafael Morfín, ejidal commissariat of Chilchota, to Lázaro Cárdenas, 13 November 1939, expediente 404.1/312, Lázaro Cárdenas, Fondo Presidentes, AGN.

47. Juan M. Santos, municipal president of Chilchota to Lázaro Cárdenas, 13 November 1939, expediente 404.1/312, Lázaro Cárdenas, Fondo Presidentes, AGN.

ciled. According to Prado's lawyer, Gustavo Gallardo González, a peacekeeping mission had gathered in Tanaquillo. Prado, his followers, Gallardo himself, a group of Prado's campesino enemies, and Ternorio Carmona, an emissary for Michoacán governor Gildardo Magaña, made up the group. Prado promised "reconciliation and good will," and his enemies spoke of their own hopes for reconciliation. Gallardo claimed that Carmona was impressed. "If you people take this plan seriously, and if the other compañeros want to come to agreement, why, everything will work out," he cried.[48] To cement the new accord, Prado's followers set off for Chilchota on foot, hoping to meet with their former enemies.

Gallardo found that peace would not come readily. Arriving at the outskirts of Chilchota, Prado's men encountered a group of soldiers who maintained "a provocative, threatening attitude." Immediately General Enrique Morfín Figueroa, the anti-Pradista municipal president, emerged from the crowd. "Listen to me, *cabrón,* don't you know that demonstrations from contrary parties are illegal? You're going to be responsible for what happens."

"But, my general," Gallardo interjected.

Figueroa cut him off, insisting there would be no "'my general.' You are a son of your fucked mother that comes defending these *cabrones bandidos.*"

In response, Gallardo pressed him. "You know, my general, that we come to patch up all of these issues for the good, and it is not possible that anything bad will happen, because the people with me are disarmed."

"They may be disarmed, but mine are going to murder more than four sons of the fucked mothers."

Seeing that the situation was more difficult than he had imagined, Gallardo said to the general, "Fine, my general, then we'll leave." But Morfín refused: "You're not leaving yet, you sons of the fucked mother, now you're going to get fucked." True to his word, Figueroa cried out, "Kill four or five sons of their fucked mothers! Seize the bandits and assassins!"

For men like Morfín, Múgica, and division commander Antonio Gómez Velasco, Gallardo's rendition of events was unimaginable.

---

48. The following representation is based on Gallardo's rendition, found in Gustavo Gallardo González to Lázaro Cárdenas, 26 January 1940, expediente 542.1/2644, Lázaro Cárdenas, Fondo Presidentes, AGN.

Developing a competing version of the Chilchota encounter, Gómez Velasco claimed that Magaña had ordered *Ingeniero* Horacio Tonorio to host a meeting in which Tarascans would iron out "old grievances based on questions of land and politics." Meeting in Chilchota, they hoped to work out their differences, when suddenly "they heard many people from Tangancícuaro arriving in Chilchota."[49]

With the arrival of Gallardo, "leading one hundred hostile Indians," the anti-Pradistas turned skittish. Morfín invited them to name a commission to participate in the meetings, "but far from obeying, they continued advancing from different parts, and as they came upon the pueblo, people recognized Tomás Bautista, a murderer, who, obeying a signal, took out his pistol and began to shoot, killing Agustín Marcus and wounding Francisco Bautista."

Though he was an outside observer, Gómez Velasco, like Gallardo, had entered a fractious world. Neighbors had come to view one another as rivals, as thieves carting off treasured possessions. It was a world in which victory was all that mattered. As only villains or innocent victims could populate such a world, Gómez Velasco, like Gallardo, hastened to designate men responsible for the shootout. For him the culprit was "Ernesto Prado, who has surrounded himself with wicked people operating in the guise of innocent peasants, and with these elements, he has dominated most of the Indians who view him with terror. The general opinion is that unless he leaves the region or is imprisoned, along with his gunmen, there will be no peace and there will continue to be butchery among the peasants."

Traces of Indian Life?

Praying for a bountiful afterlife. Wearing governmental garb. Pushing neighbors off the land into isolated ravines. Tarascans clearly could not be neatly categorized as "inoffensive Indians."

49. The following reconstruction is based principally on Antonio Gómez Velasco to Lázaro Cárdenas, 30 January 1940, expediente 542.1/2644, Lázaro Cárdenas, Fondo Presidentes, AGN. For similar points of view, see Múgica's telegram to Cárdenas, found in Francisco J. Múgica to Lázaro Cárdenas, 26 January 1940, ibid. Within his own telegram, Múgica quoted from a 24 January 1940 telegram he had received from Morfín expressing much the same perspective.

What are we to make of them, then? While the loss of life, the brutality that charged the Chilchota encounter, is arresting, a mannered image comes to mind. It seems that certain painters engage in a practice called pentimento. A concept made memorable by Lillian Hellman,[50] pentimento comes into play when painters, caught by second thoughts, paint over their initial efforts. Sometimes, though, their early intentions peak through. The pentimenti are the early attempts to weld together elements as disparate as hand and eye, brush and canvas. They reflect the painter's struggle to make a limited piece of canvas an arena displaying complex intuitions.

There is a way that pentimento suggests that beneath all the stray brush strokes there is one true image. For Cardenistas who had developed well-intentioned yet one-dimensional images of the Indians, this thought might have proved comforting. Pentimento, however, can also speak of varying interpretations. It can speak of this gesture, then that one, of an Indian eagerly sending her child to the school, then another rejecting Prado's claim to represent the revolution. As Tarascans' responses to the revolution suggest, they would sketch and resketch their own political trajectories depending on the political context. For Lázaro Cárdenas, a president suddenly forced to make an alliance with restive Indians, it would be this flexibility that would catch his eye.

50. Lillian Hellman, *Pentimento* (New York: Signet, 1973); Jon Eubank Manchip White, *Diego Velázquez, Painter and Courtier* (New York: Rand McNally, 1969), 25.

Conclusion

The Redemption of the Mexican Revolution

Even a preview suggests something of the complexity of the story's ending. It also implies the significance of what Michoacán peasants were able to do. For the story winds down with Cárdenas besieged by competing demands. He had long entrusted much of his fate in rural Michoacán to men like Ernesto Prado. Though Prado had blood on his hands, his loyalty to Cárdenas had been unshakable. Indeed, he may have considered his assaults on "clerical reactionaries" to be tokens of allegiance.[1] In the short run, the combination of loyalty and violence had proved effective, and that had once been enough for Cárdenas. But when the crunch came, Cárdenas turned on Prado. Their past together became suddenly irrelevant.

The problems run deeper than untangling seeming disloyalty to a friend. Cárdenas was able to evade the obligations of friendship and to ignore Prado's many favors because anti-Pradistas provided him with an alternative source of peasant support. Their numerous pleas and demands, here ceremonial, there almost inarticulate, amounted to a sort of guidebook to their concerns. Teaching him that murder need not be the only measure of allegiance, Michoacán peasants showed him a more effective way to reconstruct the postrevolutionary government.

1. Ernesto Prado to secretary-general, CRMDT, 11 January 1934, expediente 525.3/72, Abelardo Rodríguez, Fondo Presidentes, Archivo General de la Nación (AGN), Mexico City.

155

The trouble is, we have come to know them differently. As we know that Tarascan women made do with one, perhaps two new garments a year, how are we to see them as moved by more than economic difficulties? And campesinos who murdered neighbors in retaliation for theological skepticism would prove willing to compromise? More unsettling still, how are we to recognize the notable role Michoacán campesinos played in shaping a new government when all along their power had proved inadequate?

Because of the official story, Cárdenas himself has taken on another guise. By creating an image of Cárdenas as secular Jesus, official historians have developed a persona that could not have been plagued by misapprehensions of campesino culture. The numerous episodes in which Cárdenas and the campesinos share food, language, and physical space serve as parables confirming Cárdenas's ability to discern. In these tales of a messianic president and a grateful flock, the often baffling encounters between Cárdenas, Cardenistas, and peasants play no role. Serious conversation, questioning, painful mistakes and reformulations—all are absent from this rendition. For a man blessed with instinctive recognition of the needs of his flocks, study would have been unnecessary.[2]

There is a wistful quality to all this, for does the image of Cárdenas as benefactor, peasants as grateful beneficiaries, not betray a longing for inertia? And who among us is immune to the temptations of passivity, the hope that silence and immobility will summon a benevolent custodian prepared to take our difficulties in hand?

Nonetheless, in the end Cárdenas's Jesus-like abilities were threatened. During the last years of his presidency, disaffected landowners and foreign capitalists attempted to undermine Cárdenas's program.

2. See, e.g., Frank Tannenbaum, *Mexico: The Struggle for Peace and Bread* (New York: Knopf, 1950), 71–73; and Luis González, *Los días del presidente Cárdenas,* vol. 15 of *La historia de la revolución Mexicana,* ed. González (Mexico City: El Colegio de México, 1981), 120–21. In "Cardenismo: Juggernaut or Jalopy?" *Journal of Latin American Studies* 26 (February 1994): 73–107, Alan Knight develops a perspective on Cardenismo that appears to be in broad agreement with much of the analysis I developed in "Torching La Purísima, Dancing at the Altar: The Construction of Revolutionary Hegemony in Michoacán, 1934–1940," in *Everyday Forms of State Formation: Revolution and the Negotiation of Rule in Modern Mexico,* ed. Gilbert M. Joseph and Daniel Nugent (Durham, N.C.: Duke University Press, 1994). What remains worrisome about Knight's formulation—that in the end Cárdenas succeeded in creating an institutional shell, its core hollow of radicalism—is that the specific intellectual dynamism of Cardenistas, peasants, and the emerging state is obscured.

The Unión Nacional Sinarquista emerged in 1937. The next year U.S. companies initiated a boycott on Mexican oil sales and landlords stepped up pressure on the government.[3]

Cárdenas as failed messiah has excited relatively little scholarly attention. Still, a handful of scholars have attempted to explain Cárdenas's about-face. Taken together, their perspectives suggest a certain consensus. It goes something like this. The reemergence of the Right, in the form of sinarquismo, *acción nacional,* a bourgeoisie frightened by the land reform, and the Catholic hierarchy, forced Cárdenas to relinquish his previous positions. Notwithstanding the challenge to his superhuman capacities, Cárdenas retained a will to protect his flock. (And after all, Jesus himself was also a man.) In order to protect some portion of revolutionary gains, he did not hand the presidency to his lifelong friend Francisco J. Múgica, for Múgica would incite further right-wing activity. Rather, he tapped the safer candidate, Manuel Avila Camacho.[4]

The fact that poor people enabled Cárdenas to reconstruct the postrevolutionary state may seem prosaic, even pallid, against the hope of an untarnished hero. If we must set aside secular mysticism, it is at least partly because Michoacán campesinos' letters confronted Cárdenas with a painful truth. Cárdenas's ineffable ability to draw people to him, while real, had never been enough. For all their good-heartedness, Cárdenas and the Cardenistas had proved myopic, unable to see the worlds the peasants did, oblivious to what campesinos valued most.

Playing on Cárdenas's inadequacies (and inadvertently revealing their own), the peasants had demanded what must be called the redemption of the Mexican revolution. Although this entailed reopening the churches, it meant more than a Catholic restoration. Instead, Michoacán peasants acted in part on the Cardenista insistence that men, if not women, need not accept humility with gratitude. Still, because of the campesinos' view that invisible realities, even possibilities, deserved meticulous care, Catholic activities would have to resume their public space.

---

3. Nora Hamilton, *The Limits of State Autonomy: Post-Revolutionary Mexico* (Princeton: Princeton University Press, 1982), 236.

4. A particularly sophisticated version of this perspective can be found in Hamilton, *Limits of State Autonomy,* 275–79. See also Alicia Hernández Chávez, *La mecánica cardenista,* vol. 16 of González, *La historia de la revolución mexicana* (1979), 198–99; and Victoria Lerner, *La educación socialista,* vol. 17 of ibid. (1979), 179–80.

Whatever their trepidations, peasants had addressed Cárdenas's ignorance. And whatever his attachment to his own methods, to Prado, and to anticlericalism, Cárdenas knew when to listen. What did this taciturn, undereducated man from Jiquilpan learn? What were Michoacán campesinos to accept? When we left Cárdenas, peasants had inundated him with demands and pleas. Though they were frequently cautious about voicing their concerns, enough of the revolutionary program had spoken to them to elicit response.

It is time to conclude the story. Possessing the letters as an instruction manual, Cárdenas had before him the task of translation. For does not learning frequently imply a twofold process? First comes retention of the teacher's formula, insurance against demands for proof that the lesson has been absorbed. There is also the more difficult task of interpretation, making the teacher's words personal through reworking them.

Culling through the letters, Cárdenas became a political translator, fitting something of the peasants' understanding into his own frame of reference. Take the issue of land. The possibilities of access to land had excited marked popular hope and enthusiasm. To be sure, there had been dissent, but Cárdenas was learning to weigh and measure campesino reactions. From eluding the bank by planting garbanzos or pasturing an animal on ejidal lands to invading neighbors' lands, all could be read as the acceptance of the broad agrarian outlines he promoted. And what if some peasants refused the land? Considering the generalized insufficiency of land, that could be accommodated.

Cárdenas determined that concerns over caciques and, more generally, political domination could be played similarly. People were outraged when specific leaders—a Prado, a Cuevas, a Gutiérrez—behaved in certain ways. Pulling hair, jailing women, shooting up the countryside. Yet there was enough peasant identification with what particular caciques and, by implication, the government itself could do for them to enable Cárdenas to clip Prado's wings while retaining an authoritarian political structure.

Agreement on Indian issues proved more tenuous. For one thing, there were complex and sometimes nebulous Indian concerns to accommodate. Some Indian men had relinquished the Catholic component of their ethnicity, adopting the cultural pattern of mestizo campesinos. Others had accepted the Cardenista invitation to style themselves metaphors for revolutionary concern for Indians. Their motivations were probably varied—the paucity of governmental agrarian aid to Tarascans, a will to honor a semblance of their past, a guarded enthusiasm for the government's attention to Indian matters. Cárdenas's own response to the Indians revealed something of the complexity of the man. It also proved wrenching. To be sure, Cárdenas had demonstrated sympathy for Indians and admiration for their pre-Conquest achievements on many occasions.[5] That attitude persisted in 1939, when Secretary of Foreign Relations Eduardo Hay asked him to reconsider his plan to invite Indians to an international Indian conference to be held in Pátzcuaro in 1940. The grounds?

There is no question that most of the Indians will be unable to deliberate and to figure out ways to help the evolution of the various American Indian races of the American countries. Instead, let me suggest that you suggest that governments send competent, qualified people knowledgeable about the idiosyncrasies and needs of the various Indian races.

Were Indians ignorant of their own living conditions? Or had they developed an understanding of their lives, despite the inadequacies they suffered? Clearly toying with both perspectives, Cárdenas told Hay, "Your point is right on the mark. Even so, it would still be worthwhile to invite, along with the qualified people, one or two Indians."[6]

When Indians aligned with mestizos demanded the reinstatement of public worship, however, Cárdenas was forced to yield. The demand was too widespread, and the consensus regarding public worship included local elites, the Catholic hierarchy, the sinarquistas. While in many respects Cárdenas and the Michoacán Cardenistas had persuaded campesinos to accept governmental initiatives, Catholic fervor proved politically overwhelming.

It is true that Cárdenas's response to this demand for Catholic restoration was reluctant. For the man who refused to satisfy his future in-laws' wish that he marry in a church, this clamor for spiritual

---

5. Often these emphases merged in Cárdenas's speeches. See, e.g., a series of speeches delivered in 1934, including a Durango speech reprinted in Lázaro Cárdenas, *Palabras y documentos públicos de Lázaro Cárdenas: Mensajes, discursos, declaraciones, entrevistas y otros documentos, 1928–1940*, 3 vols. (Mexico City: Siglo XXI Editores, 1978), 132. See also Cárdenas's Oaxaca speech, in *Maestro Rural*, July 15, 1934, 4; and a February 2, 1934, Chiapas speech, transcript housed in expediente 545.2/5, Lázaro Cárdenas, Fondo Presidentes, AGN.

6. Lázaro Cárdenas to Gabino Vázquez, chief, Departamento Agrario, 25 November 1939, cartas 1938–40, Archivo Juan Gutiérrez (AJG), Zamora, Michoacán.

renewal would have been unsavory.[7] In November 1939 he wrote in his diary that "public officials participating in religious worship disorient the common people, who view the priests as the traditional enemy fighting against their freedom."[8] Moreover, until the end of his presidency, anticlericalism would play some role in policymaking, as his 1940 denial of a petition to build a new Zamora cathedral implies.[9]

Nonetheless, he had shown his flexibility as early as 1936 with his speeches rejecting blatant anticlericalism. His Guadalajara speech proved particularly important. In it he maintained that it was "not the government's role to promote antireligious campaigns, which result in nothing but sterile wastes of public servants' efforts, igniting resistance."[10] Celso Flores Zamora, the general director of the education ministry, circulated the Guadalajara message to school inspectors within the week.[11] Churches reopened their doors, and priests returned to the pulpits. By 1940 socialist education was a doomed proposition. Whatever illusions Cárdenas had harbored about his statecraft, however "unqualified" Indians might have been to deliberate about their own future, peasants had joined with him and against him to construct an altered political culture.

What had they done? From a short-term, local perspective, the peasants had collaborated with Cárdenas to resolve festering problems. The culture of purity and redemption would no longer be the same. While the church doors swung open again, and while La Purísima's message of modesty and public powerlessness was still considered potent for women, the combination of a land redistribution and a secular framework provided men with alternatives. No longer did they need to view God as celestial architect, drafting elaborate plans for landowners' homes and scribbling cramped afterthoughts to house the poor.

As for Cárdenas, he emerged armed with the information he

---

7. In his diary Cárdenas claimed that he scandalized his future wife's parents by refusing to marry within a church. See Lázaro Cárdenas, *Obras: I Apuntes,* 3 vols. (Mexico City: Universidad Nacional Autónoma de México, 1972), I: 206.

8. Cárdenas, *Apuntes,* 430.

9. Microfilm vol. 19, pt. 1, Lázaro Cárdenas, Fondo Presidentes, AGN.

10. Cárdenas, *Palabras,* 199–200.

11. Colección de circulares giradas por la Dirección General de Enseñanza Primaria de los Estados y Territorios, 1936, caja 557, Archivo Histórico de la Secretaría de Educación Pública, Mexico City.

needed to pacify the west.[12] His governorship and his presidency had been dogged by the restive behavior of the peasantry. If Mexican peasants had been persistently unable to seize power on the battlefield, they consistently distorted elite conceptions of order.

They had found resolutions to temporary problems and neighborhood spats. Yes, and they had done still more. The information the peasants offered, the compromise Cárdenas effected, amounted to a series of implicit alliances. Peasants were tacitly granting Cárdenas their allegiance. And Cárdenas? He should not be viewed in isolation. He had come into the project armed with something of Calles' cultural perspective, that of Múgica, perhaps some sense of the Zapatistas. Now drawing on the cultural expertise of the Michoacán campesinos, themselves masters at assimilating and reworking clerical and revolutionary perspectives, Cárdenas devised the makings of a governing framework that could be reproduced over time.

That framework would be what has come to be called a hegemonic framework. While hegemony has often been understood as ideological domination, it meant something far more subtle in Mexico. To be blunt, had elites mustered sufficient power to impose their will on the poor, this history would not have occurred. Moving this reflection a step further, hegemonic orders remain intact partly because the poor have carved out the space to participate in them. The dimensions of that space, whether institutions of government relegate poor people to cramped corners or amply respond to peasant concerns, are a direct reflection of the power of the poor in relationship to others.

Until now the Michoacán campesinos' role in shaping the postrevolutionary state has gone unnoticed. As Cárdenas would have been unable to reconstruct the government without the knowledge they offered him, it is important to address this error. Yet it is also important to recognize the bittersweet nature of the accomplishment.

12. Although the entire west had presented Cárdenas with a governing problem, Cárdenas's focus on Michoacán went even further than analyzed here. A sampling of Michoacán issues that engaged his attention includes problems surrounding the land redistribution discussed in Francisco J. Múgica to J. Trinidad Fuentes et al., 8 May 1935, and Ignacio García Tellez to Lázaro Cárdenas, 19 May 1938, ejido Zamora, 1935–39, AJG; the irrigation project in the Valley of Zamora, Vicente Adame to Juan Gutiérrez, 7 May 1938, ibid.; and the schooling and farming needs of Tarascans, Lázaro Cárdenas to Lic. Gonzalo Vázquez Vela, 12 December 1938, and Lázaro Cárdenas to Gildardo Magaña, 12 November 1938, expediente 151.3/1124, Lázaro Cárdenas, Fondo Presidentes, AGN.

Notwithstanding their valor, the campesinos' battlefield defeats left them unable to claim the state as their own. This left them to choose between plunging the west into bloody disarray and relinquishing their cultural knowledge to outsiders.

The government they helped to make reflected this uncomfortable position. By offering up their cultural knowledge, Michoacán campesinos did not undermine Cárdenas's one-party state. Nor did they dislodge national or international capitalist domination of the Mexican economy. Nonetheless, they taught Cárdenas that ideological conformity was not necessary for governmental control. Nor was it necessary to undermine every vestige of rural political expression. Rather, such expression could both coexist with and, because of its coexistence, fortify the postrevolutionary state. If there has been subtlety in this form of government, it is largely due to the Michoacán peasantry and their redemption of the Mexican revolution.

Select Bibliography

Primary Sources

ARCHIVES

Mexico City

Archivo General de la Nación, Fondo Presidentes
   Lázaro Cárdenas
   Abelardo Rodríguez
   Emilio Portes Gil
   Pascual Ortíz Rubio
Archivo Histórico de la Secretaría de Educación Pública
Archivo Histórico de la Secretaría de Reforma Agraria
Hemeroteca de la Ciudad Universitaria

Morelia

Archivo General del Poder Ejecutivo
Archivo Histórico del Poder Ejecutivo de Michoacán
Archivo Histórico Manuel Castañeda Ramírez
Archivo Judicial del Estado de Michoacán
Archivo del Poder Judicial
Archivo de la Secretaría de Reforma Agraria

Zamora

Archivo Municipal de Zamora
Archivo Particular de Juan Gutiérrez

Archivo Particular de José Lomelí
Archivo Particular de Ignacio Prisciliano Vargas
Archivo de la Purísima Corazón
Archivo de la Secretaría de Reforma Agraria
Colegio de Michoacán, Fondo Ramón Hernández y Hernández

Pátzcuaro

Archivo Municipal de Pátzcuaro

Jiquilpan

Centro de Estudios de la Revolución Mexicana "Lázaro Cárdenas," A.C.

Ario de Rayón

Archivo Municipal de Ario de Rayón

PUBLISHED DOCUMENTS

Cárdenas, Lázaro. *Ideario político.* Mexico City: Serie Popular Era, 1972.
———. "9 documentos inéditos." *Universidad Michoacana de San Nicolás de Hidalgo Revista Cuatrimestral,* July–October 1982, 9–25.
———. *Obras: Apuntes.* 3 vols. Mexico City: Universidad Nacional Autónoma de México, 1972.
———. *Palabras y documentos públicos de Lázaro Cárdenas: Mensajes, discursos, declaraciones, entrevistas y otros documentos, 1928–1940.* 3 vols. Mexico City: Siglo XXI Editores, 1978.
———. *Plan sexenal.* Mexico City: Partido Revolucionario Institucional Comisión Nacional Editorial, n.d.
———. *El problema indígena de México.* Mexico City: Departamento de Asuntos Indígenas, 1940.
———. *Escuela socialista y religión.* Mexico City: Talleres Gráficos de la Nación, 1936.
Corona Núñez, José. *A través de mi vida: Historia de mi pueblo.* Morelia: Universidad Michoacana de San Nicolás de Hidalgo, 1984.
Cusi, Ezio. *Memorias de un colono.* Mexico City: Editorial Jus, 1955.
Embriz Osorio, Arnulfo, and Leon García, Ricardo, eds. *Documentos para la historia del agrarismo en México.* Mexico City: Centro de Estudios Históricos del Agrarismo en México, 1982.
Fabila, Manuel, ed. *Cinco siglos de legislación agraria, 1493–1940.* Mexico City: Secretaría de Reforma Agraria/Centro de Estudios Históricos del Agrarismo en México, 1981.
Fulcheri y Pietra Santa, Ilmo. y Rev. Dn. Manuel. *Carta Pastoral del Ilmo. y Rvmo. Sr. Dr. Don Manuel Fulcheri y Pietra Santa, Obispo de Zamora.* Zamora: privately printed, 1922.

————. *Carta Pastoral del Ilmo. y Rvmo. Sr. Dr. Dn. Manuel Fulcheri y Pietra Santa, Obispo de Zamora.* Zamora, 1924.

Lucio, G. *Simiente: Libro cuarto para escuelas rurales.* Mexico City: Editorial Patria, n.d.

————. *Simiente: Libro segundo para escuelas rurales.* Mexico City: Editorial Patria, n.d.

————. *Simiente: Libro tercero para escuelas rurales.* Mexico City: Editorial Patria, n.d.

Novo, Salvador. *Jalisco, Michoacán 12 Días.* Mexico City: Imprenta Mundial, 1933.

Núñez, Ilmo. y Rmo. Sr. Obispo de Zamora, Doctor Don José Othón. *Edicto XIX del Ilmo y Rmo. Sr. Obispo de Zamora, Doctor Dn. José Othón Núñez.* Zamora, 1921.

Prelados de la provincia de Michoacán. *Carta pastoral colectiva de los prelados de la provincia de Michoacán.* Morelia: Tipografía de Agustín Martínez Mier, 1920.

————. *Carta pastoral sobre la acción social católica.* Mexico City, 1921.

Ramírez, Ignacio. *El niño campesino: Libro tercero, escuelas rurales.* Mexico City: Editorial Patria, 1939.

————. *Reglamento de la música sagrada que deberá observarse en la provincia eclesiástica de Michoacán.* Morelia: Tipografía del Agustín Martínez Mier, 1921.

Romero, José Guadalupe. *Noticias para formar la historia y la estadística del obispado de Michoacán.* Mexico City: Imprenta de Vicente García Torres, 1862.

Sáenz, Moisés. *Carapan: Bosquejo de una experiencia.* Lima: Librería e Imprenta Gil, 1936.

El sembrador: Libro primero de lectura para las escuelas rurales. Mexico City: Herrero Hermanos Sucesores, 1929.

Velázquez Bringas, Esperanza. *Lecturas populares para escuelas primarias superiores y especiales.* Mexico City: La Impresora S. Turanzas del Valle, 1935.

PERIODICALS

Actualidades: Periódico de Variedades e Información. Morelia.
Alerto: Seminario Social. Michoacán.
El Amigo de la Verdad: Bisemanal Católico y Social de Controversia. Mexico City.
El Baluarte: Periódico Doctrinario y de Defensa. Zitácuaro.
Brecha: Seminario de Combate e Información. Morelia.
El Campesino. Morelia.
El Correo de Zamora. Zamora.
Defensa Proletaria: Organo de la Federación Agraria y El Despertador. Maravatio.
Emancipación. Morelia.
Diario Oficial. Mexico City.
Firmeza: Organo del Partido Político "Junta Patriótica Liberal Benito Juárez."

El Heraldo: Seminario de Información, Literatura y Variedades. Morelia.
Heraldo Michoacano. Morelia.
La Hoja Social: Quincenal de Propaganda Católica. Zamora.
Maestro Rural. Mexico City.
Mercurio: Organo de la Sociedad de Alumnos de la Escuela de Comercio. Morelia.
El Orientador. Tacámbaro.
Orientación: Organo del Partido Liberal Avanzando del Distrito de Zitácuaro. Zitácuaro.
Para Todos. Morelia.
Periódico Oficial del Estado de Michoacán. Morelia.
La Prensa. Mexico City.
Pueblo Libre: Organo del Comité Radical Pro-Cárdenas.
Renovación: Periódico de Combate. Zitácuaro.
Restauración. Zamora.
Sindicalista del Distrito de Zitácuaro. Zitácuaro.
Tierra, Periódico del Departamento Agrario para los Ejidatarios. Mexico City.
Unificación. Uruapan.
La Verdad. Zinapécuaro.
Zitácuaro: Periódico de Combate e Información. Zitácuaro.

INTERVIEWS

Aceves, Celso. Ario de Rayón, Michoacán. 15 May 1990.
Aceves, Jesús. Ario de Rayón, Michoacán. 15 May 1990.
Acosta, Angelina. Zamora, Michoacán. 8 November 1990.
Amezcua, Luis. Ario de Rayón, Michoacán. 28 May 1990.
Arreola Cortéz, Raul. Mexico City. 20 August 1984.
Barragán, Soledad. Ario de Rayón, Michoacán. 6 June 1990.
Capilla, Eulario. Jarácuaro, Michoacán. 2 September 1985.
Cervantes, Carlos. Ario de Rayón, Michoacán. 7 June 1990.
Corona Núñez, José. Morelia, Michoacán. 12 July 1985; 11 July 1989.
Crespin Méndez, Señora. Ario de Rayón, Michoacán. 22 August 1985.
De los Angeles Verduzco Gómez, María. Ario de Rayón, Michoacán. 25 May 1990.
Elizalde, Francisco. Zamora, Michoacán. 19 July, 26 July 1985; 2 June 1988; 5 November 1990.
Espitia, Ignacio. Zamora, Michoacán. 18, 25 August 1985.
Garibay, Luis. Zamora, Michoacán. 23 August 1985.
Godínez López, Francisco. Ario de Rayón, Michoacán. 1 May 1990.
González Esquivel, Francisco. Zamora, Michoacán. 5 August 1985.
Lomelí, José. Zamora, Michoacán. 20, 26 August 1985.
López, Atiliano. Jarácuaro, Michoacán. 31 August 1985.
López, Jervacio. Jarácuaro, Michoacán. 31 August 1985.
Losornio, Enrique. Zamora, Michoacán. 24 August 1985.
Martínez, Carlos. Ario de Rayón, Michoacán. 7 September 1985.
Mayes, Julia. Morelia, Michoacán. December 1985.

Mayes Navarro, Antonio. Morelia, Michoacán. 4 December 1984.
Medina, Padre Porfirio. Zamora, Michoacán. 12 August 1985.
Méndez, Concepción. Ario de Rayón, Michoacán. 9 June, 3 November 1990.
Miranda, Padre Francisco. Zamora, Michoacán. 15 March 1990.
Múgica Martínez, Jesús. Morelia, Michoacán. 4 December 1984; 11 July
    1988; 10 July, 3 August 1989; 26 June, 3 August 1990.
Murillo, Constantino. Morelia, Michoacán. 16 July 1985; 7 March 1990.
Ochoa González, Rafael. Ario de Rayón, Michoacán. 7, 11, 12 May, 13 July,
    5 November 1990.
Padilla, Maximino. Zamora, Michoacán. 16 August 1985.
Paz, Padre Joaquín. Zamora, Michoacán. 12 August 1985.
Peña, Salvador. Ario de Rayón, Michoacán. 6 September 1985.
Pérez, Vicente. Zamora, Michoacán. 8 August 1985.
Ramírez, Celerino. Jarácuaro, Michoacán. 2 September 1985.
Reyes Garibaldi, Hilario. Morelia, Michoacán. 18 July 1985; 26 June 1990.
Rico Cano, Tomás. Morelia, Michoacán. 26 June, 3 August 1990.
Río, Santiago del. Zamora, Michoacán. 22 August 1985.
Rocha, Esperanza. Ario de Rayón, Michoacán. 13 May, 2 June, 6 July 1990.
Valadéz de García, Carmen. Ario de Rayón, Michoacán. 9 June 1990.
Valencia Ayala, Francisco. Zamora, Michoacán. 13 August 1985.
Verduzco de Peña, Mari Elena. Ario de Rayón, Michoacán. 24, 25, 27, 28, 30
    April, 25, 27 May, 12 July, 1 November 1990.
Villaseñor Espinosa, Roberto. Mexico City. 1 March 1984.

Secondary Sources

Aguilar Camín, Héctor. *La frontera nomada.* 3d ed. Mexico City: Siglo XXI
    Editores, 1981.
———. "The Relevant Tradition: Sonoran Leaders in the Revolution." In
    Brading, *Caudillo and Peasant in the Mexican Revolution,* 92–123.
———. *Saldos de la revolución.* Mexico City: Ediciones Oceano, 1984.
Agulhon, Maurice. *The Republic in the Village.* Translated by Janet Lloyd.
    Cambridge: Cambridge University Press, 1979.
Anderson, Benedict. *Imagined Communities: Reflections on the Origin and
    Spread of Nationalism.* London: Verso, 1983.
Andrade, Jesús Teja. *Zitácuaro.* Morelia: Gobierno del Estado de Michoacán,
    1978.
Anguiano, Arturo. *El estado y la política obrera del cardenismo.* Mexico City:
    Editorial Era, 1975.
Anguiano Equihua, Victoriano. *Lázaro Cárdenas, su feudo y la política
    nacional.* Mexico City: Editorial Eréndira, 1951.
Ankerson, Dudley. "Saturnino Cedillo: A Traditional Caudillo in San Luis
    Potosi." In Brading, *Caudillo and Peasant in the Mexican Revolution,*
    140–68.
Arreola Cortés, Raul. *Tacámbaro, Carácuaro, Nocupétaro, Turicato.* Morelia:
    Gobierno del Estado de Michoacán, 1979.

Ashby, Joe. *Organized Labor and the Mexican Revolution under Lázaro Cár-denas.* Chapel Hill: University of North Carolina Press, 1963.

Bailey, David. "Revisionism and the Recent Historiography of the Mexican Revolution." *Hispanic American Historical Review* 58:1 (1978): 62–79.

———. *Viva Cristo Rey! The Cristero Rebellion and the Church-State Conflict in Mexico.* Austin: University of Texas Press, 1974.

Barragán López, Esteban. "Más allá de los caminos: Los rancheros de la sierra." Master's thesis, El Colegio de Michoacán, 1986.

Barthelemy, Ricardo, and Jean Meyer. *La casa en el bosque: Las "trojes" de Michoacán.* Zamora: El Colegio de Michoacán, 1987.

Bartra, Roger. *La jaula de la melancolía: Identidad y metamorfosis del mexi-cano.* Mexico City: Editorial Grijalbo, 1987.

———. "Peasants and Political Power in Mexico: A Theoretical Model." *Latin American Perspectives* 2:2 (1975): 125–63.

Basauri, Carlos. *La población indígena de México.* 3 vols. Mexico City: Secre-taría de Educación Pública, 1940.

Bataillon, Claude. *Las regions geographiques au Mexique.* Paris: Institut des Hautes Études de L'Amerique Latine, 1967.

Bauer, Arnold J. *Chilean Rural Society from the Spanish Conquest to 1930.* Cambridge: Cambridge University Press, 1975.

Bazant, Jan. *Alienation of Church Wealth in Mexico: Social and Economic Aspects of the Liberal Revolution, 1856–1875.* Translated by Michael P. Costeloe. Cambridge: Cambridge University Press, 1971.

———. "Peones, arrendatarios y aparceros en México: 1851–1863." *Historia Mexicana* 23 (October–December 1973): 330–57.

———. "Peones, arrendatarios y aparceros en México:1868–1904." *Historia Mexicana* 24:1 (July–September 1974): 94–121.

Beals, Ralph. *Cherán: A Sierra Tarascan Village.* 2d ed. New York: Cooper Square, 1973.

Becker, Marjorie. "Black and White and Color: *Cardenismo* and the Search for a *Campesino* Ideology." *Comparative Studies in Society and History* 29 (1987): 453–65.

———. "El cardenismo y la búsqueda de una ideología campesina." *Rela-ciones: Estudios de Historia y Sociedad* 29 (winter 1987): 5–22.

———. "Cardenistas, Campesinos, and the Weapons of the Weak: The Limits of Everyday Resistance in Michoacán, Mexico, 1934–1940." *Peasant Stud-ies* 16 (summer 1989): 233–50.

———. "Lázaro Cárdenas and the Mexican Counter-Revolution: The Struggle over Culture in Michoacán, 1934–1940." Ph.D. diss., Yale University, 1988.

———. "Purity, Danger, and Revolution: The Cultural Roots of Cardenismo in Michoacán." Paper presented at the Center for U.S.-Mexican Studies, University of California, San Diego, 26 May 1991.

———. "Call Out a Posse, Gather Up Their Music, Teach Them to Sing: The Reinvention of the Indian in Post-Revolutionary Mexico." Paper presented at the Yale University Program in Agrarian Studies, New Haven, 7 Febru-ary 1992.

———. "Torching la Purísima, Dancing at the Altar: The Construction of

Revolutionary Hegemony in Michoacán, 1934–1940." In Joseph and Nugent, *Everyday Forms of State Formation.*

―――. "When I Was a Child, I Danced as a Child, but Now That I Am Old, I Think about Salvation: Soledad Barragán and a Past That Would Not Stay Put." Paper presented at "Narrating Histories: A Workshop," Division of the Humanities and Social Sciences, California Institute of Technology, Pasadena, April 1994.

Behar, Ruth. "Rage and Redemption: Reading the Life Story of a Mexican Market Woman." *Feminist Studies* 16 (summer 1990): 223–58.

Benítez, Fernando. *El agua envenenada.* Mexico City: Fondo de Cultura Económica, 1961.

Benjamin, Walter. *Illuminations.* Translated by Harry Zohn. New York: Harcourt, Brace & World, 1968.

Bierstack, Aletta. "Local Knowledge, Local History: Geertz and Beyond." In *The New Cultural History,* edited by Lynn Hunt. Berkeley: University of California Press, 1989.

Bois, Paul. *Paysans de l'ouest.* Paris: Flammarion, 1971.

Bonfil Batalla, Guillermo. *México profundo: Una civilización negada.* Mexico City: Editorial Grijalbo, 1987.

Bourdieu, Pierre. *Distinction: A Social Critique of the Judgement of Taste.* Translated by Richard Nice. Cambridge: Harvard University Press, 1984.

―――. *Outline of a Theory of Practice.* Translated by Richard Nice. Cambridge: Harvard University Press, 1977.

Boyte, Harry. *The Backyard Revolution: Understanding the New Citizen Movement.* Philadelphia: Temple University Press, 1980.

Brading, D. A., ed. *Caudillo and Peasant in the Mexican Revolution.* Cambridge: Cambridge University Press, 1980.

―――. "La estructura de la producción agrícola en el Bajío, 1700–1850." *Historia Mexicana* 23 (October–December 1973): 197–237.

Brand, Donald. *Coalcomán and Motines del Oro: An Ex-District of Michoacán Mexico.* Austin: University of Texas Press, 1960.

―――. "An Historical Sketch of Geography and Anthropology in the Tarascan Region: Part I." *New Mexico Anthropologist* 6–7 (1943): 37–108.

Brandes, Stanley. "El significado simbólico de los fuegos artificiales en la fiesta de febrero en Tzintzuntzan." In de la Peña, *Antropología social de la región purépecha,* 191–207.

Bravo Ugarte, José. *Historia sucinta de Michoacán.* Mexico City: Editorial Jus, 1964.

Bremauntz, Alberto. *La educación socialista en México: Antecedentes y fundamentos de la reforma de 1934.* Mexico City, 1943.

Brenner, Anita. *Idols behind Altars.* New York: Harcourt Brace, 1929.

Britton, John A. *Educación y radicalismo en México: Los años de Bassols (1931–1934).* Mexico City: Sepsetentas, 1976.

―――. *Educación y radicalismo en México: Los años de Cárdenas (1934–1940).* Mexico City: Sepsetentas, 1976.

Burke, Peter. *The Historical Anthropology of Early Modern Italy.* Cambridge: Cambridge University Press, 1987.

Burkhart, Louise M. *The Slippery Earth: Nahua-Christian Moral Dialogue in Sixteenth-Century Mexico*. Tucson: University of Arizona Press, 1989.

Burns, E. Bradford. *The Poverty of Progress: Latin America in the Nineteenth Century*. Berkeley: University of California Press, 1980.

Carr, Barry. "Recent Regional Studies of the Mexican Revolution." *Latin American Research Review* 15:1 (1980): 3–14.

Carrasco, Pedro. *Tarascan Folk Religion: An Analysis of Economic, Social, and Religious Interactions*. New Orleans: Middle American Research Institute, Tulane University of Louisiana, 1952.

Chamorro, Arturo. "Sincretismo y cambio en la formación de la música purépecha." In *La sociedad indígena en el centro y occidente de México*, by Pedro Carrasco et al. Zamora: El Colegio de Michoacán, 1986.

Chartier, Roger. *The Cultural Uses of Print in Early Modern France*. Translated by Lydia G. Cochrane. Princeton: Princeton University Press, 1987.

Chevalier, François. "The Ejido and Political Stability in Mexico." In *The Politics of Conformity in Latin America*, edited by Claude Veliz, 158–91. London: Oxford University Press, 1967.

Chowning, Margaret. "A Mexican Provincial Elite: Michoacán, 1810–1910." Ph.D. diss., Stanford University, 1984.

Cleland, Robert Glass, ed. *The Mexican Year Book, 1920–21*. Los Angeles: Mexican Year Book, 1922.

Clendinnen, Inga. *Ambivalent Conquests: Maya and Spaniard in Yucatán, 1517–1570*. Cambridge: Cambridge University Press, 1987.

———. *Aztecs: An Interpretation*. Cambridge: Cambridge University Press, 1991.

———. "Disciplining the Indians: Franciscan Ideology and Missionary Violence in Sixteenth-Century Yucatán." *Past and Present* 94 (February 1982): 27–48.

———. "'Fierce and Unnatural Cruelty': Cortés and the Conquest of Mexico." *Representations* 33 (1991): 65–100.

———. "Landscape and World View: The Survival of Yucatec Maya Culture under Spanish Conquest." *Comparative Studies in Society and History* 22 (1980): 374–93.

———. "Yucatec Maya Women and the Spanish Conquest: Role and Ritual in Historical Reconstruction." *Journal of Social History* 15 (1982): 427–41.

Clifford, James. *The Predicament of Culture: Twentieth Century Ethnography, Literature, and Art*. Cambridge: Harvard University Press, 1988.

Cline, Howard. *Mexico: Revolution to Evolution*. New York: Oxford University Press, 1962.

Coatsworth, John H. "Railroads, Landholding, and Agrarian Protest in the Early Porfiriato." *Hispanic American Historical Review* 54:1 (1974): 48–71.

Cockcroft, James D. *Intellectual Precursors of the Mexican Revolution 1900–1913*. Austin: University of Texas Press, 1968.

———. "El maestro de primaria en la Revolución Mexicana." *Historia Mexicana* 16 (April–June 1967): 565–88.

Córdova, Arnaldo. *La política de masas del cardenismo*. Mexico City: Serie Popular Era, 1974.

———. "La transformación del PNR en PRM: El triunfo del corporativismo en México." In *Contemporary Mexico: Papers of the IV International Congress of Mexican History*, edited by James W. Wilkie, Michael C. Meyer, and Edna Monzón de Wilkie, 204–27. Berkeley: University of California Press, 1976.

Correa Pérez, Genaro. *Geografía del estado de Michoacán*. 3 vols. Morelia: Gobierno del Estado de Michoacán, 1974.

Corrigan, Philip, and Derek Sayer. *The Great Arch: English State Formation as Cultural Revolution*. Oxford: Basil Blackwell, 1985.

Cosío Villegas, Daniel. "Mexico's Crisis." In *Is the Mexican Revolution Dead?* edited by Stanley Ross, 73–86. 2d ed. Philadelphia: Temple University Press, 1975.

———, ed. *Historia moderna de México*. 13 vols. 3d ed. Mexico City: Editorial Hermes, 1955–73.

Costeloe, Michael. *Church Wealth in Mexico: 1880–1856*. Cambridge: Cambridge University Press, 1967.

Cumberland, Charles. *Mexico: The Struggle for Modernity*. New York: Oxford University Press, 1968.

Davis, Natalie Zemon. *The Return of Martin Guerre*. Cambridge: Harvard University Press, 1983.

———. *Society and Culture in Early Modern France*. Stanford: Stanford University Press, 1975.

de Certeau, Michel. *The Practice of Everyday Life*. Translated by Steven F. Rendall. Berkeley: University of California Press, 1984.

Deere, Carmen Diana. *Household and Class Relations*. Berkeley: University of California Press, 1990.

de la Peña, Guillermo. "Ideology and Practice in Southern Jalisco: Peasants, Rancheros, and Urban Entrepreneurs." In Smith, *Kinship Ideology and Practice in Latin America*, 204–34.

———, ed. *Antropología social de la región purépecha*. Zamora: El Colegio de Michoacán, 1987.

de Lauretis, Teresa, ed. *Feminist Studies/Critical Studies*. Bloomington: Indiana University Press, 1986.

Demos, John. *The Unredeemed Captive: A Family Story*. New York: Knopf, 1994.

Diego Hernández, Manuel. *La confederación revolucionaria michoacana del trabajo*. Jiquilpan de Juárez: Centro de Estudios de la Revolución Mexicana "Lázaro Cárdenas," A.C., n.d.

Douglas, Mary. *Purity and Danger: An Analysis of the Concepts of Pollution and Taboo*. London: Ark Paperbacks, 1984.

Eckstein, Salomon. *El ejido colectivo en México*. Mexico City: Fondo de Cultura Económica, 1966.

Embriz Osorio, Arnulfo. *La liga de comunidades y sindicatos agraristas del estado de Michoacán: Práctica político-sindical, 1919–1929*. Mexico City: Centro de Estudios Históricos del Agrarismo en México, 1984.

Estados Unidos Mexicanos, Secretaría de la Economía Nacional. Dirección General de Estadística. *Primer censo agrícola ganadero de 1930.* Mexico City, 1936.

———. *Primer censo ejidal, 1935: Estado de Michoacán.* Mexico City, 1937.

———. *Quinto censo de población—15 de mayo de 1930: Estado de Michoacán.* Mexico City, 1943–1948.

———. *Segundo censo ejidal, 1940.* Mexico City, 1942.

———. *Sexto censo de población, 1940: Estado de Michoacán.* Mexico City, 1943–48.

Evans, Sara. *Personal Politics: The Roots of Women's Liberation in the Civil Rights Movement and the New Left.* New York: Knopf, 1979.

Falcón, Romana. "El surgimiento del agrarismo cardenista—una revisión de las tesis populistas." *Historia Mexicana* 27 (January–March 1978): 333–56.

Farriss, Nancy. *Crown and Clergy in Colonial Mexico, 1759–1821: The Crisis of Ecclesiastical Privilege.* London: Athlone, 1968.

Fernando, Justino. *Pátzcuaro.* Mexico City: Talleres de Imprenta de Estampillas y Valores, 1936.

Florescano, Enrique, and María del Rosario Lanzagorta. "Política económica: Antecedentes y consecuencias." In González, *La economía mexicana en la época de Juárez,* 57–107. Mexico City: Sepsetentas, 1976.

Foglio Miramontes, Fernando. *Geografía económica agrícola del estado de Michoacán.* 4 vols. Mexico City: Editorial Cultural, 1936.

Foucault, Michel. *Power/Knowledge: Selected Interviews and Other Writings, 1972–1977.* Edited by Colin Gordon. New York: Pantheon Books, 1980.

Franco, Jean. *Plotting Women.* New York: Columbia University Press, 1989.

Fraser, Donald L. "La política de desamortización en las comunidades indígenas, 1856–1872." *Historia Mexicana* 21 (April–June 1972): 615–52.

Friedlander, Judith. *Being Indian in Hueyapan: A Study of Forced Identity in Contemporary Mexico.* New York: St. Martin's, 1975.

Friedrich, Paul. *Agrarian Revolt in a Mexican Village.* 1970. Reprint. Chicago: University of Chicago Press, 1977.

———. "The Legitimacy of a Cacique." In *Local-Level Politics: Social and Cultural Perspectives,* edited by Marc J. Swartz, 243–70. Chicago: Aldine, 1968.

———. "A Mexican Cacicazgo." *Ethnology* 4 (1965): 190–209.

———. *The Princes of Naranja: An Essay in Anthrohistorical Method.* Austin: University of Texas Press, 1986.

———. "Revolutionary Politics and Communal Ritual." In *Political Anthropology,* edited by Marc J. Swartz, Victor W. Turner, and Arthur Tuden, 191–220. Chicago: Aldine, 1966.

Furet, François. *Interpreting the French Revolution.* Translated by Elborg Forster. Cambridge: Cambridge University Press, 1981.

Galván Campos, Fausto. "El problema agrario entre los tarascos." In Mendieta y Núñez, *Los tarascos,* 275–95.

García Márquez, Gabriel. "La increíble y triste historia de la cándida Eréndira y de su abuela desalmada." In *La increíble y triste historia de la cándida Eréndira y de su abuela desalmada.* Barcelona: Barral Editores, 1972.

————. *One Hundred Years of Solitude.* Translated by Gregory Rabassa. New York: Harper & Row, 1970.

García Mora, Carlos. "El conflicto agrario-religioso en la sierra tarasca." *América Indígena* 36 (January–March 1976): 115–29.

————. "Tierra y movimiento agrarista en la sierra purépecha." In *Jornadas de historia de occidente: Movimientos populares en el occidente de México, siglos XIX y XX,* 47–101. Jiquilpan de Juárez: Centro de Estudios de la Revolución Mexicana "Lázaro Cárdenas," A.C., 1981.

Geertz, Clifford. *Agricultural Involution: The Process of Ecological Change in Indonesia.* Berkeley: University of California Press, 1963.

————. "Ethos, World View, and the Analysis of Sacred Symbols." In Geertz, *The Interpretation of Cultures.*

————. *The Interpretation of Cultures.* New York: Basic Books, 1973.

Genovese, Eugene D. *Roll, Jordan, Roll: The World the Slaves Made.* New York: Vintage Books, 1976.

Gerhard, Peter. "Congregaciones de indios en la Nueva España." *Historia Mexicana* 103 (January–March 1977): 347–95.

————. *A Guide to Historical Geography of New Spain.* Cambridge: Cambridge University Press, 1972.

Gibson, Charles. *The Axtecs under Spanish Rule: A History of the Indians of the Valley of Mexico.* Stanford: Stanford University Press, 1964.

Gilly, Adolfo. *La revolución interrumpida.* Mexico City: El Caballito, 1971.

Ginzburg, Carlo. *The Cheese and the Worms: The Cosmos of a Sixteenth-Century Miller.* Translated by John Tedeschi and Anne Tedeschi. London: Routledge & Kegan Paul, 1980.

Glantz, Susana. *El ejido colectivo de Nueva Italia.* Mexico City: SEP-INAH, 1974.

Gledhill, John. "Casi Nada: Capitalism, the State, and the Campesinos of Guaracha." Ph.D. diss., University College, London, n.d.

González, Luis. *Los artífices del cardenismo.* Vol. 14 of *La historia de la revolución mexicana,* edited by Luis González. Mexico City: El Colegio de México, 1979.

————. *Los días del presidente Cárdenas.* Vol. 15 of *La historia de la revolución mexicana,* edited by Luis González. Mexico City: El Colegio de México, 1981.

————. "El match Cárdenas-Calles o la afirmación del presidencialismo mexicano." *Relaciones: Estudios de Historia y Sociedad* 1 (winter 1980): 5–33.

————. *Nueva invitación a la microhistoria.* Mexico City: Fondo de Cultura Económica, 1982.

————. *La querencia.* Morelia: Editorial SEP Michoacán, 1982.

————. *Sahuayo.* Morelia: Gobierno del Estado de Michoacán, 1979.

————. *San José de Gracia: Mexican Village in Transition.* Translated by John Upton. Austin: University of Texas Press, 1972.

————. "Tierra Caliente." In *Extremos de México: Homenaje a Don Daniel Cosío Villegas,* 115–19. Mexico City: El Colegio de México, 1971.

————. *Zamora.* 2d ed. Zamora: El Colegio de Michoacán/CONACYT, 1984.

————, ed. *La economía mexicana en la época de Juárez.* Mexico City: Sepse-tentas, 1976.

González Navarro, Moisés. *Porfiriato, vida social.* Vol. 4 of Cosío Villegas, *Historia moderna de México.*

————. "Tenencia de la tierra y población agrícola, 1877–1960." *Historia Mexicana* 19 (June–September 1969–70): 62–86.

Goodwyn, Lawrence C. *Democratic Promise: The Populist Moment in America.* New York: Oxford University Press, 1976.

Gramsci, Antonio. *Selections from the Prison Notebooks.* Edited and translated by Quintin Hoare and Geoffrey Nowell Smith. New York: International Publishers, 1971.

Greenblatt, Stephen. *Marvelous Possessions: The Wonder of the New World.* Chicago: University of Chicago Press, 1991.

Gruening, Ernest. *Mexico and Its Heritage.* New York: Century, 1928.

Guerra, François-Xavier. *México: Del Antiguo Régimen a la Revolución.* Trans-lated by Sergio Fernández Bravo. 2 vols. Mexico City: Fondo de Cultura Económica, 1988.

Guha, Ranajit, and Gayatri Chakravorty Spivak, eds. *Selected Subaltern Studies.* New York: Oxford University Press, 1988.

Gutiérrez, Angel, José Napoleon Guzmán A., and Gerardo Sánchez D. *La cuestión agraria: Revolución y contrarrevolución en Michoacán (tres ensayos).* Morelia: Universidad Michoacana de San Nicolás de Hidalgo, 1984.

Guzmán, Martín Luis. *La sombra del caudillo.* Madrid: 1929; Mexico City: Editorial Porrua, 1983.

Guzmán Avila, José Napoleon. *Michoacán y la inversión extranjera, 1880–1911.* Morelia: Universidad Michoacana de San Nicolás de Hidalgo, 1982.

Hall, Linda B. "Alvaro Obregón and the Agrarian Movement, 1912–1920." In Brading, *Caudillo and Peasant in the Mexican Revolution,* 124–39.

————. "Alvaro Obregón and the Politics of Mexican Land Reform." *His-panic American Historical Review* 60:2 (1980): 213–38.

————. *Alvaro Obregón: Power and Revolution in Mexico, 1911–1920.* College Station: Texas A&M Press, 1981.

Hamilton, Nora. *The Limits of State Autonomy: Post-Revolutionary Mexico.* Princeton: Princeton University Press, 1982.

Hansen, Roger. *The Politics of Mexican Development.* Baltimore: Johns Hop-kins Press, 1971.

Harris, Richard L. "Marxism and the Agrarian Question in Latin America." *Latin American Perspectives* 5:4 (1978): 2–26.

Hellman, Lillian. *Pentimento.* New York: Signet, 1973.

Hernández, Manuel Diego, and Alejo Maldonado Gallardo. "En torno a la historia de la Confederación Revolucionaria Michoacana del Trabajo." In *Jornadas de historia de occidente: Movimientos populares en el occidente de México, siglos XIX y XX,* 121–36. Jiquilpan de Juárez: Centro de Estudios de la Revolución Mexicana "Lázaro Cárdenas," A.C., 1981.

Hernández Chávez, Alicia. *La mecánica cardenista.* Vol. 16 of *La historia de la revolución mexicana,* edited by Luis González. Mexico City: El Colegio de México, 1979.

Herrejón Pereda, Carlos. *Tlapujahua.* Morelia: Gobierno del Estado de Michoacán, 1980.

Hobsbawm, E. J. "Peasants and Politics." *Journal of Peasant Studies* 1 (October 1973): 3–22.

—. *Primitive Rebels: Studies in Archaic Forms of Social Protest in the Nineteenth and Twentieth Centuries.* New York: W. W. Norton, 1959.

Hobsbawm, E. J., and Terence Ranger, eds. *The Invention of Tradition.* Cambridge: Cambridge University Press, 1983.

Hunt, Lynn. *Politics, Culture, and Class in the French Revolution.* Berkeley: University of California Press, 1984.

—, ed. *The New Cultural History.* Berkeley: University of California Press, 1989.

Ianni, Octavio. *El estado capitalista en la época de Cárdenas.* Translated by Ana Maria Palos. 2d ed. Mexico City: Era, 1983.

Jacobs, Ian. "Rancheros of Guerrero: The Figueroa Brothers in the Revolution." In Brading, *Caudillo and Peasant in the Mexican Revolution,* 76–91.

Joseph, Gilbert M. "On the Trail of Latin American Bandits: A Reexamination of Peasant Resistance." *Latin American Research Review* 25:3 (1990): 7–55.

—. *Rediscovering the Past at the Mexican Periphery.* University: University of Alabama Press, 1986.

—. *Revolution from Without: Yucatán, Mexico, and the United States, 1880–1924.* Cambridge: Cambridge University Press, 1982.

Joseph, Gilbert M., and Daniel Nugent, eds. *Everyday Forms of State Formation: Revolution and the Negotiation of Rule in Modern Mexico.* Durham, N.C.: Duke University Press, 1994.

Kaplan, Temma. *The Anarchists of Andalusia, 1868–1903.* Princeton: Princeton University Press, 1977.

Katz, Friedrich. "Labor Conditions on Haciendas in Porfirian Mexico: Some Trends and Tendencies." *Hispanic American Historical Review* 54:1 (1974): 1–47.

—. *The Secret War in Mexico: Europe, the United States, and the Mexican Revolution.* Chicago: University of Chicago Press, 1981.

—, ed. *Riot, Rebellion, and Revolution: Rural Social Conflict in Mexico.* Princeton: Princeton University Press, 1988.

Kelley, Joan. "The Doubled Vision of Feminist Theory: A Postscript to the 'Women and Power' Conference." *Feminist Studies* 5 (spring 1979): 216–27.

Klor de Alva, Jorge de. "Spiritual Conflict and Accommodation in New Spain: Toward a Typology of Aztec Responses to Christianity." In *The Inca and Aztec States, 1400–1800: Anthropology and History,* edited by George A. Collier, Renato I. Rosaldo, and John Wirth, 345–66. New York: Academic Press, 1982.

Knight, Alan. "Cardenismo: Juggernaut or Jalopy?" *Journal of Latin American Studies* 26 (February 1994): 73–107.

————. "El liberalismo mexicano desde la reforma hasta la revolución (una interpretación)." *Historia Mexicana* 35 (July–September 1985): 59–86.

————. *The Mexican Revolution.* 2 vols. Cambridge: Cambridge University Press, 1986.

————. "Peasant and Caudillo in Revolutionary Mexico 1910–1917." In Brading, *Caudillo and Peasant in the Mexican Revolution,* 17–58.

Krauze, Enrique, Jean Meyer, and Cayetano Reyes. *La reconstrucción económica.* Vol. 10 of *La historia de la revolución mexicana,* edited by Luis González. Mexico City: El Colegio de México, 1977.

Kuhn, Annette, and Ann Marie Wolfe, eds. *Feminism and Materialism: Women and Modes of Production.* London: Routledge & Kegan Paul, 1978.

Laclau, Ernesto, and Chantal Mouffe. *Hegemony and Socialist Strategy: Towards a Radical Democratic Politics.* New York: Verso, 1989.

Ladurie, Emmanuel Le Roy. *The Peasants of Languedoc.* Translated by John Day. Urbana: University of Illinois Press, 1974.

Landsberger, Henry A., ed. *Latin American Peasant Movements.* Ithaca: Cornell University Press, 1969.

Lears, Jackson. "The Concept of Cultural Hegemony: Problems and Possibilities." *American Historical Review* 90 (June 1985): 567–93.

Lefebvre, Georges. *The Great Fear of 1789: Rural Panic in Revolutionary France.* Translated by Joan White. New York: Pantheon Books, 1973.

Lerner, Victoria. *La educación socialista.* Vol. 17 of *La historia de la revolución mexicana,* edited by Luis González. Mexico City: El Colegio de México, 1979.

Lida, Clara. *Anarquismo y revolución en la España del XIX.* Madrid: Siglo XXI de España, 1972.

Lipset, Seymour Martin. *Political Man: The Social Bases of Politics.* Garden City, N.Y.: Doubleday, 1960.

McBride, George. *The Land Systems of Mexico.* 1923. Reprint. New York: Octagon Books, 1971.

MacCormack, Sabine. "Demons, Imaginations, and the Incas." *Representations* 33 (1991): 121–46.

Macías, Pablo. *Pátzcuaro.* Morelia: Gobierno del Estado de Michoacán, 1978.

Maldonado Gallardo, Alejo. "La CRMDT: Lázaro Cárdenas y el problema agrario en Michoacán, 1928–1932." In *IV Jornadas de historia de occidente: Ideología y praxis de la Revolución Mexicana.* Jiquilpan de Juárez: Centro de Estudios de la Revolución Mexicana "Lázaro Cárdenas," A.C., 1982.

Mallon, Florencia E. *The Defense of Community in Peru's Central Highlands: Peasant Struggle and Capitalist Transition, 1860–1940.* Princeton: Princeton University Press, 1983.

————. "Patriarchy in the Transition to Capitalism: Central Peru, 1830–1950." *Feminist Studies* 13 (summer 1987): 379–407.

————. *Peasant and Nation: The Making of Post-Colonial Mexico and Peru.* Berkeley: University of California Press, 1995.

Marcuse, Herbert. *One-Dimensional Man: Studies in the Ideology of Advanced Industrial Society.* Boston: Beacon, 1966.

Martin, Cheryl English. *Rural Society in Colonial Morelos.* Albuquerque: University of New Mexico Press, 1985.

Marx, Karl. *Pre-Capitalist Economic Formations.* Edited by E. J. Hobsbawm. Translated by Jack Cohen. New York: International Publishers, 1965.

Marx, Karl, and Frederich Engels. *The German Ideology.* Edited by C. J. Arthur. New York: International Publishers, 1970.

Menchú, Rigoberta. *I, Rigoberta Menchú: An Indian Woman in Guatemala.* Translated by Ann Wright. Edited by Elisabeth Burgos-Debray. London: Verso, 1984.

Mendieta y Núñez, Lucio, ed. *Los tarascos.* Mexico City: Universidad Nacional Autónoma de México Imprenta Universitaria, 1940.

The Mexican Yearbook, 1912. London: McConquodale, 1912.

The Mexican Yearbook, 1913. London: McConquodale, 1913.

Meyer, Jean. *The Cristero Rebellion: The Mexican People between Church and State, 1926–1929.* Translated by Richard Southern. Cambridge: Cambridge University Press, 1976.

———. *La Cristiada.* Translated by Aurelio Garzón del Camino. 2d ed. 3 vols. Mexico City: Siglo XXI Editores, 1974.

———. *Esperando a Lozada.* Zamora: El Colegio de Michoacán, 1984.

———. "Haciendas y ranchos, peones y campesinos en el Porfiriato: Algunos falacias estadísticas." *Historia Mexicana* 35 (January–March 1986): 477–509.

———. "Los Kulaki del ejido (los años '30)." *Relaciones: Estudios de Historia y Sociedad* 8 (winter 1987): 23–43.

——— *Problemas campesinos y revueltas agrarias, 1821–1910.* Mexico City: SEP, 1973.

———. *La revolution mexicaine.* Paris: Calmann Levy, 1973.

———. "La segunda (cristiada) en Michoacán." In *La cultura purhé: II coloquio de antropología e historia regionales,* edited by Francisco Miranda, 245–76. Mexico City: Colegio de Michoacán/FONAPAS Michoacán, 1981.

———. *El sinarquismo, ¿un fascismo mexicano?* Mexico City: Editorial Joaquín Mortiz, 1979.

Meyer, Jean, Enrique Krauze, and Cayetano Reyes. *Estado y sociedad con Calles.* Vol. 11 of *La historia de la revolución mexicana,* edited by Luis González. Mexico City: El Colegio de México, 1977.

Meyer, Lorenzo. *El conflicto social y los gobiernos del maximato.* Vol. 13 of *La historia de la revolución mexicana,* edited by Luis González. Mexico City: El Colegio de México, 1978.

———. "El estado mexicano contemporáneo." *Historia Mexicana* 23 (April–June 1974): 722–52.

Michaels, Albert. "The Crisis of Cardenismo." *Journal of Latin American Studies* 1:2 (May 1970): 51–79.

———. "Fascism and Sinarquismo: Popular Nationalisms against the Mexican Revolution." *Journal of Church and State* 8 (spring 1966): 234–50.

Migdal, Joel. *Peasants, Politics, and Revolution: Pressures toward Political and Social Change in the Third World.* Princeton: Princeton University Press, 1974.

Mintz, Sidney W. *Sweetness and Power: The Place of Sugar in Modern History.* New York: Viking Penguin, 1985.

Mintz, Sidney W., and Eric R. Wolf. "An Analysis of Ritual Co-parenthood (Compadrazgo)." In *Peasant Society: A Reader,* edited by Jack N. Potter, May N. Díaz, and George Foster, 174–99. Boston: Little, Brown, 1966.

Miranda, Francisco. "Ocumicho, una comunidad en fiesta." *Relaciones: Estudios de Historia y Sociedad* 16 (fall 1983): 40–41.

———. *Uruapan.* Morelia: Gobierno del Estado de Michoacán, 1979.

———. *Yurécuaro.* Morelia: Gobierno del Estado de Michoacán, 1978.

———, ed. *La cultura purhé: II coloquio de antropología e historia regionales.* Mexico City: Colegio de Michoacán/FONAPAS Michoacán, 1982.

Moheno, César. *Las historias y los hombres de San Juan.* Zamora: El Colegio de Michoacán/CONACYT, 1985.

Moreno García, Heriberto. *Cotija.* Morelia: Gobierno del Estado de Michoacán, 1979.

———. *Guaracha: Tiempos viejos, tiempos nuevos.* Mexico City: Colegio de Michoacán/FONAPAS Michoacán, 1980.

Monroy, Guadalupe Huitron. *Política educativa de la Revolución (1910–1940).* Mexico City: SEP, 1975.

Montes de Oca, Rosa Elena. "The State and the Peasants." In *Authoritarianism in Mexico,* edited by José Luis Reyna and Richard S. Weinert, 47–63. Philadelphia: Institute for the Study of Human Issues, 1977.

Moore, Barrington. *Social Origins of Dictatorship and Democracy: Lord and Peasant in the Making of the Modern World.* Boston: Beacon, 1966.

Morin, Claude. *Michoacán en la Nueva España del siglo XVIII: Crecimiento y desigualdad en una economía colonial.* Mexico City: Fondo de Cultura Económica, 1979.

Morner, Magnus. "The Spanish American Hacienda: A Survey of Recent Research and Debate." *Hispanic American Historical Review* 53:2 (1973): 183–216.

Morse, Richard. "The Heritage of Latin America." In *The Foundation of New Societies: Studies in the History of the U.S., Latin America, Southern Africa, Canada, and Australia,* edited by Louis Hartz, 123–77. New York: Harcourt, Brace & World, 1964.

Morrison, Toni. *Playing in the Dark: Whiteness and the Literary Imagination.* Cambridge: Harvard University Press, 1992.

Múgica Martínez, Jesús. *La Confederación Revolucionaria Michoacana del Trabajo.* Mexico City: EDDISA Ediciones, 1982.

Nash, June. *We Eat the Mines and the Mines Eat Us: Dependency and Exploitation in Bolivian Tin Mines.* New York: Columbia University Press, 1979.

Nash, June, and Helen I. Safa, eds. *Women and Change in Latin America.* South Hadley, Mass.: Bergin & Garvey, 1986.

———. *Sex and Class in Latin America.* New York: Praeger, 1976.

O'Brien, Jay, and William Roseberry, eds. *Golden Ages, Dark Ages: Imagining the Past in Anthropology and History.* Berkeley: University of California Press, 1991.

Ochoa, Alvaro. *Los agraristas de Atacheo.* Zamora: El Colegio de Michoacán, 1989.

———. *Jiquilpan.* Morelia: Gobierno del Estado de Michoacán, 1978.

Olivera de Bonfil, Alicia. "José Inés Chávez García 'El Indio': Bandido, revolucionario, o guerrillero?" In *Jornadas de historia de occidente: Movimientos populares en el occidente de Mexico siglos XIX y XX,* 103–113. Jiquilpan de Juárez: Centro de Estudios de la Revolución Mexicana, "Lázaro Cárdenas," A.C., 1981.

Olivera Sedano, Alicia. *Aspectos del conflicto religiosa de 1926 a 1929: Sus antecedentes y consecuencias.* Mexico City: Instituto Nacional de Antropología e Historia, 1966.

Padilla Gallo, Jesús. *Los de abajo en Michoacán.* Morelia: Tipografía de la Escuela Técnica Industrial "Alvaro Obregón," 1935.

Pagden, Anthony. *The Fall of Natural Man: The American Indian and the Origins of Comparative Ethnology.* Cambridge: Cambridge University Press, 1982.

Paz, Octavio. *The Labyrinth of Solitude: Life and Thought in Mexico.* Translated by Lysander Kemp. New York: Grove, 1961.

Pearse, Andrew. *The Latin American Peasant.* London: Frank Cass, 1975.

Pérez Sadrine, Pascale. "Cambios tecnológicos, dinámica social y sus impactos sobre la organización del espacio: Dos comunidades rurales del Valle de Zamora." Master's thesis, Colegio de Michoacán, 1989.

Phelan, John Leddy. "Neo-Aztecism in the Eighteenth Century and the Genesis of Mexican Nationalism." In *Culture and History,* edited by Stanley Diamond, 760–70. New York: Columbia University Press, 1960.

Pla, Rosa, and Moheno, Cesar. "¿Milenarianismo campesino? El sinarquismo en San Juan Parangaricutiro." *Relaciones: Estudios de Historia y Sociedad* 6 (spring 1981): 65–81.

Polanyi, Karl. *The Great Transformation.* Boston: Beacon, 1957.

Poniatowska, Elena. *La noche de Tlatelolco.* Mexico City: Biblioteca Era, 1971.

Popkin, Samuel. *The Rational Peasant: The Political Economy of Rural Society in Vietnam.* Berkeley: University of California Press, 1979.

Powell, T. G. "Los liberales, el campesinado indígena, y los problemas agrarios durante la Reforma." *Historia Mexicana* 21 (April–June 1972): 653–75.

———. "Priests and Peasants in Central Mexico: Social Conflict during La Reforma. *Hispanic American Historical Review* 57:2 (1977): 296–313.

Raby, David. *Educación y revolución social en México, 1921–1940.* Mexico City: SEP, 1974.

———. "Los maestros rurales y los conflictos sociales en México, 1931–1940." *Historica Mexicana* 18 (October–December 1968): 190–226.

———. "Los principios de la educación rural en México: El caso de Michoacán, 1915–1929." *Historia Mexicana* 22 (April–June 1973): 553–81.

Ramírez, Luis Alfonso. *Chilchota: Un pueblo al pie de la sierra.* Zamora: El Colegio de Michoacán, 1986.

Ramos Valladolid, José. *Analysis factorial del desarrollo agrícola en el estado de Michoacán (1935–1970)*. Mexico City: Instituto Politécnico Nacional, 1972.

Rebel, Hermann. "Why Not 'Old Marie'. . .or Someone Very Much Like Her? A Reassessment of the Question about the Grimms' Contributors from a Social Historical Perspective." *Social History* 13:1 (1988): 1–24.

Reddy, William. *Money and Liberty in Modern Europe: A Critique of Historical Understanding*. Cambridge: Cambridge University Press, 1987.

———. "The Spinning Jenny in France: Popular Complaints and Elite Misconceptions on the Eve of Revolution." In *Proceedings of the Consortium on Revolutionary Europe*, edited by Harold T. Parker, Louise S. Parker, and John C. White, 51–62. Athens, Ga., 1981. Photocopy.

Reina, Leticia. *Las rebeliones campesinas en México*. Mexico City: Siglo XXI Editores, 1980.

Reyes García, Cayetano. "Las condiciones materiales del campo michoacano, 1900–1940." 1987. Paper in author's possession.

———. "Resistencia al cambio tecnológico en la agricultura mexicana, 1886–1940." 1987. Paper in author's possession.

Ricard, Robert. *The Spiritual Conquest of Mexico: An Essay on the Apostolate and the Evangelizing Methods of the Mendicant Orders in New Spain, 1523–1572*. Translated by Leslie Byrd Simpson. Berkeley: University of California Press, 1966.

Rodríguez Díaz, María del Rosario. *El suroeste de Michoacán y el problema educativo, 1917–1940*. Morelia: Universidad Michoacana de San Nicolás de Hidalgo, 1984.

Rodríguez Zetina, Arturo. *Zamora: Ensayo histórico y repertorio documental*. Mexico City: Editorial Jus, 1952.

Romero, Javier. "Múgica en 1939–1940: La frustrada candidatura a la presidencia." In *VII Jornadas de historia de occidente: Francisco J. Múgica*. Jiquilpan de Juárez: Centro de Estudios de la Revolución Mexicana "Lázaro Cárdenas," A.C., 1985.

Romero Flores, Jesús. *Historia de la Revolución en Michoacán*. Mexico City: Biblioteca del Instituto Nacional de Estudios Históricos de la Revolución Mexicana, 1964.

Rose, Willie Lee. *Rehearsal for Reconstruction: The Port Royal Experiment*. New York: Oxford University Press, 1964.

Roseberry, William. *Anthropologies and Histories: Essays in Culture, History, and Political Economy*. New Brunswick, N.J.: Rutgers University Press, 1989.

Rosengarten, Theodore. *All God's Dangers: The Life of Nate Shaw*. New York: Knopf, 1974.

Rosenstone, Robert A. *The Mirror in the Shrine: American Encounters with Meiji Japan*. Cambridge: Harvard University Press, 1988.

Ross, Stanley. *Francisco I. Madero: Apostle of Mexican Democracy*. New York: Columbia University Press, 1955.

Ruíz, Ramón Eduardo. *The Great Rebellion: Mexico, 1905–1924*. New York: W. W. Norton, 1980.

Rulfo, Juan. *El llano en llamas*. 2d ed. México City: Fondo de Cultura Económica, 1980.

———. *Pedro Páramo*. Translated by Lysander Kemp. New York: Grove, 1959.

Salamini, Heather. *Agrarian Radicalism in Vera Cruz, 1920–38*. Lincoln: University of Nebraska Press, 1971.

———. "Revolutionary Caudillos in the 1920s: Francisco Múgica and Adalberto Tejeda." In Brading, *Caudillo and Peasant in the Mexican Revolution*, 169–92.

Sánchez Díaz, Gerardo. "Movimientos campesinos en la tierra caliente de Michoacán, 1869–1900." In *Jornadas de historia de occidente: Movimientos populares en el occidente de México, siglos XIX y XX*, 31–45. Jiquilpan de Juárez: Centro de Estudios de la Revolución Mexicana "Lázaro Cárdenas," A.C., 1981.

Sargent, Lydia, ed. *Women and Revolution: A Discussion of the Unhappy Marriage of Marxism and Feminism*. Boston: South End Press, 1981.

Sarmiento, Domingo. *Civilización y barbarie*. Buenos Aires: Librería El Ateneo, 1952.

Schryer, Frans J. *The Rancheros of Pisaflores: The History of a Peasant Bourgeoisie in Twentieth Century Mexico*. Toronto: University of Toronto Press, 1980.

Scott, James C. *The Moral Economy of the Peasant: Rebellion and Subsistence in Southeast Asia*. New Haven: Yale University Press, 1976.

———. "Protest and Profanation: Agrarian Revolt and the Little Tradition, Part I." *Theory and Society* 4:1 (1977): 1–38.

———. "Protest and Profanation: Agrarian Revolt and the Little Tradition, Part II." *Theory and Society* 4:2 (1977): 216.

———. *Weapons of the Weak: Everyday Forms of Peasant Resistance*. New Haven: Yale University Press, 1985.

Scott, Joan Wallach. *Gender and the Politics of History*. New York: Columbia University Press, 1988.

Sider, Gerald. "Christmas Mumming and the New Year in Outport Newfoundland." *Past and Present* 71 (May 1976): 102–25.

———. *Culture and Class in Anthropology and History: A Newfoundland Illustration*. Cambridge: Cambridge University Press, 1986.

———. "A Delicate People and Their Dogs: The Cultural Economy of Subsistence Production." Paper presented at a Yale University Anthropology Department seminar, New Haven, January 1986.

———. "The Ties That Bind: Culture and Agriculture, Property and Propriety in the Newfoundland Village Fishery." *Social History* 5:1 (1980): 1–39.

Simpson, Eyler. *The Ejido: Mexico's Way Out*. Chapel Hill: University of North Carolina Press, 1937.

Simpson, Leslie Byrd. *Many Mexicos*. 4th ed. Berkeley: University of California Press, 1966.

Skirius, John. *José Vasconcelos y la cruzada de 1929*. Translated by Felix Blanco. Mexico City: Siglo XXI Editores, 1978.

Smith, Peter. *Labyrinths of Power: Political Recruitment in Twentieth Century Mexico*. Princeton: Princeton University Press, 1979.

Smith, Raymond, ed. *Kinship Ideology and Practice in Latin America*. Chapel Hill: University of North Carolina Press, 1984.

Smith, Waldemar R. *The Fiesta System and Economic Change*. New York: Columbia University Press, 1977.

Stanislawski, Dan. *The Anatomy of Eleven Towns in Michoacán*. Austin: University of Texas Press, 1950.

Stavenhagen, Rodolfo, ed. *Agrarian Problems and Peasant Movements in Latin America*. New York: Anchor Books, 1970.

Stedman Jones, Gareth. *Languages of Class: Studies in English Working Class History, 1832–1982*. Cambridge: Cambridge University Press, 1983.

Stern, Steve J. "Feudalism, Capitalism, and the World System in the Perspective of Latin America and the Caribbean." *American Historical Review* 93 (October 1988) 829–72.

———. *Peru's Indian Peoples and the Challenge of Conquest: Huamanga to 1640*. Madison: University of Wisconsin Press, 1982.

———, ed. *Resistance, Rebellion, and Consciousness in the Andean Peasant World, Eighteenth to Twentieth Centuries*. Madison: University of Wisconsin Press, 1987.

Sunyer, Oriol Pi. *Zamora: A Regional Economy in Mexico*. New Orleans: Middle American Research Institute, 1967.

Tannenbaum, Frank. *The Mexican Agrarian Revolution*. 1929. Reprint. New York: Archon Books, 1968.

———. *Mexico: The Struggle for Peace and Bread*. New York: Knopf, 1950.

———. *Peace by Revolution: Mexico after 1910*. 1933. Reprint. New York: Columbia University Press, 1966.

Tapia Santamaría, Jesús. *Campo religioso y evolución política en el bajío zamorano*. Zamora: El Colegio de Michoacán/Gobierno del Estado de Michoacán, 1986.

———. "El culto de la Purísima: Un mito de fundación." Paper presented at VII Reunión de historiadores mexicanos y norteamericanos, Oaxaca, Mexico, 23–26 October 1985.

Taussig, Michael T. *The Devil and Commodity Fetishism in South America*. Chapel Hill: University of North Carolina Press, 1980.

Taylor, William B. *Drinking, Homicide, and Rebellion in Colonial Mexican Villages*. Stanford: Stanford University Press, 1979.

Thomas, Keith. *Religion and the Decline of Magic*. New York: Charles Scribner's Sons, 1971.

Thompson, E. P. *The Making of the English Working Class*. New York: Vintage Books, 1966.

———. "The Moral Economy of the English Crowd in the Eighteenth Century." *Past and Present* 50 (February 1971): 76–136.

Tilly, Charles. *The Vendee*. Cambridge: Cambridge University Press, 1964.

Tobler, Hans Werner. "Peasant Mobilization and the Revolution." In Brading, *Caudillo and Peasant in the Mexican Revolution*, 408–23.

Todorov, Tzvetan. *The Conquest of America: The Question of the Other*. Translated by Richard Howard. New York: Harper Colophon, 1985.

Toqueville, Alexis de. *The Old Regime and the French Revolution*. Translated by Stuart Gilbert. Garden City, N.Y.: Doubleday Anchor Books, 1955.

Townsend, William Cameron. *Lázaro Cárdenas: Mexican Democrat.* Ann Arbor: George Wahr, 1952.

Tuck, Jim. *The Holy War in Los Altos: A Regional Analysis of Mexico's Cristero Rebellion.* Tucson: University of Arizona Press, 1982.

Tutino, John. *From Insurrection to Revolution in Mexico: Social Bases of Agrarian Violence, 1750–1910.* Princeton: Princeton University Press, 1986.

Uribe Salas, José Alfredo. *La industria textil en Michoacán, 1840–1910.* Morelia: Universidad Michoacana de San Nicolás de Hidalgo, 1983.

Vanderwood, Paul. *Disorder and Progress: Bandits, Police, and Mexican Development.* DeKalb: Northern Illinois University Press, 1976.

Vaughan, Mary Kay. "Education and Class in the Mexican Revolution." *Latin American Perspectives* 2:2 (1975): 17–33.

——. *The State, Education, and Social Class in Mexico, 1880–1928.* DeKalb: Northern Illinois University Press, 1982.

Vázquez, Josefina. "La educación socialista de los años treinta." *Historia Mexicana* 13 (January–March 1969): 408–23.

——. *Nacionalismo y educación en México.* 2d ed. Mexico City: El Colegio de México, 1975.

Verduzco, Gustavo. "Zamora en el Porfiriato: Una expresión liberal de los conservadores." In *El dominio de las minorías: República restaurada y Porfiriato,* edited by Anne Staples, Gustavo Verduzco, Carmen Blázquez Domínguez, and Romana Falcón. Mexico City: El Colegio de México, 1989.

Villegas Muñoz, Griselda. *Emilia, una mujer de Jiquilpan.* Jiquilpan de Juárez: Centro de Estudios de la Revolución Mexicana "Lázaro Cárdenas," A.C., 1984.

Wallerstein, Immanuel. *The Modern World System: Capitalist Agriculture and the Origins of the European World-Economy in the Sixteenth Century.* New York: Academic Press, 1976.

Warman, Arturo. *Ensayos sobre el campesinado en México.* Mexico: Editorial Nueva Imagen, 1980.

——. *"We Come to Object": The Peasants of Morelos and the National State.* Translated by Stephen K. Ault. Baltimore: Johns Hopkins University Press, 1980.

Warner, Marina. *Alone of All Her Sex: The Myth and Cult of the Virgin Mary.* New York: Knopf, 1976.

Warren, J. Benedict. *The Conquest of Michoacán: The Spanish Domination of the Tarascan Kingdom in Western Mexico.* Norman: University of Oklahoma Press, 1985.

Weber, Eugen. *Peasants into Frenchmen: The Modernization of Rural France 1870–1914.* Stanford: Stanford University Press, 1976.

Weber, Max. *The Sociology of Religion.* Translated by Ephraim Fischoff. Boston: Beacon, 1964.

West, Robert C. *Cultural Geography of the Modern Tarascan Area.* Washington D.C.: Smithsonian Institution of Social Anthropology, 1948.

Weyl Silvia, and Nathaniel Weyl. *The Reconquest of Mexico: The Years of Lázaro Cárdenas.* New York: Oxford University Press, 1939.

White, Hayden. *Tropics of Discourse*. Baltimore: Johns Hopkins University Press, 1978.

White, Jon Eubank Manchip. *Diego Velázquez, Painter and Courtier*. New York: Rand McNally, 1969.

Wilkie, James W. "The Meaning of the Cristero Religious War against the Mexican Revolution." *A Journal of Church and State* 8 (spring 1966): 214–33.

———. *The Mexican Revolution: Federal Expenditure and Social Change since 1910*. Berkeley: University of California Press, 1970.

Williams, Raymond. *The Country and the City*. New York: Oxford University Press, 1973.

———. *Culture and Society, 1780–1950*. New York: Harper & Row, 1958.

Winn, Peter. *Weavers of Revolution: The Yarur Workers and Chile's Road to Socialism*. New York: Oxford University Press, 1986.

Wolf, Eric. *Peasant Wars of the Twentieth Century*. New York: Harper & Row, 1969.

Womack, John. "The Mexican Economy during the Revolution, 1910–1920: Historiography and Analysis." *Marxist Perspectives* 4 (winter 1978): 80–123.

———. *Zapata and the Mexican Revolution*. New York: Vintage Books, 1968.

Yáñez, Agustín. *The Edge of the Storm*. Translated by Ethel Brinton. Austin: University of Texas Press, 1963.

———. *Las tierras flacas*. 1962. Reprint. Mexico City: Joaquín Mortiz, 1982.